SONGS OF LIGHT

Reflections on the Hymns of Shinran

GEORGE GATENBY

(Volume One)

Songs of Light has been made possible through the generosity of Mr. Roy Cooke in memory of the late Rev. George Gatenby.

Copyright © 2024 by Jodo Shinshu International Office

All rights reserved. No part of this publication may be reproduced, distributed, or transmitted in any form or by any means, including photocopying, recording, or other electronic or mechanical methods, without the prior written permission of the publisher, except in the case of brief quotations embodied in critical reviews and certain other noncommercial uses permitted by copyright law. For permission requests, write to the publisher, addressed "Attention: Permissions Coordinator," at the address below.

Jodo Shinshu International Office
1710 Octavia Street
San Francisco, CA 94109

www.jsinternational.org

FOREWORD

INTRODUCTION

Volume One: Commentary on the *Jōdo Wasan*

Hymns based on Master T'an-luan's Gāthās in Praise of Amida Buddha

1: News of the Day
2: Doubt
3: The Dharma-Body
4: The Dawn
5: Attachments
6: Clouds
7: The Last Resort
8: Light in Hell
9: On Being Human
10: The Light of Compassion
11: The Source of All Evil
12: On Houses and Carts
13: Coming in from the Cold
14: Buddha of Ineffable Light
15: The Limits of Language
16: The Great Teacher
17: A Model Bodhisattva
18: A Vehicle Built for Bodhisattvas
19: The Bodhisattva that Shinran Knew in Person
20: Śākyamuni
21: The Business of the Dharma
22: The Land of Happiness
23: *Nirvāṇa*
24: On Not Falling Back
25: Hearing the Name
26: Watching Plums Ripen and Flowers Bloom
27: Cloth of Despair, Robe of Joy
28: The Supremely Difficult Thing
29: Two Truths
30: *Chōmon*
31: *Mahāsāhasra Lokadhātu*

32: *Ganga*
33: Why is Amida Buddha's Pure Land in the West?
34: The Three Treasures
35: A Safety Net?
36: The Pure One Who Broadly Grasps All Beings
37: Compassionate Means
38: The Primal Vow
39: Pure Music
40: The Religion of the Forest
41: The Complexity of Being
42: Many Lights
43: How to Spot a Buddha
44: Effulgence
45: Water
46: The Pain of Ignorance
47: Becoming Wise
48: Single-mindedness
49: The Form of Amida Buddha
50: The Infinite Debt

Hymns on the Three Pure Land Sūtras

51: Thus Have I Heard
52: Śākyamuni's Splendour
53: The Samādhi of Great Tranquility
54: When the Desert Blooms
55: The Infinite
56: The Dawn of Compassion
57: Unhindered Light
58: *Shinjin*
59: *Jñana*
60: The Absolute Equality of Women and Men
61: *Sangan Tennyū*
62: The Life of the Nineteenth Vow
63: Various Good Deeds
64: The True Gate
65: The *Amida Sūtra*
66: *Tariki*
67: *Namo Amida Butsu* is Everything

68: The Bodhisattva Vehicle
69: The Teacher
70: A Lesson from Trees
71: The True Teaching
72: The One and the Many
73: The Thunderbolt
74: The *Nirvāṇa Sūtra*
75: *Anitya*
76: On Violence
77: Outrage
78: *Upāya*
79: Introducing the 'Evil Person'
80: Drowning
81: Of Seeds and Trees
82: *Nembutsu*
83: Only the Name
84: On Going Against the Stream
85: Practicing Great Compassion
86: Many Voices

Hymns on Amida based on Various Sūtras

87: The Personality of the Dharma
88: The Transmission of the Dharma
89: When the Heart is Full
90: The Ninety-Five Wrong Paths
91: Stepping Into the Unknown
92: The Religion of the Books
93: On Being True to Ourselves
94: The Fulfilment of the Dharma
95: Fear of Religious Conviction

Hymns on Benefits in the Present

96: The *Sūtra of Golden Splendour*
97: Dengyō Daishi
98: Lightness of Being
99: Following Shinran Shōnin
100: Gods and the Dharma

101: More About the Gods
102: Unearthing the Dharma
103: *Nāgas*
104: *Yama*, the Dharma-King
105: *Māras*
106: Influence
107: On Being Naked
108: Avalokiteśvara Bodhisattva
109: True Entrusting Heart
110: The Delight of the Buddhas

Hymns in praise of Mahāsthāmaprāpta Bodhisattva

111: Courage
112: Time and the Dharma
113: Twelve Lights
114: *Samādhi*
115: Thinking on the Buddha
116: Nembutsu Saturation
117: The *Sahā* World
118: The Geniality of the Dharma

Foreword

One does not come across a work of this nature very often. What we find embodied here is a great love of the Dharma and a desire to share it with ordinary people. It represents a valiant attempt to convey the power, depth and beauty found in the *Jōdo Shinshū* school of Pure Land Buddhism (also known as *Shin*).

The author believed that the best way to do this was by introducing readers to the three-volume collection of hymns (*wasan*) written by Shinran (1173-1263) who founded this tradition. These represent a comprehensive overview of this rich teaching and, unlike his principal work (the *Kyōgyōshinshō*), the hymns are much more accessible, having originally been written in the everyday colloquial Japanese of his time, instead of the classical Chinese that was used by scholars.

The Reverend George Gatenby, who passed away in March 2021, is not widely known among many followers of Shin Buddhism, so perhaps a few words about this Australian priest are in order. Born in Sydney in 1943, Rev. Gatenby led a fascinating and unconventional life, notwithstanding its many difficulties (which were very often considerable).

While he worked successfully in the business world, he often struggled with the compromises and ruthless behaviours with which he had to contend. Being the gentle soul that he was, the cut-throat environment of commerce was hardly his true calling in life, but this did not detract from the consummate professionalism he always displayed.

Where he did find a true vocation, however, was in his spiritual journey. Before entering the world of business, Rev. Gatenby was a minister in the Anglican Church for nine years (between 1968 and 1977). He quickly became a popular pastor who was renowned for his compelling sermons.

During this time in the ministry, he joined the Oratory of the Good Shepherd, a religious order of priests and lay brothers, which satisfied the longing he had for a close-knit community of like-minded seekers, and which also gave him a contemplative refuge from the often-distracting preoccupations of a busy parish.

Rev. Gatenby often mentioned the sense of belonging and fulfilment he felt among the kindred spirits in that group. And yet, he was never entirely at home in the Christian tradition. While having come to value many of its theological and liturgical treasures, he found himself gradually drifting towards the East for greater spiritual sustenance. This was brought on by his providential encounter, around fifty years ago, with Max Müller's 19th-century translation of the *Sūtra on the Buddha of Eternal Life*. Even though his transition to Buddhism didn't happen overnight, Rev. Gatenby was already finding himself thinking in Buddhist ways, even while serving as a clergyman. Before long, however, this tension became too much and he felt the need to take decisive action.

Despite these doubts, leaving the comfort and security of a welcoming parish where he was held in such high regard would have been a difficult decision. For someone with limited previous work experience, job opportunities for ex-priests were severely restricted. Nevertheless, he finally made the break from the Church and cast himself into a world of perilous uncertainty. After a series of odd jobs and arduous challenges, he entered the mercantile realm and established himself as a sales representative with a honey manufacturer where he worked for many years.

Rev. Gatenby was also an avid broadcaster, having presented a regular program of classical music on 5MBS-FM for many years, which had quite the following. After a while, he was invited to become manager of the radio station – a position he undertook conscientiously and with great enthusiasm.

In October 1994, Rev. Gatenby and I received *tokudo* ordination together at the Nishi Hongwanji in Kyoto and, in December 2007, he became the first Australian to receive the higher ordination rank of *kyōshi*. Upon his return from Japan, he started to ramp up his teaching activities and established a little *dōjō* from his home in Adelaide which, while certainly modest in its numbers, punched way above its weight when it came to the quality and depth of this group's discussions.

Around the same time, he embarked on what was to become the great work of his life; a monumental commentary on Shinran's hymns (which amount to over 350) – a feat that has never before been attempted in English (or, I am told, even in Japanese). It took Rev. Gatenby over a decade to write these exquisite reflections, after which he spent many more years refining them.

When I first met him in 1991, I was immediately struck by his jovial nature and distinctive, irrepressible laugh – a far cry from the somber attitude often displayed by many Buddhists I had known. But what was particularly impressive was his passion for exploring the significance of our fragile and mysterious human existence. It was heartening to see such enthusiasm for the Buddha's teachings, brought alive so vividly in the daily example of this extraordinary man.

I was always moved by how much he cared for the spiritual well-being of his community, and by his desire to see them nourished by life's deeper truths. Despite the self-deprecating assessment of his own achievements, it has become quite apparent that his impact on others was more consequential than he himself could have imagined.

Rev. Gatenby had a deep understanding of people and their troubles, and was always generous with his time. His humour was infectious as was his abiding love of the Dharma, which enriched his life immensely and gave him great joy. If nothing else, he taught me the supreme value of having a sacred orientation in our all-too-brief lives on this planet.

While Rev. Gatenby was an outstanding pioneer of Shin Buddhism in his native country, he nevertheless exercised an understated yet enduring pastoral influence on a number of grateful Shin followers around the world. In many ways, he was ahead of his time yet often had to tread a lonely path, especially when faced with the misconceptions that often plague this largely unexplored tradition. And yet his courage in defending Shinran's wonderful teaching was remarkable – and an inspiration to those who sought to have their lives transformed by a liberating encounter with Amida Buddha through a life of nembutsu.

John Paraskevopoulos
Canberra
January 2023

INTRODUCTION

Opening the Book

Shinran's three collections of hymns (*Sanjō Wasan*) are a kind of Pure Land equivalent of the *Dhammapada*, for they draw on the entire corpus of its tradition, philosophy and practice. These works leave us with succinct and inspiring verses, which are memorable and accessible guides to the dharma. As we begin to discover the hymns, we often need to delve more deeply into its teaching, for we are sometimes confronted with ideas that are new and challenging.

Though they may pose a lifetime of work for the reader, the value of the hymns is that their content is elegant. The books are portable, but they also help us to cut through extraneous and irrelevant concerns to get to the essence of the dharma. When we consider our seemingly endless wandering in *samsāra* – one lifetime is a very short period indeed – the privilege of coming in contact with the dharma is so great that we cannot afford to waste a second in extraneous pursuits.

Finally, although Shinran nowhere specifically says so, the hymns are actually a manifestation of the Seventeenth Vow of Amida Buddha – the 'Vow that all Buddhas Praise My Name', such being the means by which Amida's Name is heard and beings are called to entrust themselves to the Primal Vow.

Reading the Book

Reading important and, especially, succinct works like this collection of hymns in translation can, unfortunately, be a perilous endeavour. This is all the more so when the decisive matter of our salvation is being explored. One misunderstood word can lead to critical errors in our spiritual understanding.

Fortunately, English speakers have two very good works available to them. Volumes 4, 6 & 7 of the Ryūkoku Translation Series comprise each of the three collections of hymns. Anyone who wants to study them closely will find this translation a rich resource because it has detailed footnotes and cross-references. It is advisable, however, to buy the earlier publications in this series since some references in the footnotes are to them.

The first volume of *The Collected Works of Shinran* – published by Jōdo

Shinshū Hongwanji-ha – contains all of Shinran's hymns. What I like about this translation is that it also includes his marginal notes. These are particularly valuable for clarifying Shinran's intentions.

Another very useful resource is *A Glossary of Shin Buddhist Terms*, also published by Ryūkoku University. There are very few technical words used by Shinran that are not included in this little book, which is an invaluable aid to clarifying the terminology that one finds in the hymns. The work is particularly helpful in that it uses all previous translations of Shinran's Japanese language writings as its reference.

Songs of Light

Bearing in mind everything said thus far, I would now like to take you on a marvelous journey through the three collections. Working one's way through this cycle is like flying, like tasting a world of ultimate freedom, like losing one's self in the clear blue sky, and like entering the pure and radiant house of the dharma. It's an adventure we can all take, not only by reading and studying the hymns, but also by treasuring them – even, in time, committing them to mind.

When we survey the three collections as a whole, a cosmic drama engages us, transcending the detail of each verse. It begins with a single, magnificent and decisive fact: the reality of Amida Buddha – the Dharma-Body – whose brilliance is omnipresent. At the end of the first volume, *Hymns on the Pure Land* (*Jōdo Wasan*), this light is revealed in the words of Śākyamuni who tells us of the power of his Vow as expressed in his name, *Namo Amida Butsu*.

Amida's light sweeps through history as his truth becomes more clearly known in the lives and teaching of the seven Pure Land masters. Finally, in the *Hymns on the Dharma-Ages* (*Shōzōmatsu Wasan*), Amida's light is frankly no longer evident in our dark times, but it does wondrously shine in the living *nembutsu* that springs from the hearts of those who sincerely surrender to the *shinjin* of Amida Buddha.

The beginning of everything of concern to us is Amida Buddha. Shinran's verses begin in the *Jōdo Wasan* as a reflection of the *Gāthās in Praise of Amida Buddha* by T'an-luan. A statement of intent prefaces this incandescent early section of the *Jōdo Wasan* focusing, as it does, on the light of Amida Buddha. The purpose of the hymns is made clear. They are an extension of the nembutsu, the manifestation of the Seventeenth

Vow of Amida Buddha:

> If, when I attain Buddhahood, innumerable buddhas in the lands of the ten quarters should not all praise and glorify my Name, may I not attain perfect enlightenment.[1]

These hymns carry the nembutsu's significance and are an expression of shinjin.

> Those who have Faith sincere and true,
> Uttering Amida's Name,
> With the thought of Buddha ever mindful,
> Desire to repay His Benevolence.[2]

This verse makes it clear that *shōmyō nembutsu* ('uttering Amida's Name, with thought of Buddha ever mindful') is the way in which we live out our response to the joy and relief in awakening to Amida's shinjin.

The verses that follow are permeated by the light of wisdom itself, which calls those who hear to entrust themselves. Amida's Name, therefore, is not only the expression of our debt, but the vehicle by which the Buddha's call resounds throughout the universe.

As Shinran says when explaining the nembutsu in the *Kyōgyōshinshō*:

> *Kimyō* [i.e. *Namo*] is the command of the Primal Vow calling to and summoning us.[3]

In the fiftieth verse of the *Jōdo Wasan*, Shinran again reminds us of the true meaning of nembutsu:

> I praise Amida's wisdom and virtue
> So that beings with mature conditions throughout the ten quarters may hear.
> Let those who have already realized shinjin
> Constantly respond in gratitude to the Buddha's benevolence.[4]

---

[1] Hisao Inagaki, *The Three Pure Land Sutras: A Study and Translation*, p. 243.
[2] *Jōdo Wasan*, Ryūkoku Translation Series (RTS) IV, p. 26.
[3] *The Collected Works of Shinran* (Kyoto: Jōdo Shinshū Hongwanji-ha, 1997), Volume I, p. 38 [hereafter CWS].
[4] CWS, p.337.

So far, Shinran has shown us Amida Buddha's reality, power and light. He makes clear how this light manifests itself in the hearts of those who entrust themselves. He goes on to celebrate the way in which Amida's light can be seen to shine in human history. Shinran begins the hymns on the *Triple Sūtra* with a list of those people who acted in such a way as to bring about the revelation of the Primal Vow.

Amida Buddha and his attendant bodhisattvas, Avalokiteśvara and Mahāsthāmaprāpta, are seen to act through Śākyamuni Buddha and the story of the tragedy which befell the royal household of Magadha. The event is related in the Contemplation Sūtra, and it's the first recorded instance of a person (Queen Vaidehī) awakening to the working of the Primal Vow.

Thus, the transmission of Amida Buddha's shinjin begins in this very world of suffering. Yet Shinran's hymns go back to recall the first moment in which Śākyamuni presented the teaching of Amida, as related in the Larger Sūtra. Then he extends the revelation of the Buddha's Name to other parts of the Mahāyāna canon.

Still immersed in the world of birth-and-death, the second collection of hymns recalls the ways in which the seven Pure Land masters responded to Amida's light and developed keen insights into the working of his Vow. Amida Buddha is seen as active, gradually bringing about a full understanding of his truth until, finally, a mature understanding – suitable for our times – shines forth in the life and teaching of Shinran's teacher, Hōnen Shōnin (also known as Genkū).

> As our teacher Genkū appeared in the world
> And spread the One Vehicle of the universal Vow,
> Throughout the entire country of Japan
> Favourable conditions for the Pure Land teaching emerged.[5]

At last! From deep in lost aeons, Amida's Vow and light arose, entering the world of birth-and-death in tangible form at the time of Śākyamuni. Working its way more and more deeply into human consciousness, as the need for the Vow deepened, Amida's light finally bursts forth in all its clarity and glory in Master Hōnen:

---

[5] CWS, p. 387.

> Our teacher Genkū appeared
> Through the power of the Light of Wisdom,
> And revealing the true Pure Land way,
> He taught the selected Primal Vow...[6]

In the *Shōzōmatsu Wasan*, we approach a dark age in which even the light of Amida shining forth from the heart of Hōnen has been extinguished. We enter the world of the last volume of the hymns, in which the mature, rounded and completed teaching becomes manifest, showing how Amida works in the everyday lives of ordinary people.

Our only teacher now, our only light, is the Primal Vow itself. Amida's light is no longer visible, and no teacher lives who radiates it. With the passage of time, the universe has turned cold and all that remains for us is to entrust. Referring to the power of the Vow extending even into these dark times, Shinran sings:

> It is a great torch in the long night of ignorance;
> Do not sorrow that your eyes of wisdom are dark.
> It is a ship on the vast ocean of birth-and-death;
> Do not grieve that your obstructions of karmic evil are heavy.[7]

The all-pervading theme of the third and final collection of hymns is that there is nothing left on which we can depend but the Primal Vow of Amida Buddha. We cannot rely upon our practice, the *sangha* or even Shinran.

> Karmic evil is from the beginning without real form;
> It is the result of delusional thought and invertedness.
> Mind-nature is from the beginning pure,
> But as for this world, there is no person of truth.[8]

Conclusion

The three collections of Shinran's hymns have always been a source of light and insight for me. But I cannot but be moved by the drama of the cycle itself. From the brilliant radiance of Amida Buddha's primordial enlightenment, we first observe the play of the light in our world at large, before coming to feel its irresistible call. As history unfolds, we witness

---

[6] *Ibid.*
[7] CWS, p. 407.
[8] CWS p. 423.

its power in the hearts of great and enlightened teachers until – for Shinran especially – its joyful illumination emerges from the heart of Hōnen. Finally, in the existential reality of life as we know it, Shinran clearly understood that there's nowhere we can turn any more except to the Name of the Buddha, and to that alone.

Namo Amida Butsu

VOLUME ONE:
Commentary on the *Jōdo Wasan*

Jōdo Wasan 1
Those who truly attain shinjin
As they utter Amida's Name,
Being mindful of the Buddha always,
Wish to respond to the great benevolence.

NEWS OF THE DAY

The best news to read each day is to be discovered in our immediate vicinity; those with whom we share our lives, for example, or the garden – or just by going for a rambling walk around our neighbourhood.

Needless to say, the really striking thing about the daily news, our neighbourhood, other people, our garden, and our own lives is that they all foreshadow the one immutable fact of life: change. No matter how friendly people may be one day, the next day they can become an enemy; no matter how wondrous a few mushrooms look when they emerge in the morning mist, by lunchtime they have disappeared.

Such a realization surely drives most sensitive people to an urgent quest for the infinite, and this pursuit eventually changes our focus from the illusions of the world to the wondrous and growing joy in discovering that which is unconditioned. Already, a sense of indebtedness grows within us, not just for this boundless reality but also for those evanescent things in our daily life which, themselves, paradoxically urge us to seek eternal truth.

It is natural for human beings to want to express this awe – this joy – in some way and it is something of this to which Shinran Shōnin[1] alludes when he suggests that we seek to 'respond' to that which provokes our wonder. Even so, he has something much more vital and specific in mind.

The teaching of Shinran was inherited from his predecessors, Śākyamuni Buddha and the masters of India, China and Japan. We will encounter the latter in the second volume of hymns, the *Kōsō Wasan*.

This Buddhist way is called 'the true Pure Land teaching' (*Jōdo Shinshū*),

---

[1] *Shōnin* is an honourific term that is used with Shinran's name. Its meaning is similar to the more familiar Indian term *mahātmā* or 'great soul'.

a term first used by the Chinese master Fa-chao (766-822), who was influenced by the Chinese Jōdo Shinshū patriarch Shan-tao (613-681). It is very straightforward and ultimately easy to understand, even without knowing basic Buddhist concepts.

The compassion of Amida Buddha manifests itself in the Name (*Namo Amida Butsu*),[2] which is a transliteration of the original Sanskrit phrase and means 'take refuge in Amida Buddha'. It is the call to us from the depths of reality, the Primal Vow (*hongan*).

When we assent to the call of the Vow without any misgivings, 'Other-Power' shinjin (*tariki no shinjin*) finds a secure and exclusive place in our lives, and is expressed as the nembutsu of gratitude.

The way of Jōdo Shinshū, in a nutshell, can be found in the opening words of the *Tannishō*, a famous and much-loved text:

> Saved by the inconceivable working of Amida's Vow,
> I shall realize birth in the Pure Land: the moment you entrust yourself thus to the Vow, so that the mind set upon saying the nembutsu arises within you, you are immediately brought to share in the benefit of being grasped by Amida, never to be abandoned.

These truths will be unfamiliar to people encountering the teaching for the first time. Hence, the purpose of Shinran's writings is to explain and celebrate how this comes to be, and just what it means for us. As we read his words, and listen to his voice, our understanding will grow.

The question arises as to just how we should 'repay the Buddha's benevolence': an inclination that we cannot resist when Amida Buddha's

---

[2] *Namo Amida Butsu* means 'Take refuge in Amida Buddha'. Shinran emphasized the Sanskrit term *Amitābha* ('immeasurable light') as the principal meaning of Amida. To be more precise, *Namo Amida Butsu* means to 'take refuge in the Tathāgata (Buddha) of unhindered light filling the ten quarters' and 'take refuge in the Tathāgata of inconceivable light.' Note: *The Collected Works of Shinran*, which is the source of the translation of Shinran's hymns and other writings, renders *Namo Amida Butsu* as *Namu-amida-butsu*. But, of course, there is no difference in the meaning of the phrase and they are merely alternative pronunciations of the same Chinese characters. In practice, the phrase is pronounced in various ways, for example in abbreviated form such as *Namandabu*, etc.

entrusting heart has arisen in our hearts. In one of her letters,[3] Shinran's wife Eshinni reports that he had a very clear idea regarding the matter, which can be outlined as follows:

There are two aspects to repaying the Buddha's benevolence. One is the nembutsu, saying the Name: *Namo Amida Butsu*; the other is to 'accept the teaching oneself and lead others to accept it.' *Namo Amida Butsu* means to 'take refuge (*namo*) in the infinite light and life (*amida*)[4] Buddha (*butsu*)'. We will learn to understand this better as we explore Shinran's hymns. More than anything, it is the joyful and natural cry that comes from a heart set free by the dharma of Amida Buddha.

The best way to hear and celebrate the call of the Vow is to make use of the resource that has been bequeathed to us by Shinran and his eminent successor Rennyo Shōnin (1415-1499). This is the collection of Shinran's poems or hymns in three volumes (*sanjō wasan*) – the subject of these essays. So, let us begin our quest and enjoy for ourselves these songs of light, liberation and joy.

Jōdo Shinshū: The true teaching (or school) of the Pure Land way into the bodhisattva vehicle.
Name: *Namo Amida Butsu*: 'Take refuge in the Buddha of immeasurable light'.
Nembutsu: Saying *Namo Amida Butsu*.
Primal Vow: Amida Buddha's forty-eight Vows, especially the Eighteenth, which reveal his true intention that all who trust in him will be born in the Pure Land and become buddhas at the end of this life.
Shinjin: The entrusting heart.

---

[3] *The Life of Eshinni, Wife of Shinran Shōnin* by Yoshiko Ohtani, pp. 95-6.
[4] Amida is a contraction of two Sanskrit words: *amitābha* ('immeasurable light') and *amitāyus*, ('immeasurable life'). Sanskrit, a classical Indian language, was often used to record ancient Buddhist teachings and ideas for posterity.

Jōdo Wasan 2
Those who say the Name while they doubt
The Vow beyond conceptual understanding
Attain birth and abide for five-hundred years
Vainly within a palace; so it is taught.

DOUBT

In the time of Śākyamuni Buddha,[1] people in his country – Benares, now in India – lived as many still do today: within a caste system that grades human beings into classes depending on their birth. I understand that, during that period, people generally believed that by carrying out certain rituals they could amass sufficient merit to enable them to be born into a higher caste. From a Buddhist perspective, it is said that this belief is one of the 'fetters' that bind beings to the cycle of birth-and-death.

The are many such fetters but the focus often seems to be on just three of them. These are generally understood to be:

1. belief in a self (Sk. *ātman*)
2. doubt
3. belief in the efficacy of mere ritual.

These three fetters subsist in ignorance (*mumyō*; Sk. *avidyā*) or darkness of mind. If they can be overcome, our benighted state will be vanquished and light can begin to break through.

In this verse, Shinran laments the fetter of doubt because, like the belief in self and the efficacy of ritual, it imprisons beings in a glorious world of their own creation. The dharma (the Primal Vow of Amida Buddha) is ultimately inconceivable. In other words, it cannot be fully contained in our minds as an object except as the Name (*Namo Amida Butsu*).

When the Name as nembutsu (i.e. saying *Namo Amida Butsu*) is the spontaneous expression of shinjin, it's no longer a mere ritual act, for it unshackles beings from all fetters and ends the contrivances that keeps

---

[1] 'Śākyamuni' is another name for Gautama Buddha (563-483 BCE) and means 'Sage of the Śākya nation'. Gautama was the principal founder of the cultural, philosophical, speculative and religious movement we call 'Buddhism'. It is properly known as *Buddha-dharma*.

them in the thrall of *saṃsāra*.[2]

So, what shall we do? If doubt is such a serious obstacle to the Buddhist way, how can we challenge and conquer it?

The Pure Land tradition has discovered, in the teachings handed down through the ages (and in the experience of ordinary people), that to entrust oneself to Amida Buddha in the Name (*Namo Amida Butsu*) is one way that Śākyamuni Buddha taught – and that it is tried and true. As the great Australian Buddhist thinker Marie Byles said towards the end of her long life of Buddhist practice:

> It is not easy to relax and let go, and plunge into the flood with only a simple phrase as your life-belt and the very-nature-of-things-as-they-are. It is not easy, but it is a great relief when you do so.[3]

What we see at work here is a profound wisdom – the light that informs our experience of shinjin; and it is this, and only this, that can eliminate doubt. We cannot do it on our own.

Fetters: Attachments that keep us bound to the endless course of birth-and-death.

---

[2] *saṃsāra*: literally 'wandering', this is the cycle of birth-and-death.
[3] Paul Croucher, *Buddhism in Australia* (Sydney: New South Wales University Press, 1989), p. 73.

Jōdo Wasan 3
Amida has passed through ten kalpas now,
Since realizing Buddhahood;
The Dharma-Body's wheel of light is without bound,
Shining on the blind and ignorant of the world.

THE DHARMA-BODY

When the ultimate reality assumes an accessible form, it is referred to as 'Dharma-Body of Compassionate Means'. In its essential nature, it is called 'Dharma-Body of Suchness'. In this aspect, it is formless, inconceivable and altogether beyond our cognition. It is the highest dharma; the reality of things as they truly are.

According to the *Lotus Sūtra*, the Dharma-Body appears in any form that enables it to reach into our hearts so that we can hear, and respond to, its call. The Dharma-Body breaks through the hard shell of human suffering, permeating our pain and darkness, to give us relief. In order to enter our hearts, Amida Buddha takes the form of the Name (*Namo Amida Butsu*) and light.

It is only because of the existence of light that things can be seen. The effect of light is illumination. Amida Buddha is inconceivable light itself – the wisdom-compassion that characterizes the Dharma-Body and exposes reality as it is.

All of Shinran's verses are concerned with the illumination of the world by the Buddha-dharma.

> The Dharma-Body is eternity, bliss, self and purity. It is forever free of all birth, aging, sickness, and death; of not-white and not-black, not-long and not-short, not-this and not-that, not learning and not non-learning; hence, whether the Buddha appears in the world or does not appear in the world, he is constantly unmoving and without change.[1]

> All buddhas and bodhisattvas have Dharma-bodies of two dimensions: 'Dharma-Body as Suchness' and 'Dharma-Body as Compassionate Means'. 'Dharma-Body as Compassionate Means' arises from 'Dharma-Body as Suchness', and

---

[1] CWS, p. 188.

'Dharma-Body as Suchness' emerges out of 'Dharma-Body as Compassionate Means'. Those two dimensions of Dharma-Body differ but are not separable; they are one but cannot be regarded as identical.[2]

Dharma: Ultimate, transcendent truth; the doctrine of the Buddha.

---

[2] CWS, p. 164.

Jōdo Wasan 4
The light of wisdom exceeds all measure,
And every finite living being
Receives this illumination that is like the dawn,
So take refuge in Amida, the true and real light.

THE DAWN

In entering the way of nembutsu, and awakening to shinjin, Shinran Shōnin found an altogether new life and became free.

> I, Gutoku Shinran, disciple of Śākyamuni, discarded sundry practices and took refuge in the Primal Vow in 1201.[1]

This was when Shinran at last joined the nembutsu movement led by Hōnen Shōnin. For him, it was a kind of rebirth. A passage from the writings of Nāgārjuna, which Shinran quotes in the second book of his major work (*The True Teaching, Practice and Realization of the Pure Land Way* – hereafter referred to as *Kyōgyōshinshō*[2]), reminds us that 'the person of the first fruit' in the bodhisattva way is one who is 'born into the house of tathāgatas'. Of course, the awakening of shinjin is not exactly this but is somewhat like it. For Shinran it was a new dawn.

Embracing the nembutsu life, abandoning religious practices, and trusting completely in the Primal Vow of Amida Buddha was, for Shinran (as it is for all beings), life's primary purpose. From that day in 1201, he awakened to an abiding joy in the dharma that was so infectious, it spread the love of the nembutsu way to hundreds – and ultimately millions – of other people.

In *Notes on the Inscriptions on Sacred Scrolls*, Shinran says of this awakening:

> The compassionate light of the Buddha of unhindered light always illumines and protects the person who has realized shinjin; hence the darkness of ignorance has already been cleared, and the long night of birth-and-death is already dispelled and become dawn. Let this be known. … Know that when one realizes shinjin, it is as though dawn has broken.

---
[1] CWS, p. 290.
[2] CWS, p. 19.

> A completely new chapter opens up in our lives when we abandon self-power practices and embark on the life of shinjin and nembutsu.

Since that momentous breakthrough in his life, Shinran experienced grief, knew sickness, and was afflicted with despondency; but he never despaired of the Primal Vow of Amida Buddha and its embodiment as *Namo Amida Butsu*.

Śākyamuni Buddha's enlightenment is not the same thing as shinjin in Pure Land Buddhism. Buddhas have attained enlightenment; ordinary people realize shinjin and gain enlightenment upon birth in the Pure Land. Needless to say, both enlightenment and shinjin are deeply transformative events.

Just as Śākyamuni taught his sūtras following the great awakening, all that we know and revere of Shinran is, similarly, the outcome of his own awakening to the shinjin of Amida Buddha. This is the joyful, appreciative Shinran. It is the Shinran, not of theory but of experience, not of mere dogma but of veracity – the truth, at once, of his inner reality and the glorious dawn of Amida Buddha's all-pervading and unhindered light.

Whenever Shinran alludes to the experiences in his life that led to this spiritual renewal, he always recounts it as a process of leaving things behind: 'discarding', 'departing' and 'abandoning'. He tried the Tendai Pure Land practices but discarded them; he abandoned sundry practices such as meditation, devotional exercises and rules of discipline; he rejected self-centered nembutsu, which – in his own words – was an attempt to create a stock of virtue for ourselves:

> Sages of the Mahāyāna and Hīnayāna,[3] and all good people, make the auspicious Name of the Primal Vow their own root of good; hence, they cannot give rise to shinjin and do not apprehend the Buddha's wisdom.[4]

---

[3] *Hīnayāna* ('Small Vehicle') refers to schools like the Sarvāstivāda, which is now extinct. The focus of their teaching and practice was the *Abhidharma*, an analysis of the elements of existence and of the cosmos.
[4] CWS, p. 240.

Shinran's new dawn occurred when he was twenty-nine years old. His story began at this point. Everything up to that time could only, thereafter, be described as having been relinquished, in the way a butterfly leaves behind its cocoon forever.

I believe that Shinran is the epitome of humanity – the 'light of the world' – because he found the settled shinjin that each of us really seeks. This liberation, light and peace beckons every person with a deep and quiet voice.

Along the way, we can take many wrong turns; our lives are filled with inducements to find fulfillment in superficial things – material goods, ideologies and causes – whose noise can drown out the call of our deepest wish.

Shinran took wrong turns, too, but for him the way was harder than it is for us because he was a pioneer. All we need to do is listen to his teaching, because he has already travelled the path, and reported back to us on both its perils and its joys.

Sundry practices: All practices other than the nembutsu.

Jōdo Wasan 5
The liberating wheel of light is without bound;
Each person it touches, it is taught,
Is freed from attachments to being and nonbeing,
So take refuge in Amida, the enlightenment of non-discrimination.

ATTACHMENTS

According to the longer *Sukhāvatīvyūha Sūtra* (hereafter referred to as the 'Larger Sūtra'), all buddhas glorify the Name of Amida Buddha.[1] The shorter version of this text (commonly known as the 'Amida Sūtra') tells us that this Buddha is so called because his light 'shines boundlessly and without hindrance' throughout the worlds of the ten directions.[2]

The Name, *Namo Amida Butsu*, is always with us as sound and form – it's the way we touch and taste the inconceivable light. We are not required to believe anything, do anything, or grasp at anything – we can just think, breathe and live *Namo Amida Butsu*. However, our nembutsu is no mantra or a magic formula; rather, it is true mindfulness. Shinran tells us that, for people of true shinjin, the nembutsu is

> Uttering the Buddha's Name with thought of Buddha
> ever mindful.[3]

To keep the Name in mind is to take refuge in Amida as the Buddha of Inconceivable Light.

'Suffering and the release from suffering' is the core message of the Buddha-dharma. We are bound to this realm of birth-and-death by our attachments, especially to beliefs that govern our inner reality. From them, we construct a picture of ourselves and of how things work – a 'worldview'.

It follows that if we are released from our attachments, the objectives of the Buddha-dharma will be fulfilled as we'll then enter a realm that is without suffering. Because the Name is the working of the Buddha-

---

[1] *The Larger Sukhāvatī-vyūha,* tr. by F. Max Müller, Sacred Books of the East Vol. XLIX, p. 45.
[2] *The Three Pure Land Sūtras, A Study and Translation from Chinese* by Hisao Inagaki, (Kyoto: Nagata Bunshodo, 2000), p. 355.
[3] *Jōdo Wasan*, Ryūkoku Translation Series II, p. 26.

dharma, it will liberate us from the various views that form the basis of those attachments which hold us in their thrall.

When Shinran describes the fundamental attachments of 'being' and 'non-being', he is touching on erroneous ancient Buddhist teachings, which taught that the elements of our existence (*dharmas*) were either real or illusory. In fact, neither of these basic notions are in accordance with the Buddha-dharma, which is the middle path. Neither existence nor non-existence captures the truth of things.

Our craving for existence or non-existence is hard to overcome using our innate resources – intellect, reason, contemplation and self-discipline. The middle way is the Name, the fragrance of Amida Buddha's light. It easily transcends the views to which we are attached. Once that happens, and we accept the Name in complete trust, we're on the way to the Pure Land, to Nirvāna, as the dying embers of our attachments play out in what remains of this current life, however long or short that may be.

Sukhāvatī-vyūha: literally 'adorned with bliss'; the realm of Nirvāna.

Jōdo Wasan 6
The cloud of light is unhindered, like open sky;
There is nothing that impedes it.
Every being is nurtured by this light,
So take refuge in Amida, the one beyond conception.

CLOUDS

The tenth and final of the stages, through which an aspiring Buddha must pass, is called 'Dharma Cloud'. My understanding is that, after aeons of spiritual development, a bodhisattva (one who is becoming a buddha) receives the acclamation and consecration of all buddhas throughout the universe. His body is then transformed from that of a mere human being into the body of a Buddha with its eighty-four special traits.

The Dharma Cloud is light or wisdom and, like mist, it pervades all existing things without hindrance. It fills their inner being and cocoons them. Like a cloud, it brings compassionate release and coolness from the parched desert of samsāra; like rain, it brings life and nurture to all living things.

For the people of India, as with all people who live in places that have distinct dry and wet seasons, clouds are full of significance. Before the rain comes, the ground is parched and dry from months of drought; and the building humidity and heat, as the monsoon approaches, intensifies the suffering: the pain and depression of samsāra. Anyone experiencing these last days of long, dry conditions would understand the significance of a 'dharma cloud'.

Clouds begin to build, and thunder starts to rumble, before the first drops of rain fall. Hungry to watch this wondrous event, we sit exhausted from the heat and humidity, and see first one, then two, then three, drops of cool rain stain the ground. Then, gradually the earth is wet and soon small puddles of cooling water start to form.

The rain begins to seep into the crevices in the rocks and to penetrate the aching earth, thickening the soil, releasing sweet and healing vapours into the air and causing gentle mist to rise from the baking ground. Seeds swell and ponds fill anew with fresh life; the world, in time, bursts into bloom and new green leaves, bringing joy to all living things. The blessed sound of running water can be heard everywhere; as can the singing of birds, and the bustling activity of insects and small animals on the forest floor.

One could say that this is how it is for the nembutsu, too. The first sound of *Namo Amida Butsu* wells up like a sob from beneath our hidden recesses; that distant horizon which we keep out of sight because of habitual self-centredness.

It seems to me that, in *Namo Amida Butsu*, inconceivable light, like mist, envelops beings in its compassionate embrace. It brings a quiet joy and begins to soften their parched hearts. It begins to relieve their spiritual thirst and hunger for truth and love. It sows seeds of joy which gradually begin to bear fruit until, like a huge apple tree, the first sweet blossoms of dharma – with their rich spiritual nutrients – begin to provide beings with a reason for living and a purpose in life.

The rain does not transform the world from parched desert to rich fecundity in a split second. The evidence suggests that, generally speaking, neither does the nembutsu way. Yes, there is a point at which the seeds begin to sprout after being soaked in the rain; a point-of-no-return in which the world has passed from death to life. But such a moment is imperceptible, vital and critical as this is. The nembutsu way is quite natural – nothing is forced. As we listen to the dharma, the life of shinjin begins to emerge gently: just as from a tiny seed, a huge and fruitful tree may grow.

But the wonder of it all is that when the trees are once again in full leaf, the air is brimming with the scent of flowers, and the understorey of the forest is teeming with life once more, we become aware – with blinding clarity – that all of this has happened by itself. We did not cause the thunder to peal, the rain to fall, the flowers to bloom or the seeds to burst into life.

So, the dharma clouds come in their own time. The first drops of dharma rain fall in their own way, and dharma seeds break open in their own time; the dharma blooms and bears fruit in our lives just at the right moment, and not at a time of our choosing.

Jōdo Wasan 7
The light of purity is without compare.
When a person encounters this light,
All bonds of karma fall away;
So take refuge in Amida, the ultimate shelter.

THE LAST RESORT

According to a marginal note, which Shinran Shōnin added to this hymn, 'last resort' (*hikkyōe*) is the Dharma-Body's perfect fulfilment of enlightenment. In other words, we have nowhere left to go as Amida ('Dharma-Body as Compassionate Means') has already attained Buddhahood on our behalf.

It is striking that Amida Buddha is the ultimate shelter or last resort for many seekers of truth and liberation. They turn to *Namo Amida Butsu* after a life of struggle, utter failure and suffering; or following a long journey along many blind alleys. Turning to this last resort is not our choice. For when all pretension and self-deception has been stripped away in the turbulent waters of our deluded lives, there is nothing left – except *Namo Amida Butsu*, the final refuge.

There are many places in Shinran's writing, where he makes clear that he experiences Amida Buddha as the highest reality itself – the teacher of all buddhas, whose light breaks into our hearts and settles us on the way to liberation.

The Japanese name *Amida* is a transliteration of the Sanskrit *a-mita*; a melding of two terms which, taken together, denote the negation of any possible measurement; thus, it is rendered as 'immeasurable' or 'boundless'. Originally, in India, this Buddha was identified by two names: *Amitāyus* ('Immeasurable Life') and *Amitābha* ('Immeasurable Light'). It is in the latter sense that Shinran mostly understands Amida. That is why this verse links the working of the 'pure, clean light' with the 'ultimate shelter'.

It is all very well to speak of Amida Buddha in this theoretical or doctrinal way, but we must always remember that the Buddha-dharma is never dogmatic; its ethos is empirical. When Shinran refers to Amida as 'light' – which actively brings him to the realization of shinjin – he is talking about something that he knows and has experienced.

Indeed, it is something that we can all know and experience, too.

Jōdo Wasan 8
The Buddha's light is supreme in radiance;
Thus Amida is called 'Buddha, Lord of Blazing Light.'
It dispels the darkness of the three courses of affliction,
So take refuge in Amida, the great one worthy of offerings.

LIGHT IN HELL

Karma is usually poorly understood. One hears people saying things like 'It must be my karma', when they actually mean either destiny or fate. Karma, in fact, is an aspect of the ancient Aryan worldview which predated the rise of the Buddha-dharma by many centuries.

It was originally thought that one's caste or status in society was determined by the rituals one observed, and that people had a single surviving aspect of their personalities which endured almost to eternity through many births. However, the Buddhist movement criticized this view holding, firstly, that one's degree of enlightenment would determine the extent to which we would continue our endless wandering in samsāra.

The Buddha-dharma accepts the primitive worldview of rebirth but understands that this involves neither the transmigration of an individual entity that's immutable, nor the total destruction of personality. When it comes to the exact nature of the lives which one may have previously experienced, only a Buddha or an *arhat* (an epithet for a realized sage who has attained the highest stage of the Śrāvakayana[1]) can know such things in any detail.

The only thing of which one can be certain, is that our posthumous destinies are determined by the level of awakening attained in this life, and by the integrity of our personal conduct – and that the most unremitting factor in all this is change. Instead of a unitary personality, we are made up of complex bundles (called *skandha*s) that are in constant flux at every moment.

In our modern materialistic society, much is made of the cardinal principle known – in Sanskrit – as *anātman*. There is a strong nihilistic

---

[1] *Śrāvakayana* means 'hearer vehicle'. Currently, it is represented by southern Buddhism in countries like Sri Lanka, Thailand and Burma.

flavour attached to much commentary at this time: but the truth of the matter is that *anātman* does not hold the significance given to it by the use of trivialized renderings such as 'no soul'. *Anātman* is not a dogma, for the Buddha-dharma is never dogmatic. It's an adjective used to qualify factors of existence.

In the first place, the Greek word ψυχή (*psyche*) – often translated as 'soul' or 'spirit' – may also mean 'mind' or 'heart' which, in this case, is closer to the Sanskrit term *citta* – an important part of the Sanskrit compound *prasanna-citta* that is equivalent to shinjin. There are eight consciousnesses (Sk. *vijñāna*), of which the eighth is the *ālaya-vijñāna*, the repository of karmic *bīja* or 'seeds' that bear fruit in future lives.

This is not to undermine the 'dharma seal' or cardinal principal (Sk. *lakṣana*) of *anātman*, but it is important to be aware that the Buddha-dharma is not nihilistic; that these questions are damaging if they're exaggerated or turned into slogans and hollow clichés. The nature of life's continuity and its countless inter-relations constitute a 'middle way' that is neither eternalistic (at the level of individual personality) nor entirely negative.

Above all, we ought to remember that the dharma seeks to disabuse us of our attachment to partial or opinionated 'views' (Sk. *dṛṣṭi*), so that we can 'see things as they are'.

Karma describes our deliberate actions. But along with such actions are complicating factors, such as one's state of mind, motivations and intentions. This complex and elusive set of conditions can lead to either painful, neutral or pleasant results. Hence, unenlightened beings are completely incapable of discerning the outcomes of karma.

Impersonal and collective, we experience the results of previous karma as our current existence, which constantly shifts through varying circumstances. Sometimes we are sick and in pain, or depressed; sometimes rich and sometimes poor; sometimes we are joyful, sometimes sad. And, in the midst of all this, we remain nescient, always harbouring darkness in our minds (*mumyō;* Sk. *avidyā*).

Such changes also take place in and out of endless life forms. Honest people acknowledge complete bewilderment in the face of this endless stream of possibilities. We may, for a time, find ourselves in quite extreme situations, far more painful or even deliriously happy than anything we can ever imagine in our present life with all its vicissitudes.

The intensely happy states – the delirium of power – are in the heavens, and the unspeakably wretched destinies – the misery of impotence – are described as the three courses of affliction (*sanzu*) – 'blood' (animals), 'fire' (hell) and 'sword' (hungry spirits). Any of us may very well find ourselves in these realms for considerable lengths of time!

The majestically flaming light of Amida Buddha is, however, completely unhindered. Even in hell, we can hear the call of the Buddha: *Namo Amida Butsu*.

Dharma seals: The three immutable truths of Buddhism, which are *anitya* (impermanence), *anātman* (no self) and *Nirvāṇa*.

Jōdo Wasan 9
The radiance of enlightenment, in its brilliance, transcends all limits;
Thus Amida is called 'Buddha of the Light of Purity'.
Once illuminated by this light,
We are freed of karmic defilements and attain emancipation.

ON BEING HUMAN

We have now come to the next verse in praise of the Buddha's 'twelve lights'; and 'light of purity' is the sixth epithet of the Buddha of 'inconceivable light'. Here, Shinran Shōnin (following T'an-luan) contrasts the purity of the enlightened mind with the 'dust' of our samsāric mentality. There are many karmic taints that confine us to a feedback loop which keeps us bound to the realm of birth-and-death.

The most persistent of these are blind passions (*bonnō*; Sk. *kleśas*). It is, indeed, the clarity of enlightenment – 'inconceivable light' – that makes us acutely conscious of our binding desires and other karmic taints. The awareness of our *bonnō* is the dynamic activity of the Buddha's wisdom within us. These two forms of apprehension work in synergy, whereby through the arising of one realization, we become aware of the other.

Deliverance is a source of relief and joy, but the experience of coming face-to-face with our *kleśas* – which arise from previous karma – can be a bitter and distressing experience. Yet only the clear light of the Buddha can reveal them to us. Without knowing his compassionate embrace, any deliberate introspection to uncover them is dangerous and inadvisable. This is to invite unnecessary anguish and difficulty. Even upon awakening shinjin, a life lived in the light of the Buddha's compassion does not require any preoccupation with our *bonnō*.

As blind passions are a source of suffering, some schools of Buddha-dharma have traditionally sought to remove them by a process of excision. In our current time – the final age of the dharma (*mappō*) – this is no longer possible. No matter how much effort we may put into religious exercises to that end, our disordered affections inevitably return to bite us. There are six basic forms of *bonnō*. They include such painful emotions as envy, anger, enmity and conceitedness, and they cannot be overcome by sheer force of will.

For ordinary people (*bombu*) the grief caused by mental 'dust' is a fact of life. Confronting them is the way to maturity and self-awareness; and controlling the impulses to which they give rise is the way we develop as socially responsible and ethical beings. Far from absolving us from these realities, living in the light of Amida Buddha may lead to a more acute awareness of them. In conventional language, we describe a person who comes to terms with their disturbing inner reality as someone who 'confronts their demons', and there can be no more important factor in the development of strength of character and moral courage.

Jōdo Wasan 10
The light of compassion illuminates us from afar;
Those beings it reaches, it is taught,
Attain joy of dharma,
So take refuge in Amida, the great consolation.

THE LIGHT OF COMPASSION

The Larger Sūtra is the principal text on which the Pure Land tradition is based. It describes the 'twelve lights' of Amida Buddha. What is called the 'light of compassion' (*jikō*) by Shinran Shōnin in this verse is not actually included in the list of twelve lights. But here Shinran is, in fact, following T'an-luan who characterizes *kangikō* ('joyful light') – which is one of the twelve epithets – as 'merciful light'.

The perfection of wisdom (Sk. *prajñāpāramitā*) is to realize that every *dharma* – the constituent element of thought and personality – is empty. And here we enter the sublime world of the Greater Vehicle. It's because Amida Buddha is the perfection of wisdom, which is the form of light, that he also manifests true compassion (*karuṇā*). In the Mahāyāna, wisdom and compassion are but different aspects of the same reality.[1]

> Emptiness (Sk. *śūnyatā*) is not a mere nihilism that engulfs all entities in its universal darkness, abolishing all differences and particularities. On the contrary, *śūnyatā* is the fountainhead from which the Buddha's compassionate activity flows out.[2]

Compassion is an inevitable consequence when wisdom is perfected, because then all things are seen to be empty (*śūnya*). It is this *karuṇā* that responds to our inner need; and it shows itself in the same way that our heart leaps when we fall in love, or our faces blush when we're embarrassed. This is not possible unless emptiness is the underlying reality of all things. When we hear and accept its call, our response is to take delight in the Buddha-dharma.

---

[1] An in-depth outline of the Mahāyāna is included in *Shinran: An Introduction to His Thought* by Yoshifumi Ueda and Dennis Hirota (Kyoto: Hongwanji International Centre, 1989).
[2] Gadjin M. Nagao, *Ascent and Descent: Two Directional Activity in Buddhist Thought* (Presidential Address for the 6th Conference of the International Association of Buddhist Studies, Tokyo, 1983).

Now we can see why the Mahāyāna is a path of joy. It's because the unhindered light of compassion embraces and liberates all beings, without any discrimination. What could be more wonderful than that? What could bring us greater elation?

Jōdo Wasan 11
The light dispels the darkness of ignorance;
Thus Amida is called 'Buddha of the Light of Wisdom'.
All buddhas and sages of the three vehicles
Together offer their praise.

THE SOURCE OF ALL EVIL

Ignorance (*mumyō*, Sk. *avidyā*) is the fundamental cause of all suffering and error; it causes us to become trapped in samsāra and to respond to events by simple, mindless reactions to stimuli such as attraction or aversion. Worse, it leads us to create a totally aberrant worldview which distorts reality in a radical way. It does this through a powerful tendency to conceive of people, thoughts and events as completely separate and cut off from each other when, in fact, they are not.

We do not need to plumb the depths of experience, or of our minds, to see the truth of ignorance. This is not just a mere lack of knowledge, for there is only one thing we need to know – namely, that we're steeped in this nescience.

One of the most striking examples of how ignorance works is when we look up at the starry vault above us. At this time of the year (late summer), it is still quite dark when I get up in the morning and go out to unlock the front gate. On my way back inside, I invariably take a quick glance at the sky where one of the most prominent features is the constellation known as the *Southern Cross*.

Of course, there is in fact no cross at all; just five stars. Each one is altogether unrelated to the other and they all have different dimensions. People have always envisioned animals and events out of isolated points of light in the sky. Perspective is another simple and clear example of the illusory nature embedded in our existence and yet, without it, survival would be impossible. We see distant objects as relatively small compared to nearer ones which are the same size. Illusion, in other words, is how we perceive and make sense of our world; it's integral to the way we are.

Here lies a stark clue to the truth found in the Buddha-dharma; or at least it's a starting point. The illusory nature of everyday life affords an occasion to question our assumptions. If what I see – and how I naturally tend to organize my conceptions of the world – is fundamentally misconceived, then what can I trust? I certainly cannot rely on myself. Above all, I'm unable to depend on the most insidious of all illusions: the very idea of my own separateness!

We live in a time where we find ourselves overwhelmed by knowledge, and this surely deepens our bondage to ignorance. It causes us to become grotesque in our arrogance and to believe, for example, that our generation is wiser than any in the past. But knowledge is the mere accrual of information; it's not wisdom. It will invariably be used to garner the power of our greed, anger and delusion.

The world as we perceive it isn't altogether real; it is evanescent (Sk. *anutpattika-dharma-kṣānti*). Our certainty that it's substantial is just one mark, or symptom, of the elemental ignorance which sets in motion the chain of causation (Sk. *pratītya-samutpāda*) that must be broken if we are to become free.

Even though the ephemeral nature of the world is affirmed in the Mahāyāna, such an understanding is so profound (and counter-intuitive) that I don't think it's possible for us to sustain a rational and ordered life in the full knowledge of this truth. Only a Buddha can fully fathom such an insight.

Ignorance, for us, is wholly elusive, for we always think the best of ourselves and believe we are wise. It's the incomprehension of our own *avidyā* that needs to be challenged before anything else. Because such knowledge is inherently disturbing, it's evident that we cannot observe this ignorance with a mind that is, itself, lost in a delusory chimera.

A distorted conception of everyday reality is such an integral part of being a *bombu* that the Buddha-dharma has always been at pains to breach the walls of illusion on which our existence is built. Even the *Abhidharma* acknowledges that faith (which, in its arising, signals the first chinks in our ego-centric armour) needs to be awakened by 'another'.

That famous saying, 'When the disciple is ready, the teacher appears', refers precisely to this phenomenon. According to *The Acts of the Buddha*

(Sk. *Buddhacarita*) by Aśvaghoṣa,[1] even Śākyamuni needed the gods to contrive the appearance of a sick man, a dead man and an old man so as to dispel his false awareness – and he, unlike us, was on the very cusp of enlightenment.

Shinran refers to the 'darkness of ignorance' (*mumyō no yami*) in several places and, in so doing, strengthens the religious significance of this notion. Ignorance is not just a deformed vision; it is utter nescience. It's a profound spiritual blindness that is innate to us, and which only the wisdom of the Buddha's light can uncover when shinjin is awakened – at which time we come to know that we are embraced in his undying compassion.

Ignorance: the dark mind.

---

[1] Aśvaghoṣa Bodhisattva probably compiled the *Buddhacarita* during the reign of the Kushan monarch Kanishka who, during the first century of the common era, ruled the territory that now includes much of modern Pakistan, Afghanistan, Uzbekistan, and possibly also part of the Tarim Basin. Kanishka was an enthusiastic patron of the Dharma, and convened the fourth great Buddhist council in Kashmir, which marked the ascendency of the Mahāyāna. Translations of the Buddhacarita include *Life of the Buddha by Ashvaghosha*, translated by Patrick Olivelle (New York University Press, 2008) and *The Buddha-Karita of Asvaghosa*, translated by E.B. Cowell in 'Buddhist Mahāyāna Texts', *Sacred Books of the East, Vol. 49* (Oxford University Press, 1894).

Jōdo Wasan 12
The light shines everywhere ceaselessly;
Thus Amida is called 'Buddha of Uninterrupted Light'.
Because beings hear [and apprehend] this power of light,
Their mindfulness is enduring and they attain birth.

ON HOUSES AND CARTS

'The light shines everywhere ceaselessly.' The Buddha-dharma is a universal and unconditioned law, and our engagement with it is a living process. The way of the Buddha is a vehicle. Of course, travel sometimes involves a leap or two.

> ... a shrill scream from the engine, and everybody jumped up in alarm, Alice among the rest. The Horse, who had put his head out of the window, quietly drew it in and said, 'It's only a brook we have to jump over.' Everybody seemed satisfied with this, although Alice felt a little nervous at the idea of trains jumping at all. 'However, it'll take us into the Fourth Square; that's some comfort!'[1]

In the real world, Shinran Shōnin carefully analyses his spiritual path and, drawing on precedent from Buddhist texts, classifies the Jōdo Shinshū teaching as 'crosswise transcendence'. In this experience, there is an imperceptible shift – at some point along the way – in which we suddenly flip from our wayward wanderings onto the straight path of shinjin; from the riverbank onto the raft; from the raft into the ocean.

In the academic, philosophical and theological traditions of European civilization, the task is to build structures but Buddhist literature is designed as a travel guide; it's almost never a blueprint. In fact, when the Buddha-dharma is developed into dogmas, it begins to look severe and distinctly odd. It can make people miserable when, in fact, the Buddha-dharma is a path out of suffering.

Yet, how often do we come across works which present the teachings as an edifice when, in essence, the purpose of the Buddha-dharma is to dismantle such constructions – especially the world of birth-and-death? The most wonderful dharma treatise ever written is Shinran's *Kyōgyōshinshō*. It is a constant source of joy and inspiration. However, I

---

[1] *Through the Looking-Glass and What Alice Found There* by Lewis Carroll.

am convinced that like most – if not all – Buddhist writing, it's essentially an itinerary, not some kind of grand scheme or master plan. It is an account of his experience, telling us about what the writer has encountered at first hand.

Shinran himself describes it as a 'collection of passages' about finding transcendence and having a free heart – and it certainly lives up to its name. It's a wildly exuberant collection of joyful descriptions that bear witness to the true Pure Land way.

When we read works like the *Kyōgyōshinshō*, it's important to remember that the writer doesn't intend to bring us a merely rational exposition. Dharma texts, which resemble life itself, take many unexpected and surprising turns. Although they do indeed contain some logical or conceptional analyses, all Buddhist scriptures are nothing but the authors' testament of things that they know; what they have seen and confirmed for themselves.

These writers have recorded their experience in order to share it with others. So, we read, study and contemplate their texts as participants – not simply as spectators. The Buddha-dharma is a living and dynamic reality, which only comes alive when its teachings are assimilated by those who hear them.

When the dharma is restricted to merely formal, objective and logical examination, we invariably kill it. Of course, the needs of rationality ought to be addressed in giving an account of ourselves to the extent possible, but we will always remain far too complex to be truly (or consistently) reasonable.

Placing living organisms into straight-jackets deprives them of movement, nourishment and life. We should not confuse the dharma, which is the 'highest truth' (*paramārtha-satya*) with science, which is conventional truth (*samvritti-satya*). Both realms work together, at different levels, to enrich and liberate our lives.

I still remember the moment at my ordination when I was presented with a copy of the *Kyōgyōshinshō*. Here was I, a new disciple of the Buddha, being handed the manual for discipleship, a map of the dharma terrain. It was as though I was being told: 'Here is the travel guide, enjoy the journey'. And indeed I have. These instructions are vitally important, especially when you get lost; but, in fact, they are not an end in themselves. It's the actual journey that counts.

In listening to the Buddha-dharma, then, we need to engage with it in the same way that we listen to beautiful music. We need to roll along and flow with it – we float on the stream of dharma. If we interfere with this process, by making a building out of carts, we'll become confused and unhappy.

The Buddha once declared that 'the Dharma is beautiful in the beginning, beautiful in the middle, and beautiful at the end'. Wherever it's become known, it has thrived throughout endless aeons because people love it. It brings them joy and leads to genuine and enduring freedom – and because travel is interesting and exciting.

Amida Buddha's light – his love and compassion – surrounds and supports all travellers along the way of dharma, whatever path life has chosen for them. When we hear and accept the working of the Primal Vow (as *Namo Amida Butsu*), we all become people whose nembutsu turns to praise.

Buddhist scriptures (*sūtras* and *śāstras*): Reports of things that the writers know and have experienced; travel guides for the rest of us.

Jōdo Wasan 13
The Buddha's light cannot be fathomed;
Thus Amida is called 'Buddha of Inconceivable Light'.
All the buddhas, in acclaiming a person's attainment of birth,
Extol Amida's virtues.

COMING IN FROM THE COLD

This verse describes the admiration that all buddhas have for Amida Buddha – indeed, such reverence forms the basis of the Larger Sūtra. In that scripture, Śākyamuni delivered an account of this Buddha whose supreme virtue has made possible our final deliverance from the endless round of birth-and-death, by having us entrust in his Primal Vow through the Name (*Namo Amida Butsu*). In this way, the enlightenment of all beings who take such refuge is assured.

In the Buddha-dharma, several levels (Sk. *bhūmi*) of spiritual development are realized in the movement towards the goal of liberation: ten, according to Nāgārjuna Bodhisattva, and fifty-two according to the *Avataṃsaka Sūtra*. Those who have not reached even the first stage remain 'beyond the pale'; 'foolish beings' (*bombu*), the equivalent of spiritual pariahs.

It seems to me that having a sense of belonging has more to do with who is kept out of a group, rather than who has shared values and common ties. I cannot think of an exception to this rule. Every human group and society deliberately excludes individuals who either refuse – or are unable – to conform.

Exclusion is a manifestly cruel punishment. It's such a strong argument against non-conformity that a lot of people prefer to live in misery or distress rather than endure it. In our own consumer society, for example, many long-term unemployed people show all the signs of the psychological distress that comes from exclusion. In a society which, like ours, is governed by a flowing stream of public opinion, the creation of pariah categories varies from generation to generation.

Many schools of the Buddha-dharma have willingly held onto a rule of exclusion; despite attempts by many modern proponents who claim otherwise. Ordinary people must take second place in the scheme of salvation; the value of the monastic way of life is considered the main –

if not only – focus of Buddhist practice. However, in the Larger Sūtra, Śākyamuni explains how Amida Buddha could deliver ordinary people from the round of birth-and-death by the power of his Primal Vow. This teaching – which embraces all and forsakes none (*sesshu fusha*) – has been the basis of the rich and exuberant tradition of Pure Land Buddhism.

It is no wonder then that, as he put his brush to paper to create the verse we are now considering, Shinran's heart must have been bursting with a joy which simply could not be suppressed. For he had just finished the first draft of his great masterpiece, the *Kyōgyōshinshō*, in which he had amassed written evidence to support his conviction that, thanks to Amida Buddha's Primal Vow, the hierarchical assumptions which had prevailed in the Buddhist world are not immutable – in accordance with the principle of impermanence, one of the 'Three Seals of the Dharma' (not-self, *anātman*; impermanence, *anitya*; and *Nirvāṇa*).

He showed that ordinary people – and especially women – were in fact the primary focus of the Buddhist way; that a path to liberation from birth-and-death was clearly available to all. Common folk who had taken second place in much of Buddhist history, could now come in from the cold.

In a footnote, Shinran remarks that the phrase 'Buddha of Inconceivable Light' means that the Buddha's true reality is completely beyond our apprehension. The Buddha is inconceivable, making himself know to beings in the Name, *Namo Amida Butsu*.

Jōdo Wasan 14
The majestic light, transcending form, is beyond description;
Thus Amida is called 'Buddha of Inexpressible Light'.
All the buddhas praise this light –
The cause by which Amida's Buddhahood was fulfilled.

BUDDHA OF INEFFABLE LIGHT

There are several magnificent declarations in this verse, and all of them attest to that quality of Amida Buddha which Shinran Shōnin thought was by far the most significant: inconceivable light (*fukashigikō*). Indeed, this is the primary epithet of Amida Buddha.

As we experience it, light is impossible to grasp. We only see objects that obstruct it, whereas light enables us to see the things that get in its way. When we look at stars in the sky, they appear to us as flecks of light. We see them because their luminescence originates at points in the cosmos that are very far away.

Amida is not such a light. This Buddha's luminosity does not travel across space because it already bathes everything that exists throughout the universe; nor is it darkened by anything. This is the light of dharma; it is *prajñā* – the wisdom that fills all things.

Shinran's teaching is sometimes spoken of as a 'Buddhism of compassion', but it is more awe-inspiring than this warm and gentle radiance. Its source is 'majestic light' (*jinkō*). It's a light that causes us to acknowledge its marvellous brilliance, which leaves us speechless with wonder and joy. Shinran's Buddha-dharma is a pristine wisdom that envelops every single person who accepts its bidding.

Obviously, Amida's light is quite different to electromagnetic radiation in the physical universe. Radio waves, for example, can be deflected by various obstructions.

The wisdom of the Buddha, however, 'pervades the countless worlds; it fills the hearts and minds of the ocean of all beings.'[1] It's a living force that conveys enlightenment itself – a metaphysical reality that surpasses

---

[1] CWS, p. 461.

every other kind of light.

Clearly, of all Amida Buddha's attributes, this is the one that Shinran loves the most. He almost invariably describes Amida in terms of light.

The notes that Shinran made alongside this verse indicate that he was also moved by the *ineffable* nature of this light. He tells us that it is formless and altogether impossible to explain; that it's completely beyond verbal expression. Amida Buddha, then, is the essential, unconditioned truth that suffuses all things – one who is praised by all other buddhas; the supreme teacher and leader of the wise.

Jōdo Wasan 15
The light is more luminous than the heavenly bodies;
Thus Amida is called 'Light that Surpasses the Sun and Moon'.
Even Śākyamuni's praise cannot exhaust its virtues,
So take refuge in the one without equal.

THE LIMITS OF LANGUAGE

> The Buddha said to Ānanda and Vaidehī, 'Listen carefully, listen carefully and ponder deeply. I will expound for you the method of removing suffering. Bear my words in mind and explain them to the multitude of beings'.
>
> When these words were spoken, Amitāyus appeared above them, attended on his left and right by the two mahāsattvas, Avalokiteśvara and Mahāsthāmaprāpta. So brilliant was their radiance that it was impossible to see them in detail. They could not be compared even to a hundred thousand nuggets of gold from the Jambu River.[1]

We see here a perfect example of the way in which dharma breaches our deluded minds. The Buddha has been explaining to Vaidehī a method of contemplating the Pure Land. Then, as soon as Śākyamuni says 'Listen carefully, listen carefully and ponder deeply', he is telling Vaidehī to listen to words and ideas that have, as yet, no form. In that moment, Vaidehī is free of conceptualization and open to the dharma. This then takes form as the emptiness of the sky's blue vacuity, causing Vaidehī to fall to her knees and call the Buddha's name – 'World Honoured One!' she cries out.

In the Pure Land tradition, the way in which the dharma emerges from formlessness into a form that can be conceived is by this very means: 'Listen carefully, listen carefully and ponder deeply'. When this hearing deepens, as it were – in that profound expectation that occurs before something is said – the formless takes form as *Namo Amida Butsu*; either as an image or a sound.

This listening is fuelled by absorption of the teaching – as in Vaidehī's case when she heard the vivid descriptions of the Pure Land – that remains

---

[1] *The Three Pure Land Sūtras*, tr. Hisao Inagaki (Revised Second Edition, Numata Center for Buddhist Translation and Research, 2003), p. 83.

dormant like a seed, but which then sprouts and penetrates our awareness in an anticipatory moment that is free of all *self*-consciousness; writing itself, as it were, on the primordial emptiness, which is like a clear, blue sky.

Language is a necessity for human beings[2]. Hence, even people whose hearing or speech are impaired need to create sign language. Over and over again, we become ensnared in a net of words. Usually the Buddha-dharma is paradoxical; it uses language to transcend language. But many people turn language into a concrete 'thing', in which case it becomes idolatrous; they can never transcend words and will thus wander even further in the endless stream of birth-and-death.

The worst degradation of the dharma is when language is taken as the subject of its reference. We should allow words to settle down first and then let go of them; that is, get on with life while we 'listen carefully, listen carefully'.

---

[2] For an account of Jōdo Shinshū as a Buddhist path to realization through engagement with language, see *Asura's Harp: Engagement with Language as Buddhist Path* by Dennis Hirota (Heidelberg: Universitätsverlag, 2006).

Jōdo Wasan 16
When Amida, on becoming a Buddha, first taught the dharma,
The sages present were numerous beyond reckoning;
All who aspire to be born in the Pure Land,
Take refuge in Amida of the vast assembly.

THE GREAT TEACHER

> The Buddha said to Ānanda, 'The number of śrāvakas in the first assembly of the Buddha is beyond reckoning. So is it with the number of bodhisattvas.'[1]

Following this brief quote from the Larger Sūtra, the Buddha and Ānanda commence a wonderful repartee about mathematical magnitudes, deciding finally that the number of people at Amida's first sermon was fairly close to infinite. It's a delightful passage, one of several in this sūtra that exhibits a sense of humour. One can almost hear the Buddha and Ānanda chuckling to themselves as they try to outdo each other in hyperbole.

Śākyamuni concludes that, even though the number of people at Amida Buddha's first sermon was almost incalculable, the number of sages 'yet to be counted' is greater still. However, all these overstatements have a purpose and are not mere rhetoric or hubris. They imply that Amida Buddha is the teacher (*zenjishiki*) of the countless beings who have ever lived, and also of those who have yet to appear.

In this verse, Shinran Shōnin exhorts us to 'take refuge in Amida of the vast assembly'. He calls on all of us to listen to Amida's sermon. In doing so, we join the massive throng of the Buddha's disciples.

The Pure Land school is a universal brotherhood, supported by the presence and power of Amida. It is thus to the Buddha's assembly that we should go, and in him alone that we should take our refuge.

---

[1] *The Three Pure Land Sūtras*, tr. Hisao Inagaki (Revised Second Edition, Numata Center for Buddhist Translation and Research, 2003), p. 38.

Jōdo Wasan 17
The countless great bodhisattvas of the land of happiness,
Have reached 'succession to Buddhahood after one lifetime';
Entering the compassionate activity of Samantabhadra,
They unfailingly work to save beings in defiled worlds.

A MODEL BODHISATTVA

> The Buddha said to Ānanda, 'The bodhisattvas of that land all fulfil the attainment of Buddhahood after one lifetime, except those who, for the sake of sentient beings, have established their own original vows and, thus adorning themselves with the virtues of universal vows, seek to bring all to emancipation.'[1]

There are two kinds of bodhisattvas: those who seek simply to become buddhas like Śākyamuni and teach the Four Noble Truths and the Noble Eightfold Path; or those who, like Amida, resolve to actively cultivate merit which they transfer for the purpose of saving all sentient beings, irrespective of their capacity to practice the precepts and live a monastic life.

As Shinran makes clear in this verse, Samantabhadra Bodhisattva (Jp. *Fugen Bosatsu*) is a hero. He is the perfect example of a bodhisattva who sets out to achieve universal salvation. As the sūtra *Vows of Virtuous Conduct* makes clear, the bodhisattva seeks nothing less than to become fully awakened to a universe of totally interdependent phenomena which manifest Buddha. Either that or, as a means to this realization, birth in Amida's Pure Land.

That is why Shinran insists, repeatedly, that the goal of such birth (*ōsō*) is a return (*gensō*) to the realm of samsāra. All existing things are integral to the whole and the whole is contained in the parts. In this way, the Pure Land is a clearing house for our full integration into ultimate reality.

Samantabhadra is famous for taking ten vows which exemplify the universally oriented bodhisattva. They include the embrace of all universes, and the development of powers to help all beings and provide them with spiritual shelter; in short, becoming one with all and a refuge for all.

---

[1] *ibid.*, pp. 59ff.

Surely no religious teaching has accomplished such monumental heights of compassionate fervour and a heart-wrenching love of all beings – and it is this ethos to which the Pure Land tradition belongs. As ordinary *bombu*, we remain unenlightened recipients of this great compassionate work. Awakening to Amida's mind surely prompts in us the longing to become a part of this far-reaching salvific endeavour.

The *Sūtra of Meditation on the Bodhisattva Universal Virtue* relates that Samantabhadra rides on an elephant with six tusks and seven legs. This means that he has conquered those things that the elephant stands for:

- the heavy burden of karmic evil;
- six tusks suggest the six sense organs[2] which play a role as the vehicle of karmic affliction;
- and the seven legs of the elephant suggest the burden imposed by the seven elements of evil.[3]

Samantabhadra, therefore, represents the highest aspirations of those who follow the Jōdo Shinshū path.

Bodhisattva: Beings whose aspiration, like that of Śākyamuni Buddha before his enlightenment, is to become a Buddha in order to transcend the realm of birth-and-death for their own benefit and that of others.

---

[2] The six sense organs are: eyes, ears, nose, tongue, body and mind.
[3] The seven elements of evil are the opposite of the seven elements of virtue, which are faith, repentance, shamefulness, hearing the dharma, effort, mindfulness and wisdom.

Jōdo Wasan 18
Amassing a stock of virtues from the buddhas
For sentient beings of the ten quarters,
They bring them to entrust themselves to the universal Primal Vow;
So take refuge in Amida, the ocean-like great mind.

A VEHICLE BUILT FOR BODHISATTVAS

This verse continues the theme of the previous hymn. Shinran Shōnin does not consider himself to be the creator of a new perspective within his tradition. His use of 'true' (*shin*) as an adjective qualifying 'Pure Land' (*jōdo*)[1] is not an attempt to delineate a teaching which is, in any way, a departure from his predecessors. Rather, Shinran seeks only to bear clear witness to his teacher Hōnen.

Jōdo Shinshū seeks to steer the entire gamut of humanity onto the path of Buddhahood. Those who do not know its teachings well sometimes characterize them as 'devotional', but their real purpose is to bring about the enlightenment of all beings. In the *Kyōgyōshinshō*, Shinran suggests that those who 'carefully assess their capacity', take refuge in the Pure Land way to achieve this end. There can be little doubt that he saw it in that light.

In returning to this traditional emphasis, Shinran was trying to correct a persistent tendency to lapse into an exclusive concern for one's own liberation. In so doing, he was bringing back into its rightful focus the thought of Vasubandhu Bodhisattva and his commentator, T'an-luan.

Shinran's *Kyōgyōshinshō* takes us on a long, wonderful and intricate journey to the threshold of our spiritual emancipation. As we approach the end of this magnificent treatise, he quotes a final passage which distills his vision of universal salvation.

> A verse in the *Garland Sūtra* says:
>
> On seeing a bodhisattva perform various practices,
> Some give rise to a good mind, and others to a mind of evil;
> But the bodhisattva embraces them all.[2]

---

[1] The term *Jōdo Shinshū* or 'True Teaching of the Pure Land' was first coined by Fa-chao (766-822). Originally, it was not the name of a religious organization.
[2] CWS, p. 292.

Jōdo Wasan 19
Avalokiteśvara and Mahāsthāmaprāpta
Together illuminate the world with the light of compassion,
Never resting even for a moment
From bringing to Nirvāṇa those with mature conditions.

THE BODHISATTVA THAT SHINRAN KNEW IN PERSON

Not only is Pure Land Buddhism the gateway that leads to our participation in the bodhisattva vehicle, but we also benefit from the friendship of those who have gone before – especially Avalokiteśvara and Mahāsthāmaprāpta. These two bodhisattvas are Amida Buddha's assistants and, since they have the power to take any form which can assist in helping us to spiritual maturity and awakening, it's possible that we may also one day meet them in person.

Of the two bodhisattvas, I imagine that the one of most importance to Shinran was Mahāsthāmaprāpta. In the *Jōdo Wasan*, he alludes to him twice as often compared to Avalokiteśvara. This is not only because Mahāsthāmaprāpta epitomizes Shinran's favourite epithet of the Buddha, which is light; not because the *Śūraṅgama Sūtra* tells us that Mahāsthāmaprāpta attained enlightenment by following the nembutsu *samādhi*; or that, in his iconography, he holds a lotus flower which opens one's heart to the Buddha's wisdom; neither is it just because Mahāsthāmaprāpta is especially concerned to help people suffering in hell, or with the plight of fighting spirits or animals. It is because, in fact, Shinran knew Mahāsthāmaprāpta in person.

> Furthermore, when we were at a place called Sakai-no-go in Shimotsuma of Hitachi province, I had the following dream. The scene appeared to be a dedication ceremony for a recently completed temple. The temple faced east, and it must have been an evening festival, for the light from the candle stands was burning brightly in the front. But to the west of the candle stands, and in front of the temple, there was a piece of wood placed horizontally, as if it were a *torii* on which were hung the images of Buddha.
>
> One did not even have the ordinary face of the Buddha – all was light, and the center seemed to emanate from the head of the Buddha – and I could not see any figure. There was nothing but rays of light. The other image clearly showed the

face of the Buddha, so I asked: 'What is the name of this Buddha?' I didn't know who answered, but there was a reply: 'That one which shows only rays of light is Hōnen Shōnin. He is none other than Mahāsthāmaprāpta Bodhisattva.' So I asked again: 'Of whom then is the other image?' 'That is Avalokiteśvara Bodhisattva. He is none other than [Shinran].'

As soon as I heard these words, my eyes opened and I realized that it was all a dream. But I had heard that such dreams should never be revealed to others, and I also thought that no one would believe it, even if I had related it, so I did not tell anyone. I did tell your father [Shinran], however, about Hōnen Shōnin in my dream and he said: 'There are various kinds of dreams, but this is a very telling one which reveals what is true and real. The dream that reveals Hōnen Shōnin to be [a birth] of Mahāsthāmaprāpta Bodhisattva is frequently reported from various places. Mahāsthāmaprāpta is *unexcelled* wisdom itself, and that wisdom is manifested in the form of light.'[1]

Thanks to this letter, we know what Shinran thought of his teacher, Hōnen Shōnin. This knowledge puts paid to any idea that Shinran saw himself as his master's equal.

Reflection on the fact that Shinran had no doubt that Hōnen was Mahāsthāmaprāpta Bodhisattva certainly gives us pause to reflect. One can only bow one's head in reverence and respect before this awesome truth, and feel grateful that we also receive help on the way from such generous bodhisattvas.

---

[1] *The Life of Eshinni, Wife of Shinran Shōnin* by Yoshiko Ohtani, pp.92ff.

Jōdo Wasan 20
Those who reach the Pure Land of happiness
Return to this evil world of the five defilements,
Where, like the Buddha Śākyamuni,
They benefit sentient beings without limit.

ŚĀKYAMUNI

> *... like the Buddha Śākyamuni,*
> *They benefit sentient beings without limit.*

'Śākyamuni' is the popular name given to Gautama Buddha, who set in motion the wheel of dharma some 2,400 years ago. It means 'wise one of the Śākya clan'.

In great movements of thought and affective insight – like the one attributed to Śākyamuni – the stark personality of the founder is lost as soon as he breathes his last. This is surely something that you would expect in this case; especially of one who had attained Nirvāna!

Śākyamuni will not conform to an image that doesn't take account of his own sense of transcendence – certainly not that of a secular and materialistic culture like ours. In some traditions of the dharma, especially those that are based on the *Lotus Sūtra*, Śākyamuni is eternally enlightened and is not constrained to any limited historical perspective. He's always teaching and guiding those who seek his light; and those inspired by him (even through many generations) eventually compile an account of what they have heard.

Śākyamuni's discourses begin with the refrain 'Thus have I heard at one time' (Sk. *evam maya shrutam ekasmin samaye*).

Sūtras are 'heard' rather than 'taught'. They are, in fact, the lived practice and experience of Śākyamuni's disciples that are eventually passed on in writing. These scriptures gain their authority by being lived, cherished, followed and heard – not just by being uttered. Hence, as Shan-tao says, '[The phrase] "Thus [have I heard]" *is meant to clarify* what the Buddha taught'.[1] Śākyamuni is the vessel for the dharma which takes root in our hearts. It is then up to the disciples to say just what it is that they once heard.

---

[1] CWS, p. 214 (italics added).

In Jōdo Shinshū, Amida ...

> ... who attained Buddhahood in the infinite past,
> Full of compassion for foolish beings of the five defilements,
> Took the form of Śākyamuni Buddha
> And appeared in Gayā.[2]

Shinran Shōnin is here saying that Śākyamuni benefits sentient beings without limit because, after his enlightenment at Bōdh Gayā, he delivered the Larger Sūtra which – the Buddha assured us – will remain in the world long after the disappearance of all other Buddhist teachings.

---

[2] CWS, p. 349.

Jōdo Wasan 21
The free working of their supernatural powers
Cannot be fathomed,
For they are possessed of virtues that surpass conception;
So take refuge in Amida, the supremely honoured one.

THE BUSINESS OF THE DHARMA

This is the last of five verses which describe the bodhisattva life of the Pure Land path. Here, Shinran Shōnin celebrates the way bodhisattvas use their powers to praise and serve all buddhas of the universe, thereby propagating the dharma.

These verses always convey to me the vast scope of the Buddhist teachings; one might say – the business of the dharma. There is a real sense of bustle and activity, like the grand vision of universal salvation revealed in the *Garland Sūtra*. To participate in this great cosmic work is exciting and jubilant. What an extraordinary privilege it is to find ourselves a part of it. So, what is this great work? What exactly is the *business* of the dharma? Let me remind you again of that ancient adage, affirmed by all the buddhas,

> I teach suffering and the relief of suffering.

Because this task is so vital and urgent – so important – no stone can be left unturned; no opportunity allowed to pass. The dharma is busy, active and tireless in its endeavours. Hence the Buddhist community has always celebrated the great variety of teachings laid down by the buddhas.

Śākyamuni gave us the tools, leaving nothing out, and we are given the joyful responsibility of putting them to use. He provides the hammer, the saw, the level, the plane and we, his sincere followers, make the furniture: for those suffering to rest upon and gain relief. The Buddha gives us a general diagnosis but there is work for us to do. We ourselves must awaken to the truth of his teaching, and then take it up with single-minded courage and determination.

Hence, the history of the Buddha-dharma is an uplifting celebration whereby we enjoy the efforts of others. Many schools of dharma 'medicine' have sprung up. Very soon after Śākyamuni's demise, a divergence of strategies and therapies began to emerge. The dharma has always been gloriously sectarian. We Buddhists love and celebrate our diversity, we rejoice in the work being undertaken by others, we are friendly and kind in our rivalry – if, in fact, rivalry there be.

Let us then put our shoulder to the wheel.

Jōdo Wasan 22

In the land of happiness, śrāvakas, bodhisattvas,
Human beings, and devas all possess luminous wisdom,
And their bodily features and adornments are all the same;
Different terms are used for them only in accord with the forms
   of existence in other worlds.

THE LAND OF HAPPINESS

Another name for the Pure Land (*Jōdo*) is 'land of happiness' (*anraku*). The original Sanskrit term – *sukhāvatī* – literally means 'adorned with bliss' so it's clearly a synonym for Nirvāna, which is the goal of all Buddhist practice.

We should not confuse the Pure Land with a heavenly realm. Heavens[1] belong to the round of birth-and-death (Sk. *samsāra*) and are included in the sphere of desire (Sk. *kāma-dhātu*), where human beings are found. Hence, such heavens bear no relationship to the Pure Land – the land of happiness or Nirvāna – which completely transcends the existence that we experience now; whether it be as a denizen of hell, a human being, an animal, a heavenly being, or a hungry ghost.

'Happiness' needs to be understood carefully because, in our parlance, it's sometimes used in a frivolous way; whereas, as a synonym for Nirvāna, it means immense joy, utter felicity, total mental clarity, truth and ultimate freedom. Some people are troubled by the elaborate descriptions of the pure lands which we encounter in the sūtras. However, all of these features notably point to two distinctive aspects of Buddha-realms. The first is that they are places completely saturated by dharma; and, secondly, that they are permanent and unconditioned; in other words, Nirvāna itself (often symbolized by the prevalence of indestructible jewels in that environment).

---

[1] The source I use for Buddhist cosmology is the *Abhidharmakośa-bhāṣyam* by Vasubandhu Bodhisattva (Chapter 3, 'The World'). The opening verse says: '*Kāma-dhātu* (the realm of desire) consists of hell, *pretas*, animals, humans, and the six heavens.' In Buddhism, cosmology is not integral to the scheme of liberation, so Vasubandhu derived his ideas from existing Indian sources. In the *Kyōgyōshinshō*, Shinran Shōnin draws on the teaching of the buddhas to show that the powers that govern the universe – including the forces of evil – have undergone a conversion process, which ensures that they're amenable to the influence of compassionate principles, and to protecting the Buddha-dharma.

In all traditions of the Buddha-dharma, purified abodes have always been either way-stations or final destinations in the quest for liberation from the round of birth-and-death.

Jōdo Wasan 23
Their countenances, dignified and wonderful, are beyond compare;
Their bodies, delicate and subtle, are neither human nor deva.
Theirs is the body of emptiness, the body of boundlessness,
So take refuge in Amida, the power of non-discrimination.

NIRVĀṆA

Non-discrimination cannot arise by means of our self-induced calculation because 'self' is ultimately an illusion. It has no actual power except to ensnare us. When 'no self' – emptiness – is in play, Buddha-nature is able to function spontaneously (*jinen*) according to its inherent tendency. The attainment of Nirvāna – the body of emptiness or boundlessness – represents the fulfilment of Amida's shinjin, which is alive in all beings and leads them to enlightenment.

The nature of this dharma is free and spontaneous. It actually walks the path for us if only we will let it by abandoning our own conceits. Its natural activity is the underlying theme in all of Shinran's writing, especially in the hymns. We become intensely aware of this as we draw closer to them.

It's impossible not to notice that these verses were composed by one whose heart was full with the joy of shinjin and the nembutsu of adoration. In singing these praises, Shinran was completely open to the dharma and free of his own self. As a manifestation of the Seventeenth Vow of Amida Buddha,[2] the hymns also serve as vehicles that help free us from our self-absorption.

From the time that beings awaken to the first glimmers of inconceivable light, until the dawning of Nirvāna itself, each step is taken by that which is other than 'self' – Amida's shinjin or Buddha-nature. This can be heard in the sound that bursts forth from within us as *Namo Amida Butsu*.

---

[2] "If, when I attain Buddhahood, the countless buddhas throughout the worlds in the ten quarters do not all praise and say my Name, may I not attain supreme enlightenment." (CWS, p. 13).

Jōdo Wasan 24
People who aspire for the land of happiness
Dwell in the stage of the truly settled.
None in that land are falsely settled or unsettled;
Therefore, the Buddhas offer Amida their praise.

ON NOT FALLING BACK

The 'rightly established state' (*shōjōju*) is the most significant feature of the first bodhisattva stage. There are ten stages, although there's another system that enumerates fifty-two. In that case, this stage is the forty-first. The first stage is also called the 'stage of the truly settled' and the 'stage of joy'. The objective of a Mahāyāna Buddhist is the attainment of this first stage for, once it has been reached, realization of Nirvāna is assured.

A striking example of this focus can be found in the *Discourse on the Ten Stages* (*Daśabhūmika Vibhāṣā*) by Nāgārjuna Bodhisattva, which is almost entirely concerned with the first stage (Sk. *bhūmi*) and the practice necessary to attain it. Nāgārjuna does briefly mention the second stage but goes little further, despite the title of his work.

Chapter 3 of the *Discourse* lists the features of the first stage as follows:

> The bodhisattvas of the First Stage manifest forbearance:
> They do not like disputes; their hearts are full of joy and
> happiness; They always seek purity of heart;
> They compassionately pity sentient beings;
> And they have no anger and enmity.[1]

One of the signs of forbearance that Nāgārjuna refers to is 'no fear of falling into hell', which is very revealing:

> (*The bodhisattva's reply to Māra*)
> In order to perform the act of giving, I fall into the hell of shrieking;
> Those who receive my gifts shall attain rebirth in the heavens;
> If so, I will perform more acts of giving continuously;
> Let sentient beings dwell in the heavens, while I receive pain in

---

[1] *Nāgārjuna's Discourse on the Ten Stages*, translation and commentary by Hisao Inagaki (Ryūkoku Translation Series V, p. 20).

the hell of shrieking.[2]

I can't imagine a more succinct summary of the bodhisattva path, and of the significance of generosity as the fundamental practical aspect of 'emptiness' – true compassion.

The rest of the *Discourse* addresses the correct disposition we ought to have towards attaining the first *bhūmi*. It is brilliant and lucid, giving a superb insight into the whole ethos of the Mahāyāna. Much of its content is really an extension of earlier teaching, and all of it is faithful to the sūtras. While it's a conservative document, by reading it one can glimpse the genius of Nāgārjuna.

The path outlined in the *Daśabhūmika Vibhāṣā* is extremely rigorous, even for lay people. Yet much prejudice current at the time is turned on its head; for example, when Nāgārjuna points out that *dāna* given to an ordinary person is of greater merit than that given to an arhat.

Yet, what about the 'foolish being'? Is there a way that people like us, who are lacking in virtue and unable to carry out rigorous practices, can make progress in the dharma?

In addressing this question, Nāgārjuna says:

> There are innumerable modes of entry into the Buddha's teaching. Just as there are, in the world, difficult and easy paths – travelling on foot by land is full of hardship, and travelling in a boat by sea is pleasant – so it is among the paths of bodhisattvas. Some exert themselves diligently, while others quickly enter non-retrogression by the easy path based on shinjin.[3]

It was Shinran Shōnin who first clearly discerned the relationship between *shōjōju* and the awakening of shinjin. The person who accepts Amida Buddha's shinjin thus attains the 'stage of the truly settled' at that very moment.

---

[2] *op. cit.* p. 22.
[3] *op.cit.* p. 139.

Jōdo Wasan 25
When sentient beings in the various forms of existence throughout
  the ten quarters
On hearing Amida's Name of transcendent virtues,
Come to attain true and real shinjin,
They greatly rejoice at what they have heard.

HEARING THE NAME

In the *Kyōgyōshinshō* ('Chapter on Practice'), Shinran Shōnin carries out an exhaustive etymological analysis of the first word (*namo*) of the nembutsu in its classical Chinese cognate (*kimyō*) and concludes:

> *Kimyō*, therefore, is the command of the Primal Vow, summoning us to trust it.

This is a powerful statement because it leaves no room for us to do anything except respond.

Bodhisattvas make vows in the same way that we, at a certain point in our development as adults, plan a course of study or action with a view to attaining certain objectives in life. However, before any vows are expressed, an inner aspiration or motive has already formed itself. It is this deep intention that's equivalent to the Primal Vow.

Because we are all prey to the influence of our previous actions, we're often thwarted in our plans, but the bodhisattva's career is so selfless and sublime that it attains cosmic proportions, and its virtue is able to ultimately overcome karmic hindrances.

A bodhisattva makes certain vows and then strives to live up to them. Eventually they are fulfilled when, like Śākyamuni, the bodhisattva successfully imparts the content of enlightenment – and the fruit of those vows – to those who hear his voice. The Primal Vow of Amida Buddha refers, at once, to the totality of his vows and, in particular, to the Eighteenth:

> If all sentient beings, hearing the Name and rejoicing in faith even once – through the Buddha's sincere endowment – desire to be born in His Land, they can obtain birth instantaneously and dwell in the non-retrogressive Stage ...

This verse stands alone, and its power prevails over its antecedents.

> The word *hear* ... means that sentient beings, having heard how the Buddha's Vow arose – its origin and fulfilment – are altogether free of doubt.[1]

This hearing is profound, visceral and primordial; simple, but not at a time or in a way of our choosing; its momentary subliminal occurrence is not capable of isolation for retrospective analysis; its existence can only be known as the total abandonment of self-effort – and in the wish to manipulate events to suit our needs through magic or petitionary prayer. In other words, it's the arising of unshakable absolute trust, which emerges from this profound awakening – and of a heart that sometimes sings in serene joy.

In Shinran's thinking, the Primal Vow was initiated by the highest reality itself, which comes to be manifested in a discernable form. Moving within the law of karma – and in a way that creatures like us can comprehend – it directly lifts us out of the round of birth-and-death, the suffering existence that binds us.

This model of action is reflected in how Śākyamuni forsook the high ground of his enlightenment and moved into the tumult of the marketplace to approach people who could hear his voice and gain the same freedom that he already knew. The Primal Vow is the prototype of this yearning to liberate the suffering masses. It only differs in the important sense that it's not bound by time or circumstance, transcending both.

However, it is the 'Name' (*myōgō*) that lies at the heart of this realization because, as something concrete and knowable, it gives focus to 'the origin and fulfilment of the Vow'. As we continue our reflections on Shinran's hymns, we'll discover how, in hearing the *myōgō*, shinjin blooms for us in the here and now.

---

[1] CWS, p. 112.

<u>Jōdo Wasan 26</u>
Because of the Vow, 'If they should not be born...,'
When the moment of genuine entrusting has come
And people attain the one thought-moment of joy,
Their birth becomes completely settled.

WATCHING PLUMS RIPEN AND FLOWERS BLOOM

The title of this essay is prompted by the following phrase in *Jōdo Wasan* 26:

> When the moment of genuine entrusting has come...

There is a developmental phase in the awakening of shinjin. In Shinran Shōnin's experience, this realization is spontaneous; as natural as waking from sleep. But this again reminds us of a tendency that we have as consumers in a production-oriented society: a passion for immediacy and control.

We are deliberately out of step with the natural rhythms of life – something that is powerfully evidenced, for instance, by how we often don't allow ourselves to awaken naturally from sleep. Rather, the rest we need is truncated by artificial means at a time of our choosing. This is but one example of our habituation to a pattern of disruption. When it comes to religion, we are also hungry for control. We're not satisfied with simply allowing serene shinjin to arise in its own time; instead, we find ourselves striving to force it.

In this verse, Shinran speaks of Amida's shinjin in the same way we describe fruit as ripening:

- or a foetus growing in the womb;
- or a flower coming into bud;
- or the tide rising;
- or a cloud forming and dropping cooling and soothing rain;
- or meeting our lover for the first time;
- or awakening from a long restful sleep to a sunny day of freedom;
- or coming to graceful old age;
- or of a smile shared between old friends who complement each other like a pair of gloves;

- or the creamy bitter-sweet feel, texture and taste of beautifully brewed coffee;
- or a sea breeze rising at noon on a hot day;
- or being taken by surprise by the scent of gardenias;
- or the feel of soft warm sand on our feet;
- or a sigh;
- or the gasp of delight that comes from seeing a noble and gnarled old tree;
- or lying on our back observing the clouds;
- or that first taste of a ripe plum that we have been watching swell on the tree;
- or the rush of spring when suddenly the world bursts into bloom;
- or a crack of lightning during a thunderstorm at night; illuminating, in a flash, the world around us and – on plunging back into darkness – leaving an image in our minds of what we saw, forever.

These things all happen while we are getting on with life. None of them can be induced; if we're not the same after the encounter, we will remember them. Do you keep feeling your pulse to see if you are alive? If our pulse is not functioning, we are not going to be able to feel it anyway.

What matters is living and not worrying about whether we're alive or not. Give up everything, abandon worry. Place everything in Amida Buddha's hands and live freely and with happiness – while just saying the Name, *Namo Amida Butsu*.

Jōdo Wasan 27
The two kinds of fulfillment of the Buddha land of happiness
  – the beings and adornments
Were formed through the power of Dharmākara's Vow.
They have no equal in the heavens or on earth,
So take refuge in Amida, the power of the great mind.

CLOTH OF DESPAIR, ROBE OF JOY

In his preface to the *Kyōgyōshinshō*, Shinran Shōnin alludes to the dramatic occasion on which the Pure Land teaching came to be delivered by Śākyamuni:

> Thus it is that, when conditions for the teaching of birth in the Pure Land had matured, Devadatta provoked Ajātaśatru to commit grave crimes. And when the opportunity arose to explain the pure act by which birth is settled, Śākyamuni led Vaidehī to select the land of peace. In their selfless love, these incarnated ones – Devadatta, Ajātaśatru, Vaidehī – all aspired to save the multitudes of beings from pain and affliction, and in his compassion, Śākyamuni, the great hero, sought indeed to bless those committing the five grave offences, those slandering the dharma, and those lacking the seed of Buddhahood (Sk. *icchantikas*).[1]

The first sentence refers to the tragedy at Rājagṛha Castle, which is described in the *Contemplation Sūtra* and the *Nirvāṇa Sūtra*.[2] The crown prince, Ajātaśatru, was enticed by his friend Devadatta (Śākyamuni's cousin), to usurp the throne. To that end, Ajātaśatru imprisoned his father the king (Bimbisāra).

The king's consort was Vaidehī. She was deeply devoted to the king and smuggled food to him in an attempt to save his life because it was intended that the king should starve to death. Bimbisāra was a devout follower of the Buddha, and two important monks called daily to visit him. Eventually, the prince found out about his mother's attempts to keep the king alive and threw her into jail as well. As might be expected, the

---

[1] CWS p. 3.
[2] This, and the previous quote, are from *The Three Pure Land Sūtras, Volume I: The Amida Sūtra and the Contemplation Sūtra*, Shin Buddhism Translation Series, pp. 20 & 22.

queen at this point reached the depths of anguish:

> Then Vaidehī, having been confined, became emaciated with grief and despair.

Her agony was not just over her own predicament. It was also because, in trying to help her king, she had actually made matters far worse.

Śākyamuni sent the two monks, Mahāmaudgalyāyana and Ānanda, to see her. At the time of their visit, she also saw Śākyamuni in a vision and, in the midst of her despair, she cried:

> I beseech you, World-Honoured One, please explain to me, in detail, a place that is free of sorrow and affliction. I wish to be born there. I do not want to live in this defiled world of *Jambudvīpa* filled with beings in hell, hungry spirits and animals, and where there are many vile beings. I wish that, henceforth, I may hear no evil words and may see no evil people. ... For what I truly desire, Sun-like Buddha, is that you teach me how to visualize a place perfected by pure and undefiled acts.[3]

In this verse, Shinran's reference to the 'two kinds of fulfillment of the Buddha land of happiness – the beings and adornments' is to this aspect of the Pure Land; a realm of pure karmic perfection which stands in sharp contrast to life as we experience it.

Our lives in samsāra are nourished by the three roots of evil: greed, wrath and folly. Instead, the Pure Land has emerged from the pure karma of enlightenment: non-greed, non-wrath and non-folly. It's a place made especially for those of us who, in this life, despair of ever being able to practice the dharma and who are thwarted constantly by our conditions – whether through our own ineptitude or the nature of our circumstances. Among us are those who may even, as Shinran says in his preface, be 'without any potential for good'.

Although Vaidehī's situation appears to be the result of events that were out of her control, an insight into one's own condition may seem subjective to outsiders but it's very real nevertheless. Coming to the conclusion that one is totally bereft of any capacity to practice the dharma,

---

[3] *ibid.*

of realizing enlightenment or – worse – of becoming a person of any positive value to others, is unfashionable these days but it can also be profoundly truthful and realistic. It may be an extremely bitter awakening, but accepting even hard truths can be a source of joy and invigoration.

It's in this very moment of despair that the Pure Land way is forged. Imagine the misery of Vaidehī's situation. And do not we, ourselves, also know that kind of despair? Especially when we try to do the right thing but discover that the 'good' we contribute has only led to greater harm – a life spent in altruistic works can be brought not just to naught, but may actually serve as the occasion for unthinkable evil. Such was Vaidehī's grief and despair. A world turned not just upside down, but inside out.

Although Vaidehī could say that she was the victim of circumstances, such is not the way we explain things in the Buddha-dharma. Underlying our lives is a vast profusion of ignorant errors, mistaken moves, wrong turns, thoughtless reactions, anger, perplexity and confusion; a mesh of karmic cloth from which we can never extricate ourselves.

It's not possible to contrive an authentic awareness that we are *bombu* (Sk. *pṛthagjana*) – unwise beings – for we're so steeped in self-deception that even this can be bent to serve our ego. Such an awakening can only come to us by 'the power of another'.

It's often at a time of terrible loss, or disappointment, that the light dawns and the pain of our existential hopelessness is finally revealed to us. So, inevitably, it is the state of our lives that forces us to look at ourselves honestly when things go awry.

The Buddha-dharma is founded on the Four Noble Truths. The first of these is 'the truth of suffering'. Unless one's very being resonates with this truth, it's not possible to follow the path in any meaningful way. Shinran's introduction to the *Kyōgyōshinshō* – along with the palace rebellion in Rājagṛha – shows that the first plank of Pure Land Buddhism is despair.

Few of us have the stamina or courage to confront demons by ourselves; it is usually events that compel us to face them. But when we do so and – like Queen Vaidehī – turn to the Buddha, a tiny seed of joy may well begin to germinate in our hearts.

It's not only that moment of profound relief (in which we know that we don't need to pretend to others and to ourselves anymore) that waters this little fragile seed of shinjin. The same light which, from its pure karma wove the happy land of enlightenment specifically for despairing people like us, also brings it to our awareness.

Jōdo Wasan 28
Śākyamuni Buddha states
That even with his unhindered eloquence,
The adornments of the land of happiness cannot be fully expounded;
So take refuge in Amida, the inexpressible Buddha.

THE SUPREMELY DIFFICULT THING

Shinran Shōnin urges us to take refuge in the inconceivable Buddha, Amida – whose realm is beyond description. In matters relating to dharma, a point is always reached beyond which words cannot take us.

Indeed, a short time following his enlightenment, Śākyamuni decided that it wasn't really worth the effort of trying to share the dharma because it was too subtle for most people to understand.

> The dharma to which I have awakened is truly difficult to awaken to. It is quiescent and unexcelled, and hard to attain through ordinary reason. Deep and profound, only the wise man is able to know and attain it. How can the people of this world, who are addicted to the pleasures of desire, know such truths?[1]

The gods, alarmed at the news that Śākyamuni was having these thoughts, appointed Brahmā to persuade him to change his mind. Moved by compassion for suffering beings, Śākyamuni reflected on their diversity and saw that some might be amenable to his teachings – much like a lake filled with lotuses. Some are blue, yellow, red or white in colour. Some sprout in the water and never break the surface. Others grow in the water and remain on its surface, while a few rise above the water and yet are never touched by it. Then the World-Honoured One answered Brahmā with a verse:

> Oh Brahmā, perceiving the futility of it all, I refrained from expounding the teaching to the people. However, those who have ears to hear will attain a heart of faith. I shall open the doors of immortality.[2]

'The dharma to which I have awakened is ... quiescent and unexcelled,

---
[1] *Vinaya Piṭaka: Mahā-vagga.*
[2] *ibid.*

and hard to attain through ordinary reason.' Śākyamuni's lament is a recurring feature in the transmission of the dharma from person to person, and from generation to generation. It is even so in the Pure Land way. Down through the ages, the observation we find at the end of the Larger Sūtra is re-affirmed repeatedly by the tradition's masters, including Shinran:

> It is difficult to meet and difficult to hear the teaching of the Buddhas. It is difficult to hear the excellent teachings of the bodhisattvas – the *pāramitās*. It is also difficult to meet a true teacher, hear the teaching, and put it into practice.[3]

Śākyamuni was often reduced to silence, sometimes because he didn't think certain topics were relevant – for example, how the world was created or the 'range' of karma. At other times, he remained reticent when something was too profound or ineffable.

This is certainly the case when it comes to the Pure Land. It too is described as being filled with different coloured lotuses, reflecting the same diversity which was described by Śākyamuni as he pondered the question of how to propagate the dharma, just a few weeks after his enlightenment. The adornments of the Pure Land testify to its perfection as the realm of eternal dharma, transcending anything we can know. Even the most awe-inspiring eloquence cannot convey its full reality.

Although, from Nāgārjuna's time, the Pure Land way has been described as 'the easy path', it has never really been so. Certainly, it is easy to be born in the Pure Land – that is not where the difficulty lies. It's not even the scepticism and derision that often greets followers of this tradition. The predicament presents itself in the concept of 'practice'. People are used to the idea of practice as a set of precepts or tasks which, when carried out, bring about certain results.

There are no such blueprints in the Pure Land approach, where the only tangible spiritual reality is the Name (*myōgō*) – *Namo Amida Butsu*. Furthermore, the Name is the vehicle by which we hear the dharma and awaken to Amida Buddha's shinjin – the cause of ultimate liberation. Having awakened to shinjin, the Name then takes on a new significance: as the expression of shinjin, and as a mark of gratitude.

---

[3] *The Three Pure Land Sūtras (Volume II): The Sūtra of the Buddha of Immeasurable Life*, Shin Buddhism Translation Series, 2009, p.102.

It is extremely rare for this to be immediately obvious to those who seek the Buddha-dharma – hence the difficulty. Yet if this challenge can be surmounted, often through perseverance, the reward is inexpressible and the Jōdo Shinshū way of nembutsu-shinjin can then clearly seen as true, remarkable and unsurpassed.

In order to 'hear' the Name, we need to listen (*chōmon*) carefully, and with dedication – through reading and attending dharma talks, and by thinking about life as we actually experience it, rather than harbouring an idealized image of the way things are supposed to be.

Without doubt, Shinran provided a most skillful vehicle for hearing the Name in these three volumes of verses.

Jōdo Wasan 29
Beings born in the Pure Land in the past, present and future
Are not solely from this world;
They come from buddha-lands throughout the ten quarters
And are countless, innumerable and beyond calculation.

TWO TRUTHS

The phrase 'past, present and future' presents a challenge. For samsāra is ultimately illusory; in reality, neither the past nor the future exist. However, when we understand the Buddhist concept of 'two truths', we can accept that in a conventional, practical and objective sense, the world of time and illusion is tangible, since we are enmeshed in it. Indeed, Nāgārjuna Bodhisattva wrote that the highest truth (*paramārtha-satya*) cannot be expounded unless we have recourse to conventional truth (*saṃvṛti-satya*). All the same, he also said that Nirvāna cannot be realized apart from the highest, transcendent truth.[1]

Time belongs to the realm of conventional truth; the true and fulfilled Pure Land does not. Scientific investigation, technology and social movements – such as the European Enlightenment – may well belong to *saṃvṛti-satya* while having a tenuous relationship to *paramārtha-satya*. It is ridiculous, of course, to dismiss 'worldly truth' as of no value. While it's not 'ultimate', it nevertheless embodies 'truth' of immense practical significance. A good example of this is the science of medicine, which works very much in parallel with the ultimate values of a bodhisattva.

Throughout his writings, Shinran Shōnin constantly alludes to stages of development, especially in his own experience – of ascending from one plane of awareness to another. In doing this, he continues the tradition of working within these 'two truths' at the same time, and moving between them.

---

[1] *Madhyamakāvatāra*, VI, 10. My exposition here is obviously over-simplified. The concept of two truths was expounded by Nāgārjuna Bodhisattva. It is suggested that those who wish to study his thought in greater depth begin with *Nāgārjuna's Philosophy* by K. Venkata Ramanan (Charles E. Tuttle, 1966), recently re-issued by Motlilal Barnasidass.

It can be said that Shin Buddhism belongs to *paramārtha-satya* as ultimate, spiritual truth, in that it certainly leads to transcendence – the Pure Land is 'other-worldly' and untainted by conventional truth. There is nothing illusory about it, although it sometimes seems to lack any objective reality to people without shinjin. That is because it's not possible to know it except by means of the Primal Vow. The fact that it seems very real to us, in contrast to our own evanescent lives, is testimony to the power of Amida's unhindered light (*mugekō*).

And what of those from the 'past, present and future' who enter the Pure Land? Well, with unmatched eloquence, that very phrase testifies to the transition from illusion to enlightenment.

Jōdo Wasan 30
Those who, on hearing Amida Buddha's Name,
Rejoice in it with reverence and praise,
Receive its treasure of virtues;
The great benefit acquired with one utterance is supreme.

CHŌMON

This verse is based on the following passage from the Larger Sūtra:

> The Buddha said to Maitreya: 'If there are persons who, having heard the name of that Buddha, leap and dance with joy, and are mindful of the Buddha even once, know that they receive the great benefit; that is, they acquire the unexcelled virtues'.[1]

The 'great benefit' is, of course, Nirvāṇa. 'Hearing' the Name means that we come to understand that the Name is the call of the Vow of Amida Buddha from the 'other shore' of enlightenment. Becoming aware of our entrapment in the round of birth-and-death, we respond to this call in accepting Amida Buddha's shinjin: the mind that is 'single'. Hearing is, therefore, a vital aspect of the Pure Land way.

The condition that assists us to this end is 'deep hearing' (*chōmon*). This facilitates our engagement with the teaching – both intellectually and emotionally – by having us read reflectively, listen attentively to dharma talks, and even struggle with the teaching.

In Jōdo Shinshū, we repeatedly read, recite and contemplate the writings of Shinran, the letters and sayings of Rennyo Shōnin, and the writings of our contemporaries – women and men of shinjin. This does not necessarily imply erudition but, rather, devotion to the task of assimilating the dharma. We may not have access to a temple, owing to isolation or disability, but we can always read.

Chōmon has a clear purpose, and that is to 'hear the Name' disclosed to us by the Primal Vow.

---

[1] *The Three Pure Land Sūtras*, tr. Hisao Inagaki (Revised Second Edition, Numata Center for Buddhist Translation and Research, 2003), p. 101.

> 'Hearing the Name' is not simply hearing it in the ordinary sense of the term. It should be remembered that, when you meet a good spiritual teacher and hear, with deep understanding, the six-character word, *na-mo-a-mi-da-butsu*, this is the entrusting heart of Other-Power, through which you attain birth in the fulfilled land.[2]

Over time, hearing the dharma awakens an engagement, a 'holding fast' to the Name: adoring it, saying it, contemplating it, and living it.

'Holding fast to the Name' is not mere repetition, but signifies the working of the Buddha's virtue, along with the power of the Vow:

> The *Smaller Sūtra* states: 'Hold steadfast to [the Name]'. 'Steadfast' means that the mind is firm and unchanging. 'Hold' means not being distracted and not letting go. Hence the sense of 'never becoming confused'. 'Hold steadfast' is thus the mind that is single. The mind that is single is shinjin.[3]

Having 'heard' the Name, we find ourselves saying it. Hearing – *shinjin* – bursts forth from us as *Namo Amida Butsu*; an expression of the adoration and trust that fills our hearts.

---

[2] *Letters of Rennyo. A Translation of Rennyo's Gobunshō*, Shin Buddhism Translation Series, Hongwanji International Center, 2000, p. 51.
[3] CWS, p. 315.

Jōdo Wasan 31
*Those who hear the Buddha's Name –
Going even through flames that fill
The great thousandfold world to do so –
Attain forever the stage of non-retrogression.*

MAHĀSĀHASRA LOKADHĀTU

The great thousand-fold cosmos (Sk. *mahāsāhasra lokadhātu*) refers to the entire universe which is on fire because of the thirst (Sk. *tṛṣṇā*) fuelled by our ignorance (Sk. *avidyā*). This is experienced as suffering (Sk. *duḥkha*) and few of us need to be convinced about this.

We are reminded in this verse of the *Fire Sermon*[1], which was made popular by the American poet Thomas Stearnes Eliot, in a poem of that name. It refers to the popular *Āgama*[2] collection of sūtras in which the Buddha taught that our minds, bodies and the world are on fire. This is especially poignant because the imagery used is a powerful metaphor for the destructive nature of greed and anger.

The Larger Sūtra describes the 'five burnings' which result from the way in which we get trapped in a world of greed, anger and folly. This is not a moral judgement but a patent truth. We cannot escape the fact that we are net consumers. We cannot live but by using more resources than we put back.

To live we must take life. For example, if we are infected with bacteria which threaten our lives, our body's immune system destroys these living organisms in their billions. Our very existence is a consuming blaze. Seeing how hard it is for us to put out a fire when we, ourselves, are aflame, Amida Buddha contrived to become the Name so as to reach into our burning hearts and douse them – like cooling rain does to a raging wildfire.

---

[1] "O monks, everything is burning ... With what is it burning? It is burning with the fire of passion, the fire of hatred, the fire of delusion. I declare that it is burning with the fire of birth, decay, death, grief, lamentation, pain, sorrow and despair." *Saṃyutta Nikāya* (IV.19).
[2] The *Āgama* sutras are a collection of short discourses from the Sarvāstivāda school, which is no longer extant.

Namo Amida Butsu – the soothing breeze of the dharma whispering to us to trust in the Buddha, so that the fire's progress is arrested. This then allows the residual fuel of our karma to exhaust itself and, when it's all burnt away, it leaves behind only the serene pure joy of Nirvāna.

Jōdo Wasan 32
The Buddhas, infinite in number, all praise Amida,
Whose majestic powers are boundless;
From the eastern Buddha lands, countless as the sands of the Ganges,
Innumerable bodhisattvas go to pay homage.

GANGA

The Ganga is a great river of the plains of northern India. Although officially, as well as popularly, called *Ganga* – both in Hindi and in other Indian languages – internationally it is known by its Anglicized name, 'the Ganges'. From time immemorial, it has been the holy river of the Hindus. For most of its course, it is a wide and sluggish stream, flowing through one of the most fertile and densely populated tracts of territory in the world. Despite its importance, its length of 1,560 miles (2,510 kilometres) makes it relatively short by both world and Asian standards.

Rising in the Himalayas and emptying into the Bay of Bengal, it drains a quarter of the territory of India, while its basin supports an immense concentration of people. The Gangetic Plain, across which it flows, is the heartland of the region known as Hindustan and has been the cradle of successive civilizations from the kingdom of Aśoka in the 3rd century BC, down to the Mughal Empire, founded in the 16th century.

For most of its course the Ganges flows through Indian territory, although its large delta in the Bengal area lies mostly in Bangladesh. The general direction of the river's flow is from north-northwest to southeast. At its delta, the flow is generally southward.[1]

Everyone knows the Ganges, even if we have not been to visit it. In Buddhist teaching, its sandy shores are a popular metaphor for calculations that are close to infinite. It's a rather unremarkable river but it has sustained the cradle of the civilization that gave us the Buddha-dharma, to say nothing of its venerable history. The Ganges are the great hero in the saga of the subcontinent's settlement by Indo-Europeans moving in from the Caucasus. The other branch of these ethnic groups invaded most of Europe and became the Slavic, Germanic and Celtic (Gallic) civilizations.

---

[1] 'Ganges River', *Encyclopædia Britannica*.

In the centuries leading up to the time of Śākyamuni, the terrain stretching from the banks of the river into the Himalayas was the arena for the development of Upanishadic thought. This laid the foundation of not only later Hinduism – now one of the largest religions in the world – but also of our own Buddhist movement.

The Ganges is a telling symbol for it serves to remind us of the two great impulses in religion. The first is the tendency towards ritual. This is seen in the belief that carrying out ritual acts absolves the soul from enduring karmic liability, and frees it from endless entanglement in samsāra. The classic example is ritual bathing. Countless devotees find spiritual relief in such actions and it's not for us to gainsay them.

However, the way of the Buddha repudiates all ritual practices. Indeed, it was Śākyamuni who mused aloud that if water of the Ganges had the power to remove evil karma, then even tortoises and fish would soon find liberation.

The Buddha-dharma is a religion of the heart and mind. It's not so much what we do that is of primary importance, but how we think and feel.

> Preceded by perception are mental states,
> For them is perception supreme,
> From perception have they sprung.
> If, with perception polluted,[2] one speaks or acts,
> Thence suffering follows
> As a wheel the draught ox's foot.
>
> Preceded by perception are mental states,
> For them is perception supreme,
> From perception they have sprung.
> If, with tranquil perception, one speaks or acts,
> Thence ease follows
> As a shadow that never departs.[3]

Words, ritual, accidents of birth – none of these can break the thrall of samsāra. Only Amida Buddha's shinjin can strike at the ingrained illusions that govern our lives.

---

[2] 'Polluted' is also translated as 'blind passions'; the *akuśala kleśas* which include anger, greed and folly.
[3] *The Dhammapada*, Oxford World's Classics, p. 3.

Jōdo Wasan 33
Bodhisattvas of the Buddha lands in the nine other quarters
Likewise go to pay homage to Amida;
Śākyamuni Tathāgata has taught in verse
The praise of the Buddha's immeasurable virtues.

WHY IS AMIDA BUDDHA'S PURE LAND IN THE WEST?

Amida Buddha is the ultimate refuge of all beings – even of bodhisattvas and other Buddhas – and is always spoken of as being in the 'western quarter'. Is this a primitive view of the cosmos based on the naïve ideas of pre-scientific peoples?

> Contemplating the features of that world, I see that it transcends the three realms.[1] It is infinite, like space, vast and boundless.[2]

The Pure Land is not a heaven of any kind as it transcends the world of desire (Sk. *kāma-dhātu*) where the heavens are found. It does not belong to anything the unenlightened can know, except to the extent that it's described in visual terms which represent deathless values. The graphic descriptions of the 'transformed Buddha-lands', as found in the sūtras, are intended to dismantle our prejudices and lead us to truth by way of attraction. This is simply the obverse of the negative methodology which is used in other schools of the dharma.

> Monks and laypeople of this latter age, and the masters of these days, drowned in the concepts of 'one's self-nature [being identical with Buddha]' and '[all that exists is in] one's mind,' despise true enlightenment in the Pure Land.[3]

Why then is the Pure Land of Amida Buddha repeatedly described as being specifically in the west?

Śākyamuni exhorted his disciples to begin each day by paying reverence

---

[1] The three realms are: (i) *ārūpya-dhātu* (the 'realm of no form'), which includes boundless space; (ii) *rūpa-dhātu* (the 'realm of subtle form'), which includes the *dhyānas*, or meditative states; and (iii) *kāma-dhātu* (the 'realm of desire'), which includes human beings, heavens, gods, fighting spirits and the hells.
[2] Vasubandhu Bodhisattva, CWS, p.191.
[3] *Kyōgyōshinshō: On Teaching, Practice, Faith, and Enlightenment* by Shinran, tr. Hisao Inagaki, BDK English Tripiṭaka, p. 83.

to the four directions of the compass, along with the zenith and nadir. Each of these directions, it is said, represents a particular kind of human relationship. North, for example, is 'the way of a man and his friend'.

The west, however, is the direction which reminds us of domestic or conjugal relationships. Does Amida Buddha stand in the west because his way is that of householders? It is doubtful, since the Larger Sūtra itself is addressed to *sthaviras* ('elders' or senior monks) as well as to bodhisattvas.

If we had the time, we would find our answer by standing outside and looking at the sky for twenty-four hours. Assuming it is clear, and we started watching in the morning, we would see the sun rise before moving towards the west. Then the great and glorious procession of the moon, planets, stars and galaxies also begin to move westwards.

Amida's Pure Land is in the west. This verse celebrates the Larger Sūtra's description of all enlightened beings – and those on the path – moving like the sun, the stars and the moon, inexorably towards the west. Likewise, the ultimate destination of the entire mass of uncountable beings is Amida Buddha's Pure Land which, for Shinran, is tantamount to Nirvāna.

It seems to me that the idea of Nirvāna as the inexorable, inevitable, natural and ultimate destiny of all beings has its antecedents in the ancient ultra-orthodox school of Buddha-dharma known as the 'Completion of Truth' (Sk. *satyasiddhi*). Although extinct now, this school is considered to have been deeply faithful to the very earliest teaching of the Buddha.

Like the planets (from the Greek *planetai*, 'wanderers'; *saṃsāra* also means 'wandering') we may go on being lost indefinitely but, sooner or later, we'll arrive at the Pure Land. If, in this life, Amida Buddha's shinjin becomes settled for us, this event will only be a heartbeat away.

Jōdo Wasan 34
The countless bodhisattvas throughout the ten quarters,
To cultivate roots of virtue,
Revere and praise Amida in song;
Let us all take refuge in the Bhagavat.

THE THREE TREASURES

Whoever we are, if we truly appreciate the extraordinary power of Amida's dharma, it is impossible not to praise him. Amida Buddha is the object of our refuge.

Followers of each of the '84,000' dharma paths take refuge in the Buddha (the awakened one), the dharma (the teaching) and the sangha (the community of monks and nuns). In a community like ours, which even transcends the 84,000 paths, and does not have a monastic clergy, how are we to interpret this?

Obviously, the Buddha is Amida. Perhaps we could say that the dharma is that which proclaims his Primal Vow (*hongan*); namely, the three Pure Land sūtras. Our sangha could be seen to comprise the teachers of the lineage – awakened sages known as the 'seven dharma masters'. They are Nāgārjuna (c. 2nd–3rd century), Vasubandhu (4th century), T'an-luan (476-572), Tao-ch'o (562–645), Shan-tao (613–681), Genshin (942–1017) and Hōnen (1133–1202). When we adore the Buddha, we can see ourselves as taking refuge in the dharma and this sangha as well.

In modern times, the word 'sangha' has come to be used, in the broader sense, for a group of like-minded people who follow the dharma. This is probably because that was, indeed, its original meaning, which did not have an exclusively religious significance. However, in the Buddhist context, its use is traditionally limited to the order of monks and nuns; more specifically, to enlightened sages (Sk. *arhats*).

When the government attempted to suppress the nembutsu in 1207, Shinran was given a layman's name and officially excluded from the sangha. Thereafter, he declared himself to be 'neither a monk, nor one in worldly life'[1]. In keeping with the tradition he established, Jōdo Shinshū

---

[1] CWS, p. 289.

clergy are not usually monks or nuns. They are men and women who are destined to lead congregations as their ministers.

There are also ordinary lay people, like me, who wish to make a deeper personal – but formal – commitment to study and teach the way handed down by Shinran Shōnin. These latter are potentially qualified to lead congregations, if called upon to do so, but may choose a life committed to the dharma while holding down another occupation, profession or trade.

Shinran married and raised a family, not I think in deliberate violation of the precepts, but because he had become aware of the universal relevance of the Pure Land way and that it was appropriate to live as an 'ordinary person' (Sk. *bombu*, Sk. *pṛthagjana*).[2] Rather than being a sangha, the Jōdo Shinshū order is effectively a lay community (*kyōdan*).

Shinran himself tends to use the term *sangha* in its traditional Buddhist sense, meaning the monastic order – not in connection with fellow followers on the nembutsu path (*on-dōbō, on-dōgyō*):

> The three treasures are: first the Buddha-treasure; second, the dharma-treasure; third, the sangha-treasure. The present 'Pure Land school' belongs to the Buddha-treasure.[3]

The use of an elite concept like 'sangha' to describe our *kyōdan* does not sit well with the fine sense of equality, common humanity and fellowship that prevails amongst those *bombu* who know and share the embrace of Amida Buddha's compassion.

---

[2] According to Professor Peter Masefield's study of the *Nikāyas* in *Divine Revelation in Pāli Buddhism* (London: George Allen and Unwin, 1986), Śākyamuni's original intention for the sangha was to establish a group of elite or superior (Sk. *aryan*) sages that did not include *pṛthagjanas*.
[3] CWS, p. 534.

Jōdo Wasan 35
The hall and bodhi-tree of seven precious materials
Belong to the Pure Land of the transformed Buddha-body,
  a provisional means;
Numberless are the beings born there from throughout the ten quarters,
So pay homage to the sacred hall and bodhi-tree.

A SAFETY NET?

Thus, Shinran Shōnin calls upon us to offer our appreciation for the existence of *keshindo* – the transformed land. This is a realm in which the ineffable light of the real Buddha cannot be directly apprehended. The true Pure Land (*Nirvāṇa*) is the destination of those for whom Amida Buddha's shinjin has become settled. Instead of being something unstable, dependent on the vicissitudes of mood and limited capacity, it's a joyful, firm and settled entrusting – clearly not of our making.

True shinjin is, frankly, impossible for ordinary people. Unshakeable belief can be an immature neurotic clinging to 'views' – a reinforcement of identity and self-centredness. When settled entrusting arises in us, we are touched by Amida's wisdom, our birth in the fulfilled land is settled here and now, our take on life is transformed and – although we may not become better or more intelligent – we eventually pass on to the true Pure Land. It's as difficult for us to awaken true shinjin as it is to conceive of the Buddha's realm of immeasurable light.

The *keshindo* is described in fine detail in the Contemplation Sūtra, one of the foundational Pure Land texts. Its quasi-physical features – such as jewelled bodhi trees, celestial music, and a myriad delicate fragrances – are presented as splendidly magnificent. Yet this realm is not the true Buddha-land; but neither is it false or unreal. Since true shinjin cannot be generated by such imperfect and unwise beings as us, it's where most of us will end up by default.

There are two ways in which to be born there. One is by means of the Nineteenth Vow of Amida Buddha, which is outlined – according to Shinran – in the Contemplation Sūtra. This includes both meditative and non-meditative good, such as practicing generosity and avoiding the ten bad actions. Then there is the path of the Twentieth Vow (the 'True Gate'), which is the exclusive recitation of the nembutsu with a self-power attitude. From the point of view of the Buddha-dharma, there is simply no way to transcend samsāra except by overcoming our 'self' – which is ultimately illusory and false. Yet it's in our nature to think that by doing something we can initiate a particular outcome that's favourable to us. Indeed, this is the law of cause and effect which is central to the Buddha's teaching. However, Śākyamuni also taught that 'if there is no cause, there can be no result' and 'seeds not sown do not bear fruit.' So, we continue in our practices and striving, and decline the offer extended to us by Amida Buddha. The exclusive practice of nembutsu does not bring release if it's still 'our' practice:

> Truly we know that those who perform single praxis with a combined mind do not attain great joy. Hence, the master [Shan-tao] states:
>
> 'Such people do not realize the Buddha's benevolence and do not respond in gratitude to it; though they perform practices, they give rise to contempt and arrogance in their hearts. For they act always for the sake of fame and profit; they have been enveloped in self-attachment unawares, and do not approach fellow practicers and true teachers; preferring to involve themselves in worldly affairs, they obstruct themselves and block others from the right practice for birth.'[1]

The *keshindo* or 'temporary' Pure Land is certainly an option; especially for those who simply cannot bring themselves to abandon all self-effort, including – paradoxically – their own beliefs. But it's a pity not to accept the means, made available by Amida Buddha, so that we may leave behind this world of birth-and-death. Thanks to the efforts of Shinran, the choice is clearly laid out before us. The temporary Pure Land is a kind of prison that accommodates our trepidation; but it impedes our complete abandonment to the Primal Vow, and thwarts our intended spiritual destiny.

---

[1] CWS, p. 239.

Jōdo Wasan 36
The wondrous land, vast beyond measurement,
Is made up of adornments fulfilled through the Primal Vow;
So bow down to and take refuge in Amida,
The pure one who broadly grasps all beings.

THE PURE ONE WHO BROADLY GRASPS ALL BEINGS

In this verse, Shinran Shōnin is turning his attention to the 'true land' (*shindo*) in contrast to the 'transformed land' (*keshindo*). For him, the true land is exquisite because it's the realm of pure light. Those born there realize ultimate truth, wisdom (Sk. *prajñā*) and freedom (Sk. *mokṣa*).

> With regard to the true land, the Larger Sūtra says, 'Land of Immeasurable Light'. Also, another sūtra[1] says, 'Land of Wisdom'. The discourse [by T'an-luan] says, 'infinite like space, broad and boundless'.

> With regard to birth, the Larger Sūtra says: 'All enjoy the body of naturalness and voidness, and the body of limitlessness.'[2]

There can be no doubt that Shinran's understanding of what the Pure Land really is, as expounded throughout the centuries, convinced him that it was, in fact, synonymous with Nirvāna. After all, he speaks of it in terms such as 'exquisite', 'vast', 'immense' and 'limitless'. Such an attainment is only possible for those who have reached the highest stages of realization. And yet, at the moment shinjin is settled – because of its transcendent freedom from self – aspirants are certain of this same realization, in spite of their penetrating awareness of themselves as base and lowly, destined for the realm of hell (*jigoku*).

The true buddha land is boundless, reflecting the immeasurable condition of voidness (*śūnyatā*); it accommodates a countless multitudes of beings, as we shall see in the next two verses. The 'pure, magnanimous embracer'[3] has provided an infinitely vast realm for all – taking in every being, no matter how defiled they may be.

---

[1] *Nirvāna Sūtra*
[2] Ryūkoku Translation Series V, p.156.
[3] *Gāthā in Praise of Amida Buddha* (No.33) by T'an-luan.

When the light that is Amida brings us to see the truth of own reality, it often happens that only then are we completely free to accept the Buddha's embrace. Stripped of prejudices, and naked before our own ugliness, we come to know a warm, expansive love and compassion at the heart of life which envelops and takes us in, despite our broken condition.

Nothing is needed – just acceptance of this encompassing, benevolent light. At that point, despair becomes joy and light fills our lives; the Pure Land then becomes a genuine reality which we love to contemplate.

> In the *Hymns [on the Samādhi] of All Buddhas' Presence*, Shan-tao, the Master of Kuang-ming temple, explains that the heart of the person of shinjin already and always resides in the Pure Land.[4]

---

[4] CWS, p.528.

Jōdo Wasan 37
*Amida's self-benefit and benefit of others have been perfectly fulfilled as
  the Pure Land,
The compassionate means skillfully adorned to lead us to take refuge.
It cannot be grasped by the mind or by words,
So take refuge in the Honoured-one beyond conceptual understanding.*

COMPASSIONATE MEANS

The Buddha-dharma is ultimate truth. The features of the Pure Land we find detailed in the sūtras all signify aspects of the dharma and unconditioned reality.

> For example, some hear the sound of 'Buddha', some hear the sound of 'Dharma', some 'Sangha'; others hear 'tranquility', 'emptiness and non-self', 'great compassion', '*pāramitā*', 'ten powers', 'fearlessness', 'special qualities', 'supernatural powers', 'non-activity', 'neither arising nor perishing', 'insight into the non-arising of all dharmas' ... [1]

The Buddha's method – 'compassionate means' – is to awaken us from our stupor and to have us face, in a gentle way, those things we may not want to hear. For these teachings do confront us with unpleasant realities. Take the four seals of the dharma, for example. These are the basic 'facts of life': non-self (*anātman*), impermanence (*anitya*), suffering (*duḥkha*), and that complete felicity can only be found in *Nirvāṇa*.

These are not, usually, palatable ideas. Do we like to be told, when we're happy, that everything is fleeting?

Truth is very often unwelcome, but there's nothing more important for our own spiritual, mental and sometimes even physical health. Indeed, it's common for us to go into denial when faced with insights that are unsettling.

The adornments of the Pure Land are not its essential reality. They are presented in such a manner so as to depict Nirvāna – its eternity and bliss – in ways that are familiar to ordinary people. Hence, it is the essential

---

[1] Hisao Inagaki, *The Three Pure Land Sūtras: A Study and Translation* (Kyoto: Nagata Bunshodo, 2000), p. 262.

nature of the Pure Land – Nirvāna – that matters, and it's from the call of the Primal Vow that our hope of being born there arises.

Jōdo Wasan 38
The Buddha's majestic power and Primal Vow –
Fulfilled, luminous, resolute and ultimate –
Are means of compassion beyond conceptual understanding,
So take refuge in Amida, the truly immeasurable one.

THE PRIMAL VOW

This verse is the second time we encounter a reference to the Primal Vow (*hongan*, Sk. *pūrva-praṇidhāna*). It is 'primal' because it's fundamental to Amida Buddha's *raison d'être*; because it's inherent to the 'scheme of things'; because it's the enunciation of wisdom and compassion; because it's the first bodhisattva vow ever made; because it's the 'model' vow; because it arose as a coeval response to the root causes of suffering and to our samsāric bondage; and, not least, because it's in keeping with truth.

The Primal Vow is the natural response to our existential distress; it drove Śākyamuni Buddha to seek enlightenment; it moved the gods to plead with him to teach what he had found by having him return to suffering humanity; it's the power and motive that caused him to rise up from the enjoyment of his enlightenment and return to the world of anguish for the sake of all beings; it's the reason why we seek religion; it's the impulse and longing that we experience when, after striving for countless aeons, we come at last to seek birth in the Pure Land.

Eventually, the Primal Vow emerges in our consciousness as *Namo Amida Butsu*; it confers entrusting in the Name that foreshadows our ultimate enlightenment.

The universe has no creator apart from its constituent parts; when the wheel of karma is set in motion, so may its antidote arise. There is nothing but cause-and-effect (Sk. *pratītya-samutpāda*). It is a natural law of being and consciousness.

The Primal Vow was disclosed by Śākyamuni Buddha in the Larger Sūtra, and is detailed – in all its fullness – through the forty-eight vows of Amida Buddha. The Eighteenth Vow is considered to encapsulate their quintessence. In order to demonstrate the precise import of the Primal Vow, Shinran Shōnin identified five of the forty-eight Vows as the epitome of them all.

- **Vow 11**: If, when I attain Buddhahood, the humans and devas in my land should not dwell in the stage of the truly settled and necessarily attain Nirvāna, may I not attain the perfect enlightenment.
- **Vow 12**: If, when I attain Buddhahood, my light should be finite, not illuminating even a hundred thousand *koṭis* of *nayutas* of Buddha-lands, may I not attain the perfect enlightenment.
- **Vow 13**: If, when I attain Buddhahood, my life should be finite, limited even to a hundred thousand *koṭis* of *nayutas* of *kalpas*, may I not attain the perfect enlightenment.
- **Vow 17**: If when I attain Buddhahood, the countless Buddhas throughout the worlds in the ten quarters should not all glorify and praise my name, may I not attain the perfect enlightenment.
- **Vow 18**: If, when I attain Buddhahood, the sentient beings of the ten quarters who, with sincere and entrusting heart, aspire to be born in my land and say my name even ten times, should not be born there, may I not attain the perfect enlightenment. Excluded are those who commit the five grave offences and who slander the right Dharma.[1]

Bodhisattva vows are made by all who aspire to become buddhas. The *Daśabhūmika Vibhāṣā* of Nāgārjuna outlines the process. There are ten formal vows and bodhisattvas may add their own special vows. On doing so, they awaken the enlightening mind (*bodhicitta*), leave the state of an ordinary person (*bombu*), and enter the 'stage of joy' (*pramuditā*). On departing this life, they commence an existence that transcends samsāra. All this arises from having realized the 'equality of all dharmas' – emptiness – which is absolute and universal compassion.

Such a selfless awakening for us ordinary beings is unfathomable, because its power is unlimited. Before it we can only stand in awe, abandon all our conceit, and entrust ourselves to its embrace.

---

[1] *The Three Pure Land Sūtras (Volume II): The Sūtra of the Buddha of Immeasurable Life*, Shin Buddhism Translation Series, 2009, pp. 21-22.

Jōdo Wasan 39

The delicate, wondrous sounds of jewel-trees in the jewel-forests
Produce natural music, serene and consonant;
Unexcelled in subtlety, pathos, grace and elegance.
So take refuge in the Music of Purity.

PURE MUSIC

Perhaps *saṃvṛti-satya* – the worldly aspect of the 'two truths' – affords an opportunity to assist us in the movement towards liberation. The two truths work in a synergy. The dharma constantly descends into the world of illusion and wandering for the sake of suffering beings. So music, too, has a place in the scheme of salvation and liberation. In keeping with the sūtras, Shinran here expounds the meaning of the transformed land (*keshindo*), which represents the ideal realm of dharma. And music is one of these instruments of spiritual awakening.

In the world, music describes a plethora of genres: classical, jazz, rap, rock, dance, and swing, all of which have a huge repertoire of sounds and structures. In the Buddha-dharma, however, the purpose of music is to encourage in us a reflective, calm and joyful disposition so that we can deepen our understanding.

Much music of the nineteenth century (the 'romantic' era) is delightful and very much to be celebrated. Those of us who love music are fortunate that – as well as the stirring, enchanting and moving pieces that we so much enjoy – there is also a class of music within our very own tradition that resembles the description of music in the Pure Land: 'natural' and 'serene', replete with 'pathos', 'grace' and 'elegance'.

The music of Johann Sebastian Bach (1685-1750) comes close in the sense that it is calm, balanced, harmonious, joyful and conducive to introspection. In our times, the music of Philip Glass (b. 1937) strikes me as being both exquisite and contemplative; it always prompts me to reflect on my *bonnō* and on the distance that separates us from the pure music of *keshindo* while, at the same time, helping me to focus my heart and mind on something ineffable.

The primary musical form in the Buddhist dispensation is the chanting of the Buddha's teachings (and those of other sages in the tradition). Sometimes musical instruments are used in Buddhist orchestras to convey the same themes that we find in the sūtras: emptiness, not-self, compassion, peace, harmony and joy.

Jōdo Wasan 40
Trees of seven precious materials fill the land,
Mutually reflecting each other's brilliance;
The flowers, fruits, branches, and leaves all shine thus,
So take refuge in Amida, the store of virtues fulfilled through the Primal Vow.

THE RELIGION OF THE FOREST

Long before the appearance of Śākyamuni almost 2,500 years ago, Indian religion had become the religion of the forest. Those who revealed the *Upanishads* – to which the yogic tradition that became the Buddha-dharma owes its foundation – were sages who had withdrawn from conventional society. Contemplation, education, music, medicine and the arts were pursued in the sacred depths of a forest. Śākyamuni realized the dharma and attained enlightenment beneath the leafy branches of a forest tree.

Usually, it is held that civilization belongs to the sophisticated life of cities but, in keeping with its Indian antecedents, the Buddha-dharma views this kind of 'civilization' with suspicion. The life of cities is noisy, unbalanced, subject to artificial forms of control: places of corruption, vice and disease. True cultivation takes place in the depth of shady forests, in relative solitude and silence.

Śākyamuni always taught out in wild places, such as forests, or in a garden (the latter in which he himself was born). When the time came for him to seek the truth, he left the city and went to live away from the artifice and distractions of urban life.

Throughout its history, the Buddhist sangha has always preferred the forest as its home, emerging into the villages and towns only occasionally but always forsaking these places as a home. It is the place to which those embroiled in the derangement of the city – 'civilized' life – go for refuge. If it's not possible to be removed from the city, Buddhist sanghas will usually surround themselves with reminders of the wilderness by creating leafy, shady gardens. Trees form the great symbols of the dharma. The bodhi tree under which Śākyamuni sat, when he was enlightened, has been planted throughout the Buddhist world for 25 centuries. Other trees, like tamarisk and ginkgo, are also associated with the dharma.

Seven hundred years ago, however, the sangha suffered a fatal degeneration – at least that is how Shinran saw it. Thanks to Amida Buddha's Primal Vow, the dharma now became, through the nembutsu, accessible to all: monks, nuns, laywomen and laymen ... even those who fell completely outside the dharma. The way of the city had become unavoidable, and we had lost the pristine and hallowed precinct of the sacred forest.

In the nembutsu, the Buddha calls to us wherever we are – no matter how busy, no matter how caught up in secular life. Shin temples can be found at the heart of city and village life, reaching into the confusion, noise and often vicious environment of such places. Proving that the Buddha's light is indeed 'unhindered throughout the ten quarters'.

Jōdo Wasan 41
Pure winds blow in the jewel-trees,
Producing the five tones of the scale.
As those sounds are harmonious and spontaneous,
Pay homage to Amida, the one imbued with purity.

THE COMPLEXITY OF BEING

The way we see or hear things – our disposition when confronted with ideas, events and people – can have profound repercussions. Our spontaneous reactions can rebound not only throughout our own lives, but also in those of countless others.

Many people suffer indelible scars because a particular occurrence caught them at a vulnerable moment. The same circumstance can induce a reaction in us of either attraction or repulsion, just because of the mood we are in or as a result of other factors such as smell, sound, ill-health or irritability. The same 'innocent' remark from a friend can sometimes cause us to respond with anger or laughter, depending on how we may feel about ourselves at the time. Like a chime of bells, we're each made up of complex variants that sometimes mesh and, at other times, clash. We all tend to move gently between 'highs' and 'lows'.

The *five notes* may be seen as an allegory for the transformation of the 'five aggregates' or *skandhas*. The first is *rūpa-skandha* – form. It comprises all material objects, including the great elements of earth, water, air, fire and their derivatives. The second is *vedanā* – sensation. This is the 'interface' between the external world and our consciousness. Then there is *saṃjñā-skandha*, which is perception; the way sensations are received and interpreted. It is where errors of judgement give rise to mistaken reactions. Fourth is *saṃskāra* or the will. It is at this point that karma is produced. In themselves, sensations and perception do not generate karmic results – it is how we respond to them that matters. Finally, the fifth group is called *vijñāna-skandha* or consciousness.

In the transformed Pure Land (*keshindo*), the 'hot' complexities of personality – warmed up as they are by greed, anger and folly – are assuaged by the pure breeze of the dharma, as Shinran describes it in this *wasan*.

One of the most striking things about the transformed Pure Land is how it sets up an image of ultimate reality, an environment in which the dharma holds total sway. It is completely absent of greed, anger and folly and so the perception of forms (and the resultant response) is entirely sweet and harmonious – infused with wisdom and compassion. This likeness serves to make clear to us that our current existence in samsāra is entirely discordant and inharmonious, both within the confines of our own being and of our environment.

The dharma realm of the Pure Land is truthful and harmonious, whereas the world of our current experience is replete with lies, illusion, distortion and hostile competing interests.

Jōdo Wasan 42
Beams of light, thirty-six hundred
Thousand billion in number,
Shine brilliantly from within each flower;
There is no place they do not reach.

MANY LIGHTS

The rays of light streaming from the flowers in the transformed Pure Land show how its effects extend beyond its transcendent nature and out into our realm of desire and ignorance. We see here one way in which the inconceivable karmic power of the Buddha – resulting from his Vow and aeons of pure practices – can overcome the snares of this illusory world in which we find ourselves. *Light*, as we already know, is the wisdom of the Buddha making itself manifest in the lives of the unenlightened.

The metaphor of flowers – as the source of the light beams – reveals to us the countless ways in which the dharma is apprehended, as well as the limitless variety of people who listen and respond.

A prime example of the complex and specific nature of the dharma's approach to us is Shinran Shōnin. He explains his personal path in the final section of the *Kyōgyōshinshō*, which we know as 'turning through three vows' (*sangan tennyū*). Yet, there is only one *shinjin* ('entrusting heart') and one enlightenment, so the endpoint is always the same despite the diversity of ways in which the dharma nurtures us.

Sangan tennyū describes how we work through the Nineteenth, Twentieth and Eighteenth vows of Amida Buddha. We will consider this in more depth when we encounter it again, later in the *Jōdo Wasan*. For the moment, it serves to illustrate the way in which the Primal Vow accommodates different levels of spiritual development.

In Shinran's view, the Nineteenth Vow is explicitly outlined in the Contemplation Sūtra. This is the 'essential gate' of good behaviour and meditation. Shinran began his quest as a diligent monk but eventually abandoned this approach, turning instead to the 'true way' of the Twentieth Vow, which conforms to the requirements of the Amida Sūtra (based on reciting the nembutsu with effort).

Shinran locates his arrival at the threshold of the Eighteenth – and ultimate – Vow in the year 1201, which is when he met Hōnen Shōnin. This is the 'Vow of shinjin' since nembutsu and it are inseparable. Shinran however, did not advocate *sangan tennyū* as a formal undertaking. In fact, he encourages us to abandon the first two ways because they are provisional and expedient, leading to birth in transformed pure lands – not the 'birthless birth' of the true Pure Land of Nirvāna.

The course by which Shinran moved towards the ultimacy of this 'Great Vow of Merit Transference' (abandoning self-effort) does not necessarily have to be our journey in this life. On the other hand, perhaps it could be said that our circumstances have led us to hear the call of the Primal Vow as a result of the fact that, at some stage – either in this life or in the boundless past – we followed the way of the Nineteenth Vow. The dharma approaches us in accordance with our nature and circumstances, just as it drew near to Shinran in his monastic setting where he began to realize that all his efforts were to no avail.

The variety of spiritual methods and human temperaments is measureless, just like the colours of flowers and rays of light in the transformed Pure Land. There are many lights and many ways of seeing.

Jōdo Wasan 43
Buddha-bodies, equal in number
To the thirty-six hundred thousand billion
Beams of light, emerge from each flower;
Their features and marks are like mountains of gold.

HOW TO SPOT A BUDDHA

Generally speaking, mainstream traditions of the Buddha-dharma make a clear distinction between a *pṛthagjana* – an ordinary human being who is steeped in the illusion of samsāra – and a Buddha, who has a threefold knowledge which distinguishes him from average people like us.

It is said that a Buddha

1. sees the details of his own previous births;
2. knows the history of the births and deaths of all other sentient beings; and
3. has gained the liberating insight that brings final release from the whole miserable process of wandering in samsāra.

An ordinary person does not have this knowledge. Furthermore, so that we can know that a Buddha is genuine, he is said to be distinguished by certain external marks and signs. This idea reflects the fact that our mental state is often evident in our outward expression and demeanour.

In this verse, Shinran Shōnin is referring to the 'thirty-two characteristics of a great man' and the 'eighty subordinate marks' of a buddha. Followers of the dharma have never regarded buddhas as common, for they have transcended the limitations of mundane existence. From the very beginning, Śākyamuni was regarded as extraordinary. For about three centuries following the *parinirvāṇa*, his words were not recorded, and his image was not represented.

These features point to exquisite physical beauty and excellent deportment such as a voice like Brahmā's, broad shoulders, well-proportioned and slender legs, and a straight back. The only striking differences, compared to a regular human form, are the *chōjō-nikkei* (Sk. *uṣṇīṣa-śīrṣa*, a slight protuberance on the head), the *miken-byakugō* (Sk. *ūrṇā-keśa*, a twist of hair between the eyebrows which is sometimes mistakenly represented as a 'third eye'), and impressions on his hands and feet that resemble

1. the *svastika*, a well-known and ancient decorative symbol, so sadly misused in the twentieth century;
2. a cruciform flower; and
3. the *nandyāvarta*, a symbol of happiness and joy.

The description of these characteristics and marks may seem rather fanciful. They can, no doubt, only be seen with the eyes of faith, but the idea serves to remind us of the superlative nature of buddhas. So it is that such signs testify to their enlightenment, reliability and trustworthiness.

Jōdo Wasan 44
Each feature and mark releases, throughout the ten quarters,
A hundred thousand beams of light;
Thus the Buddhas constantly teach and spread the excellent dharma
And lead beings onto the Buddha's path.

EFFULGENCE

This verse continues the description of the all-encompassing radiance of the Buddha – and Land – of Immeasurable Light. In addition to the rays of light, which emanate from the flowers in the transformed Pure Land, the 'signs and marks' of the buddhas emerging from these flowers are also radiant with its effulgence. Once again, these are features that pervade the entire illusory realm of samsāra.

As we have already seen, light is wisdom (Sk. *prajñā*) and there is a reason for this seeming hyperbole. It conveys the sheer power of the light in question. Though it is inconceivable, it reaches even into the darkest recesses of ignorance (Sk. *avidyā*), which keeps us bound to samsāra. Wisdom, in the Buddhist sense, is to see this world of birth-and-death as it really is: empty, void and transitory.

Light as a physical reality is not something we can see. What we do see are the things illuminated by it. If there were no objects on which it alighted, its existence would be meaningless. It's not so much that the light itself is relevant to us but, rather, what it discloses. This seems also to be the case for the spiritual life. The light of the Pure Land is so far-reaching that there's nothing in our hearts and minds that it cannot throw into stark relief. If we open ourselves to this light – in the form of the Name (*Namo Amida Butsu*) – a time will come when there'll arise an acute awareness of what we really are. Then, like Shinran, we will relinquish everything about us that's false, entrusting ourselves wholly to the power of the Primal Vow.

> 'To abandon the mind of self-power' admonishes the various and diverse kinds of people – masters of Hīnayāna or Mahāyāna, ignorant beings good or evil – to abandon the conviction that one is good, to cease relying on the self, to stop reflecting knowingly on one's evil heart, and further to stop the judging of people as good or bad. When such shackled foolish beings ... thus wholly entrust themselves to the name

embodying great wisdom, the inconceivable Vow of the
Buddha of unhindered light, then while burdened as they are
with blind passion, they attain the supreme Nirvāna.[1]

To my mind, this passage gives a perfect account of the way in which the ephemeral self is abandoned when it's exposed by the immeasurable light of Amida Buddha. Such awareness is not possible as a result of merely asserting an idea; an imposition from above, as it were. It can only come from a deep-seated realization. A person enmeshed in illusion cannot apprehend the evanescence and futility of the false self by means of their own benighted insight. Only the Buddha's effulgent wisdom, which fills the universe, can bring us to such an understanding.

---

[1] CWS, p.459.

Jōdo Wasan 45
*The jewel-ponds, formed of seven precious materials, are limpid
And brimming with waters of eight excellent qualities;*[1]
*The undefiled adornments of the land surpass conceptual understanding,
So take refuge in Amida, the treasury of virtues.*

WATER

One of the 'three poisons' that mark our existence is greed. It is so powerful that it very often persists even when we've already had more than enough. While most people in the world today are hungry, many of us are gorging ourselves to death. If there is food to be had, then we will have it. The 'pleasure principle' induces us to re-live enjoyable experiences. Modern research has also shown that our survival instinct inclines us to eat just because food is available, even though we may not really need it.

Occasionally people do become aware that 'more is not better'. Some of us realize that acting on greed may exceed a level of satisfaction, to the extent that it causes more suffering. The discomfort of overeating, for example, may feel worse than mild hunger pangs. We may readily stop drinking wine just as we begin to feel that we're losing control, or recall the unpleasantness of a hangover.

In a small way, restraint based on the effects of over-consumption touches on what Śākyamuni meant when he said that 'all existence is suffering' – this includes pleasure. He was reminding us of lessons we already know from experience (but often forget to apply): that craving for what is pleasant can become a prison; it can ensnare us. Unable to resist our urges, we come to lose self-control. This is a form of emotional pain, even if it's not physical.

The Buddha-dharma does not reject pleasure, or enjoyable experiences, but it does warn against the uncontrolled quest for gratification when it becomes an addiction.

The *Fire Sermon*, which we've mentioned earlier, gives a graphic account of the way in which we can become consumed by our desires. Greed is a

---

[1] The eight merits of the water are: good to the stomach, good to the throat, of sweet taste, cool temperature, soft texture, comforting to the senses and pure.

'hot' emotion, and so is anger, for the two are inextricably linked. The failure to satisfy greed leads to anger or, in seeking to assuage it, we strive to eliminate (sometimes violently) whatever gets in the way of us doing so.

The water described in this verse signifies the way in which the realm of Nirvāna serves to quell the hot and raging fires of the heart. And yet these vehement emotions cannot be fully subdued in this life, even though the water of 'eight virtues' can alleviate the worst of their effects. Undeniably, ordinary beings (*bombu*) like us live in a world consumed by greed and anger; something of which we become aware when the light of Amida allows us – with growing acuity – to see ourselves as we truly are.

Jōdo Wasan 46
The afflictions of the three evil courses are forever eliminated,
And only spontaneous, delightful sounds are heard.
For this reason the Buddha's land is called 'Happiness';
So take refuge in Amida, the ultimately honored one.

THE PAIN OF IGNORANCE

This verse tells us that the tormenting nature of the three evil courses (or 'mires') will not be found in the Pure Land. These are the paths of *fire*, *blood* and *sword*. 'Fire' is the realm of hell; 'blood', the realm of animals; and 'sword' refers to the world of hungry spirits.

Unlike our human world – in which it's possible for us, given the right karmic conditions, to come into contact with the wonderful dharma – these mires are totally steeped in ignorance. They are also part of the natural order, and beings such as 'hungry spirits' are living organisms just like us. And yet, they are completely at the mercy of their desires. They represent 'nature red in tooth and claw' to quote the English poet, Alfred Lord Tennyson (1809–1892).

Although some people are squeamish about the idea of hell, I see no reason to suppose that it's an allegorical contrivance. Most major religions espouse an infernal destination after death. And it's not really satisfying either to suggest, as some do, that it's just a metaphor for the ordeals of this (human) existence. Suffering in our realm is bad enough (except, perhaps, for the privileged few whose comfortable circumstances allow them to think that they've somehow escaped it) but existence in hell is far harder to endure because – like animal life and that of hungry spirits – it is steeped in unmitigated spiritual and ethical blindness.

The Buddha-dharma does not necessarily maintain a benign view of the so-called natural world. In fact, it seems to me that the romantic view of nature (which characterizes the European Enlightenment) has become even more entrenched in our time, and betrays the fact that most of us live in cities and have little contact with it.

People who live close to nature have a more realistic view. Nature, like hell, is savage and brutal; ruthless and without mercy. It might be awesome, majestic and complex, but it's certainly not benign.

You only have to watch a female spider consume her offspring, or see the appalling injuries that a playful kitten can inflict on a helpless bird or mouse, or observe a python swallow whole a bleating lamb, or watch the ravages of disease and climatic catastrophes – witness Lake Eyre in central Australia move through its periodic drying phase as innumerable wetland birds and fish gradually starve, dehydrate and suffocate in the unremitting heat. Farmers and pastoralists are all too familiar with the ferocious cruelties of nature.

This, of course, is not to say that we shouldn't respect and revere the wilderness. The dharma urges us to develop compassion for all living things. Buddhists are famous for their kindness to animals, plants – and hungry spirits. In traditional Buddhist countries, such practice is deeply entrenched. In places like Thailand and Sri Lanka, people are eager to feed even hungry spirits in an act of wonderful generosity. Indeed, for the very reason that the 'afflictions of the three evil courses' are so abysmal, our compassion is called upon all the more.

Needless to say, the Buddha-dharma understands the breadth and extent of these afflictions. The central motivation for the Buddha's epic quest to find a 'way out of suffering' is fundamentally driven by a dread of this vast stock of endless suffering – both in terms of time and dimension.

There are many reasons that can prompt us to seek the deliverance offered by the great vehicle of the Dharma; and fortunate are those among us who are blessed with such a powerful dread.

Jōdo Wasan 47
Those of immeasurable wisdom throughout the ten quarters
– past, present, and future –
All, without exception, having grounded themselves in oneness,
Equally attain the enlightenment of perfection in the two aspects of wisdom;
Their salvation of beings according to conditions is beyond conception.

BECOMING WISE

Oneness has many synonyms and we've already encountered most of them in Shinran Shōnin's hymns. Two of these are 'Dharma-nature' and 'Suchness'. Shinran is, of course, referring to the highest reality or things as they are in themselves; not some kind of separate being that's remote from us. In the Pure Land tradition, this is Amida Buddha who is the 'Dharma-Body as Suchness'.[1] All buddhas throughout the universe emerge from this source. Amida is the teacher of all buddhas and, by definition, the well-spring of wisdom and compassion.

Through the perfection of wisdom (*prajñāpāramitā*), buddhas can know ultimate reality and manifest it to others. This vast comprehension extends across the entire range of existing things, beliefs, tendencies and characteristics – in such a way as to identify fully with them, and to disseminate the dharma in the world for the liberation of suffering beings. This is what compassion means in Buddhism.

Those that follow the Path of Sages; that is, who are seeking – or who have awakened – *bodhicitta* (the 'mind of enlightenment') and are entering *pramuditā*, (the first stage of joy), have an obligation to understand the world at large and to grow in transcendent wisdom.

On the Pure Land path, however, true spiritual growth leads to a deepening awareness of our status as *pṛthagjana* – ordinary people who

---

[1] 'In order to make us realize that true Buddhahood is without form, it is expressly called Amida Buddha.' (Ryūkoku Translation Series, Vol VII, p. 117). This is a passage from the *Jinen Hōni Shō*, a letter Shinran wrote late in his life (1258). Here he attests to the identity of Amida Buddha with both the 'Dharma-Body as Suchness' and the 'Dharma-Body as Compassionate Means' (the latter aspect having become the fulfilled body of the Buddha) in several places in his collection of hymns. Amida is both 'supreme Buddha' (Dharma-Body as Suchness), and the 'Buddha with form' (Dharma-Body as Compassionate Means).

are *not* sages. Paradoxically, the wisdom that comes from living in the light of the Buddha and the nembutsu way, is to recognize the full depth of our ignorance. To acknowledge our absolute dependence on the wisdom of the Buddhas, through the power of the Primal Vow, is to be genuinely wise. It is to know the blessedness of deep veracity, and the fulfilment of true insight.

> ... to say that Buddhism does not possess any fixed doctrine is not to say that it has no philosophy. Despite the fact that the content of [Śākyamuni Buddha's] enlightenment has been passed down in a variety of forms, those forms all lead back to one point. Buddhism attempts to bring people to a state of spiritual serenity by having them see themselves as they actually are, not by forcing them to maintain an established creed and dogma, and by enabling them to experience the Dharma in terms of practical existence.[2]

---

[2] *Gotama Buddha: A Biography Based on the Most Reliable Texts* by Hajime Nakamura (Tokyo: Kosei Publishing), Volume 1, p.213.

<u>Jōdo Wasan 48</u>
When we take refuge in the Pure Land of Amida,
We take refuge in all the Buddhas.
To praise the one Buddha, Amida, with the mind that is single
Is to praise all the unhindered ones.

SINGLE-MINDEDNESS

Shinran Shōnin assures us here that we only need to take refuge in Amida Buddha. In doing so, he asserts that all other buddhas are served and praised concurrently. This is because they share the same enlightenment.

The many buddhas signify the universal wisdom and compassion that saturates the universe. The dharma is filled with compassion and support for people of shinjin. Shinran celebrates the fact that nembutsu followers are free to trust entirely in *Namo Amida Butsu*. We do not need to concern ourselves with our 'fate', seeing as our most essential needs have been taken care of since the long-distant past.

Most Buddhists know about the three bodies of the Buddha (Sk. *trikāya*). These are the 'Dharma-Body' (*Dharmakāya*), the 'fulfilled body' (*Saṃbhogakāya*), and the 'accommodated body' (*Nirmāṇakāya*). The Dharma-Body is without colour or form, the fulfilled body can be conceptualized, and the accommodated body is a physical manifestation in our everyday world (such as Śākyamuni Buddha). According to T'an-luan, buddhas have two dharma bodies: the 'Dharma-Body as Suchness' and the 'Dharma-Body as Compassionate Means'. The latter may become a 'fulfilled' or an 'accommodated' body.

Shinran tells us that Amida Buddha is both the Dharma-Body as Suchness (without form) and the Dharma-Body as Compassionate Means, which took form and made vows to liberate beings through the Name. That is why Amida – as the supreme Buddha without form or colour – is the teacher of all buddhas. That is why, if we take refuge in Amida, we are also seeking refuge in all other Buddhas by extension.

The Pure Land tradition has always urged us to wholeheartedly and single-mindedly entrust ourselves to the dharma – to *Namo Amida Butsu* alone. This is a compassionate exhortation given for the sake of our emotional and spiritual health.

The nembutsu way is so spiritually satisfying, emotionally supportive and intellectually rewarding, that Shinran's encouragement to take this path is but an acclamation of an established fact. It's clear to me that he is not scolding but, rather, reassuring us. Those who live according to the nembutsu way do not have an interest in any other form of spiritual life. Shinran is, in effect, saying: "Don't worry, Amida is all that matters". By taking refuge in this Buddha, all our spiritual needs are fulfilled.

Jōdo Wasan 49
When, in even a single thought-moment of sincere mind,
You have attained shinjin and joy, gladdened by what you have heard,
Bow down in homage at the feet
Of the Buddha of Inconceivable Light!

THE FORM OF AMIDA BUDDHA

Human beings are not disembodied spirits. We're a composite of various physical and mental characteristics that are constantly in flux. We also have a natural sense of continuity – which is, paradoxically, integral to our mental well-being. There is nothing we could or should do about it. Since we are foolish beings (*bombu*, Sk. *pṛthagjana*) we need Amida Buddha's entrusting heart as the cause of our rebirth (*ōjō*) – Nirvāna – precisely because we clearly see our limited and unenlightened state. Illusion is not an objective flaw that we acknowledge. It is what we are; it's our reality.

Therefore, we find ourselves incapable of functioning at a purely ethereal or unearthly level. The Pure Land path, especially, recognizes that we cannot be reached by truth itself unless the Dharma-Body takes a form which we can comprehend; in other words, we need an 'embodied' buddha.

Communication with others remains incomplete without the physical presence of those to whom we wish to speak. Facial expressions, voice, demeanour and posture convey much of what we understand the intentions of others to be. Literature has a very important role to play but it's a special form of communication that requires readers to exercise their imagination. There is a considerable gulf between writing and face-to-face contact, which is why the Dharma-Body takes form as *Namo Amida Butsu*.

We all know the power of emotions. Intense anger can break out in violence, desire craves physical contact, gratitude a gift, awe a gasp, happiness a smile. And joy? When we're deeply touched by the unconditional compassion of Amida Buddha; when wonder and gratitude well up in our hearts, what are we to do? As embodied beings we have no other option. In our hearts and voices, Amida Buddha emerges as the Name – *Namo Amida Butsu*. Our hands come together in *gasshō* (Sk. *añjali*), that ageless gesture of adoration that is common to all people.

This sense of joy can be so overwhelming that we want to dance but perhaps, too, our heads will bow in reverence.

And our eyes need to see. The 'principal object' (*honzon*) in Shin Buddhist temples is a form that can be viewed – for example, the image of the Name in ten characters: *ki-myō-jin-jip-pō-mu-ge-kō-nyo-rai* ('Homage to the Tathāgata whose light is unhindered throughout the ten quarters'). It is the focus of veneration; it can be cherished and enjoyed. In this way, the infinite reaches into the intimate domain of creatures like us, who are uniquely characterized by complex speech and language.

Overwhelmed by joy, we call the Buddha to mind, raise our voices to say nembutsu, and join our hands in adoration.

Jōdo Wasan 50
*I praise Amida's wisdom and virtue
So that beings with mature conditions throughout the ten quarters may hear.
Let those who have already realized shinjin,
Constantly respond in gratitude to the Buddha's benevolence.*

THE INFINITE DEBT

When Shinran Shōnin set out to write the *Jōdo Wasan*, he did so from the fullness of his heart. He had already completed his most important work – *Ken Jōdo Shinjitsu Kyōgyōsho Monrui* ('The True Teaching, Practice and Realization of the Pure Land Way'), also known as *Kyōgyōshinshō* and *Honden*. In writing these hymns (*wasan*), Shinran is taking up his brush to compose – not only a personal expression of his joy in the teachings – but also a liturgical form for the use of his followers. Surely then, Shinran intended these hymns to be the main vehicle by which he passed down the Pure Land dharma to posterity.

The hymns were written in the common language of his day and framed in the genre of popular music. They were cast in a rudimentary poetic form, which could easily be committed to memory by ordinary people. The *Kyōgyōshinshō*, on the other hand, is written in the scholarly language of his location and period – literary Chinese, the language of the Buddhist canon.

Not only are the hymns intended for the common folk, but they're full of ideas and concepts that compel our attention. They are not simplistic, child-like verses that pander to intellectual laziness or to a lack of curiosity. They don't necessarily make the dharma 'easy to understand'. They are demanding, and with good reason.

Shinran's teacher, Hōnen, is renowned for an exchange in which he observed that those with whom he discussed the dharma – who were well-educated and sophisticated – were going to have great difficulty in attaining birth in the Pure Land, whereas those with few claims to scholarship and academic achievement were far more likely to awaken shinjin. Furthermore, the Pure Land way – as I have often pointed out – embraces ordinary and foolish people.

Those who truly understand how unwise, morally frail and ignorant they really are, will respond – or so it seems to me – by undertaking a quest for greater wisdom, personal growth and increased awareness. Just like children, we start every day fresh and open to new ideas; always ready to accept change and hungry for more knowledge.

The Pure Land tradition is repeatedly described as 'the way of easy practice' (*igyōbon*) but, in the Larger Sūtra, it's spoken of as 'the most difficult of all things difficult'. However challenging this path may be at first, one's joy and sense of indebtedness is palpable. This feeling of gratitude is, in a sense, the 'practice of shinjin'.

> Those who have already attained Faith
> Should always try to repay His Benevolence.

How is such a debt repaid? Essentially, it is impossible to do so. But, during a troubled time in his life, Shinran developed a very clear understanding of just precisely what form such repayment should take. His wife, Eshin-ni, relates this incident in one of her letters, now preserved in a collection rediscovered in 1923, titled *Eshinni Monjo*.

> From about noon of the 14th day of the fourth month, 3rd year of Kangi, Shinran felt a cold coming on and went to bed in the evening. He became quite ill, but did not let anyone massage his back or legs, and would not let anyone nurse him. He just lay quietly, but when I touched his body, it was burning with fever. He also had a severe headache, something beyond the normal. On the dawn of the fourth day, passed in such a condition, he said in the midst of his great discomfort, 'It must be truly so'. So I asked him, 'What is the matter? Did you say something in your delirium?'
>
> Then he replied, 'No, it's not delirium. Two days after I came to bed, I read the Larger Pure Land Sūtra continuously. Even when I closed my eyes, I could see each character of the sūtra very clearly. How strange, I thought. Thinking that there should be nothing on my mind beside true entrusting, born out of the joy of the nembutsu, I carefully thought about the matter. Then I remembered an incident which occurred seventeen or eighteen years ago, when I began reading the Pure Land sūtras faithfully a thousand times for the benefit of sentient beings. I suddenly realized the grave mistake I was making for, while I truly felt that **the repayment of the Buddha's blessing is to believe the teaching for oneself and then to teach others to believe, as in the saying, 'To believe**

the teaching oneself and make others believe [*ji shin kyō ninshin*] is the most difficult of all difficulties', yet I attempted to read the sūtra as if to complement the saying of the nembutsu which should have been sufficient by itself.

Thus, I stopped reading the sūtra. A similar thought must still have remained, lingering in my mind. Once people begin thinking like this, it's difficult to change. When I realized how difficult it is to get rid of self-generated faith and vowed to be constantly alert about it, there was no longer any need to read the sūtra. And so, on the dawn of the first day in bed, I said 'It must be truly so'. Soon after explaining all this, he perspired profusely and became well.[1]

This account of Shinran's profound physical and spiritual crisis is extremely revealing. The breaking of his fever at the moment he realized that he could now abandon an old habit (i.e. self-power nembutsu) and simply accept Amida Buddha's shinjin, is a remarkable metaphor for his sense of spiritual relief. This passage also clarifies a number of other issues; for one, that saying the nembutsu is the way in which we respond to Amida Buddha's blessing.

---

[1] *The Life of Eshinni, Wife of Shinran Shōnin* by Yoshiko Ōtani – emphasis mine.

Jōdo Wasan 51
Venerable Ānanda, rising from his seat,
Beheld the majestic radiance of the World-honored one;
Amazed, with a rare feeling of wonder emerging in him,
He realized he had never witnessed such radiance before.

THUS HAVE I HEARD

Shinran Shōnin's verses, based on the *San Amida Butsu Ge* of T'an-luan, ended with the fiftieth verse in the *Jōdo Wasan* collection. He now begins a series of hymns based on the three Pure Land sūtras, and some other texts, which throw light on the nembutsu teaching. The next three hymns describe the way in which the Larger Sūtra came to be delivered.

The three Pure Land sūtras (*Jōdo sambukkyō*) were selected by Shinran's teacher, Hōnen Shōnin. They comprise only a very small fraction of the total number of sūtras that deal with Amida Buddha and his Pure Land. In his principal works of exegesis,[1] Shinran makes it clear that the Larger Sūtra contains the key vows of Amida Buddha, especially the Eighteenth or Primal Vow. It also reports on the fulfillment of those vows.

Needless to say, Shinran draws on a wide pool of classical Buddhist literature in his works and does not restrict himself to the textual legacy that he received from Hōnen. In fact, Shinran ventures well beyond the conventional limits of the three Pure Land sūtras. When it comes to the *Sūtra of Contemplation on the Buddha of Immeasurable Life* (Contemplation Sūtra) and the *Sūtra on Amida Buddha* (Smaller Sūtra), he discloses that their meaning is more subtle than is apparent from their literal expression.

In the Larger Sūtra, the vows are considered the 'birth story' (Sk. *jātaka*) of Amida Buddha. Such stories make up a significant part of traditional Buddhist literature and their principal purpose is to affirm, from experience, the working of the law of cause-and-effect[2] and to

---

[1] Shinran's principal systematic works of exegesis are: *Ken Jōdo shinjitsu kyōgyōsho monrui* or 'The True Teaching, Practice and Realization of the Pure Land Way' (more commonly known as *Kyōgyōshinshō*) which was completed in 1247; *Jōdo monrui jushō* or 'Passages on the Pure Land Way' (1255); and *Sangyō ōjō monrui* or 'A Collection of Passages on the Types of Birth in the Three Pure Land Sūtras' (1255).
[2] This law is a cardinal principle of the dharma, without which a teaching cannot be

demonstrate, in a practical sense, how we can become emancipated. In the classical literature, no fewer than fifteen sūtras include a variety of *jātaka* stories concerning the origins of Amida Buddha.

When we read this genre of texts, it's important to remember that the 'validation' of current empirical experience is the starting point. Then the explanatory *jātaka* is derived by working backwards in ways that are constrained by the law of karma. This means that, in the *samādhi* he entered into before delivering the Larger Sūtra, Śākyamuni recalled Amida Buddha, contemplated his characteristics, and then discerned the causes that led to his manifestation.

Until the intrusion of secular humanist ideas into the Buddha-dharma at the behest of nineteenth-century Europeans and Americans, the *jātaka* tales (along with the broader *avadāna* genre) are thought to have been by far the most important kinds of literature. Unless a religious path is validated in a practical sense – as it is in these stories – it remains mere doctrine or philosophy, disengaged from living human experience.

Ānanda was the first person to recite sūtras for approval at the initial Buddhist council (consisting of five hundred enlightened monks) just after Śākyamuni's entry into *parinirvāṇa*. He was the Buddha's cousin and a very important figure in the early Buddhist movement, given his significance as a reliable source regarding its teachings.

The two most important factors in the transmission of sūtras are hearing and receiving. Whether or not they are the actual words of Śākyamuni cannot be determined with complete certainty. In any case, some sūtras would have been based on a form of transcendent realization or mind-to-mind transmission, between the Buddha and his disciples, known as *samādhi*; or on an idea which only had its germ in one of Śākyamuni's sermons; or even a gesture on his part! Furthermore, some sūtras were initially delivered by one or other of Śākyamuni's disciples, after which they were subsequently approved by the Buddha.

So it was that, from the first council onwards, sūtras became part of the Buddhist canon only by being ratified by liberated *arhats*. This process

---

considered Buddhist: 'Good acts bring good results and evil acts bring bad results.' [Contemplation Sūtra, tr. HIC 2003, p. 24.]

did not end with the first council but carried on down through time as more sūtras came into use. Some texts, which are popular even now, were rejected because they had not been formally approved at a council.[3]

The Larger Sūtra is authentic because it was 'heard and received' in keeping with the process just outlined. Many enlightened sages, especially most of the Jōdo Shinshū dharma masters, received the Larger Sūtra which is an integral part of the Chinese Buddhist canon. This sūtra begins with the phrase 'Thus have I heard', and Ānanda himself played a key role in its delivery. The significance of this is that the Larger Sūtra reveals the seminal ideas of, not only Śākyamuni's teaching, but also of his enlightenment experience.

---

[3] An example is the *Ullambana Sūtra*, which is the basis of the most popular Buddhist festival in East Asia. For a detailed discussion, see *Buddhist Sūtras: Origin, Development, Transmission* by Kogen Mizuno (Kôsei, 1982).

Jōdo Wasan 52
Śākyamuni's splendour was rare and auspicious;
Ananda, rejoicing immensely,
Asked its meaning, whereupon the Buddha revealed
The fundamental intent of his appearance in the world.

ŚĀKYAMUNI'S SPLENDOUR

In the first chapter of the *Kyōgyōshinshō*, Shinran Shōnin announces that the true teaching is the Larger Sūtra. Its message is sharp and unequivocal:

> ... To teach the Tathāgata's Primal Vow is the true intent of this sūtra; the Name of the Buddha is its essence.[1]

This is a marvellous summary. A single sentence encompasses the entire scope of both the sūtra and Jōdo Shinshū. This is all that needs to be said about it; the rest is padding. Apart from the circumstantial evidence for the intrinsic value of this text, Shinran only quotes passages from it when they serve to elucidate these two ideas.

Shinran is not just promoting his own theory here, or making a random selection of the sūtra to suit his own expectations. He seeks evidence for its importance by considering the events that surrounded its delivery.

> How is it known that this was the great matter for which Śākyamuni appeared in the world?

Shinran then quotes from four sources that call attention to the majestic appearance of Śākyamuni Buddha, and the uniqueness of the occasion on which he delivered the Larger Sūtra.

There seems to be no precedent for the significance Shinran assigns to the Buddha's radiant splendour. He cites it as evidence of the special role that this sūtra plays in Śākyamuni's dharma. It is true that such a glorious demeanour is not a common observation in the context of sūtra deliveries, but is such an event evidence enough? Could it really be the case that this scripture is, in fact, the essential reason for the birth of the historical Buddha?

---

[1] CWS p. 7.

The claim that the Larger Sūtra was the primary reason for Śākyamuni's appearance is legitimate because it has universal relevance. By this I mean that its core message – which is the call to 'hear the Name of Amida Buddha' – embraces everyone. It does not require special knowledge, a list of rules to be observed, or special attributes like intelligence or moral excellence. A person who is physically impaired is not excluded; neither do our everyday hopes and expectations have anything to do with our ability to hear the Name.

If there is one central principle in the Buddha-dharma, it is expressed in the practice of the 'four *vihāras*' whereby goodwill, friendliness, joy and peace are extended to all living beings without exception. Such unequivocal compassion is the message of the Larger Sūtra. However, the thing that matters most is its core message – the Primal Vow and the Name – which reflect the four *vihāras* at their deepest, most universal level. What more do we need to know about it?

When we read the opening passages of the *Kyōgyōshinshō*, and ponder Shinran's happiness in proclaiming the significance of Śākyamuni's radiant exuberance and joy – as he prepares to tell us about the Primal Vow that is revealed in the Larger Sūtra – we cannot but cherish this marvellous work of sacred literature. Whatever else we may admire and love about this scripture, its central purport is the source of any ultimate value that the sūtra has for us.

Jōdo Wasan 53
Having entered the samādhi of great tranquility,
The Buddha's countenance was wondrous in its radiance;
Observing the depth of Ananda's discernment,
He praised him for his insightful question.

THE *SAMĀDHI* OF GREAT TRANQUILITY

In the verse which we now have before us, Shinran Shōnin relates the opening of the Larger Sūtra in which Śākyamuni's appearance became radiant because of his meditative state. In this event, we see a telling juxtaposition between the single-minded absorption of *samādhi*, tranquility and joy which is manifested in Śākyamuni's appearance.

Samādhi occurs when the mind is firmly fixed and unwavering in complete union with the object of its concentration. It forms a component of the Noble Eightfold Path, and is a deeper state than *dhyāna*, which is essentially complete mental detachment from perception and sense-reactions. *Dhyāna* is the word often used in the titles of meditative schools in both the southern and northern traditions of Buddhism.

The Chinese school of that name is called *Ch'an*, and its Japanese counterpart is *Zen*. Yet one needs to pass beyond *dhyāna* into the transcendent realm of *samādhi*, from which it is possible to finally resolve all conflicting dharmas (constituent elements of existence) and attain enlightenment. *Samādhi* was a more or less natural frame of mind for Śākyamuni following his enlightenment; just as confusion is a natural state for us, since we are not fully awakened.

In another translation of the Larger Sūtra, we read that Śākyamuni's *samādhi* was called 'Great Tranquility' – this was none other than complete immersion in Nirvāna itself which, of course, is synonymous with Amida Buddha.

> When this Buddhahood appears with form, it is not called supreme Nirvāna. In order to make us realize that true Buddhahood is without form, it is expressly called 'Amida Buddha'; so I have been taught.[1]

---
[1] *Shōzōmatsu Wasan*, Ryūkoku Translation Series VII, 1980, p. 117.

Shinran makes the following remark in a marginal note:

> *samādhi of great tranquility:* the reason for the Buddha's inner stillness and quietude, which is now more excellent than usual, is that he has appeared in the world solely to teach the Name of Amida; thus, his particularly excellent and auspicious features.[2]

So, Ānanda is drawn to Śākyamuni's radiant appearance and asks what its cause may be. The answer? 'The reason for my appearance in the world is to reveal teachings of the Way and to save multitudes of beings by endowing them with true benefits'. Shinran understands this to be the nembutsu – *Namo Amida Butsu*.

Clearly Śākyamuni's radiance is that of exultation. As Ānanda says, '... today all your senses are radiant with joy'. In Buddhist experience, joy is associated with tranquility. Indeed, in some contexts, 'joy' and 'serenity' are interchangeable. This is in marked contrast with how 'joy' is often understood in modern usage, for it's sometimes associated with passion and strong emotions. But, in the religious sense, it is always profoundly peaceful and deeply serene. It's a delicate, limpid and gentle state of mind. And it is the condition of those who first attain *pramuditā* and enter the stream in the process of becoming bodhisattvas.

In 'endowing [us] with the true benefit', Śākyamuni shares with us the elation that comes with 'tasting' a hint of his *samādhi*. In accepting and entrusting ourselves to the Name, we encounter the joy which has been waiting for us since the eternal past, the consummation of which is our final destiny.

---

[2] CWS, p. 339.

Jōdo Wasan 54
The fundamental intent for which the Buddha appeared in the world
Was to reveal the truth and reality of the Primal Vow.
He taught that to encounter or behold a Buddha
Is as rare as the blossoming of the uḍumbara.

WHEN THE DESERT BLOOMS

I have never seen an uḍumbara blossom. In his marginal note, Shinran describes it thus:

> *uḍumbara:* This is called 'the mysterious, auspicious flower (*zuio*).' The uḍumbara tree always bears fruit, but the flower blossoms very rarely. Since a Buddha's appearance in the world occurs only with extreme rarity, it is likened to the uḍumbara flower.[1]

Indeed, the uḍumbara is *Ficus glomerata*. As a fig, of course, the flower is contained within the fruit and never visible. It is fertilized by a type of wasp which is specific to this species of fig. The wasps reside in the nascent fruit and figs do not need to produce a visible flower.[2] So the analogy – that it's as rare for a fig to flower as it is to be born in the time of a buddha – is apt.[3]

One of the things we find difficult to face up to is that a painstaking search for light might just end in futility. Sometimes we are ready to settle for second best when we know that we haven't found what we're really looking for. Searching for 'truth' and 'light' is a natural outcome for those of us who feel a profound unease and dissatisfaction with things.

Such is the first of the Four Noble Truths: all is suffering (Sk. *duḥkha* – 'discomfort'). People who come to this point in their lives set out in search of reality. They have a hunger to understand; to find a centre in themselves that portends harmony, meaning and peace of mind.

---

[1] CWS p. 340.
[2] Colin Tudge, *The Secret Life of Trees, How They Live and Why They Matter* (Penguin, 2005), pp. 329-337.
[3] In the *Kyōgyōshinshō* ('Chapter on True Teaching'), Shinran quotes from the *Sūtra of the Enlightenment of Ultimate Equality*, which reminds us that the uḍumbara (*Ficus glomerata*) 'bears fruit but no flowers'. A Buddha's appearance in the world is so rare as to be quite improbable.

In August 1970, I set out with two friends on a trip to the northern desert regions of my state. In the south-west and central parts of Australia, winter (June-August) usually brings rain to agricultural areas – and, in a good year, it extends into the drier, inland pastoral districts. We had been planning on a visit to this locality because where we live, near the coast, had experienced a very wet winter, and so we assumed that the desert would be 'blooming'. The trip is difficult and perilous but, on the spur of the moment, we decided to make it.

As we drove north, we were delighted by the green countryside and the dense fields of emerging grain crops, which promised a rich harvest in around December (late spring). But suddenly, within a few kilometres, the greenery turned to brown, dry earth. At the first town we came to, we learned that no rain had fallen at all that winter. Indeed, little rain had fallen for several years. We were disappointed, having made our way so far north to no avail, but decided to push on further into the desert.

The barrenness of the countryside was indescribable. I had never experienced anything so extreme and we began to worry about our safety. What if we ran out of water? What if our car broke down? Sensibly, we turned south to return home again. I decided, after that experience, that the desert was not for me. If it wasn't going to bloom this year, I would put it out of my mind forever. The barren, harsh desert was just that and it would never be better than this.

Three years ago, I had cause to fly across similar dry country on my way to Singapore. Having flown out of the farming areas that I know well because I had travelled there often for work, I began to feel sleepy. As I turned to pull down the shutter on the window, I was almost blinded by the brilliance of the flowers and the lush greenery that was riotously evident so far below. I could see small lakes and even tiny specs of wildlife – pelicans and flocks of birds. Was this the same country that I had visited with friends so many years ago?

I checked and yes it was. The sight of such abundant life was breathtakingly beautiful and so miraculously wonderful that I was reduced to tears. How joyous! How sublime! If I had never seen this transformation, I would never have believed it possible.

> Wherever the Buddha comes to stay, there is no state, town or
> village which is not blessed by his virtues. The whole country

reposes in peace and harmony. The sun and the moon shine with pure brilliance; wind arises and rain falls at the right time. There is no calamity or epidemic, and so the country becomes wealthy, and its people enjoy peace. Soldiers and weapons become useless; and people esteem virtue, practice benevolence, and diligently cultivate courteous modesty.[4]

From this passage we know that, like the experience I had with my friends in 1970, we have 'missed the rain' of the Buddha's blessing. We live in a world unlike the one we could expect under his dispensation. But we do still have the teachings of Śākyamuni as handed down to us, with great difficulty, through the ages. Though we may not see a Buddha in person, we can rejoice in his dharma, even at a distance.

Eventually, this teaching will also fall out of view. We are people in a cycle of time that is well past midnight. Yet the Larger Sūtra is still with us. Like the last bus out of a deserted city, it awaits to take us home.

---

[4] *TPLS* p. 304. It is interesting that the sūtra should make such a claim. In fact, Śākyamuni Buddha lived in a time of notable armed conflict (*Gotama Buddha, A Biography Based on the Most Reliable Texts* by Hajime Nakamura, Volume 1, pp. 379-84).

Jōdo Wasan 55
It is taught that ten kalpas have now passed
Since Amida attained Buddhahood,
But he seems a Buddha more ancient
Than kalpas countless as particles.

THE INFINITE

This is an extremely interesting and important verse. At first sight, it seems rather innocent, but it carries deeply significant insights into how Shinran Shōnin understands Amida Buddha.

But first, a small digression; and that is to point out that Shinran avoids a rigidly literal interpretation of sacred texts. He approaches them with reverence but with reason as well. In the *Kyōgyōshinshō*, for example, he draws on a broad reservoir of textual and commentarial resources. His hermeneutics are those of a thinker who uses the full spectrum of developed ideas. These are, after all, the outcome of accumulated spiritual wisdom spanning millennia.

Sacred texts can have no value or meaning unless they are 'proven' on the anvil of human experience. Shinran is, therefore, empirical in his approach and I think that those who take the trouble to actually read his more scholarly work will come to see him as a surprisingly 'modern' thinker. He argues in such a way as to be convincing to us in the twenty-first century.

Shinran also goes to great lengths to seek out the opinion of writers whom he considers to be authoritative, and always tries to uncover the full meaning of the texts he uses. He is an exegete of formidable skill. Hence, in the *Kyōgyōshinshō*, he quotes approvingly Nāgārjuna's exhortation to rely 'not on words but on meaning'. Following this quote, he is most emphatic about the need for a clarity that's based on an awareness of this and other similar counsel by Nāgārjuna.[1]

In this verse, Shinran alludes to a statement in the Pure Land sūtras which asserts that Amida has been a Buddha for 'ten kalpas'. A *kalpa* is an extremely protracted period of cyclical cosmic time (often described to the point of extravagance). 'Ten kalpas' is thus a phrase that combines

---
[1] CWS, p. 241ff.

immense duration with an additional multiplier; so it's altogether something beyond imagination or calculating thought.

In any case, Shinran considers that the juxtaposition of 'ten kalpas' (*jikkō*) and the name 'Amida Buddha' is an oxymoron. This is because, in Sanskrit, *amita* means literally 'immeasurable', since *mita* – a unit of measurement (it has the same grammatical origins as *metre*) – is negated by the addition of the Indo-European prefix *a*, (equivalent, of course, to *un-* in English). How can the infinite be a mere 'ten kalpas' old? Shinran actually satirizes the whole idea in a marginal note in which he extends this period of time to 'kalpas countless as mote particles' (*jinden kuongō*) – and goes on to say that Amida Buddha is 'older' *even than this*. The Buddha of Immeasurable Life (*Amitāyus*) transcends time since he is older than time itself; Amida is the source of enlightenment and thus of all buddhas.

For Shinran – following the Pure Land tradition – there is ultimately no reality except Amida Buddha and the spontaneous working of his spiritual influence. If resisted, the wisdom and compassion of this reality can never be known to us.

Jōdo Wasan 56
The Buddha of Inconceivable Light, under Lokeśvararāja Buddha,
Selected the best qualities from among
All the pure lands of the ten quarters
To establish the Primal Vow.

THE DAWN OF COMPASSION

Namo Fukashigikō Butsu – 'I take refuge in the Buddha of Inconceivable Light!' This is a stirring way to begin a verse like this: one that recounts the story in the Larger Sūtra, which tells how Amida Buddha chose the Primal Vow, proclaimed the transfer of his virtue to us in his Name, and set us on the path to Nirvāna. The *Shōshin Nembutsu Ge*, which many Shin Buddhists recite every day, similarly begins with 'I take refuge in the Inconceivable Light'.

In his accounts of this story, it's for good reason that Shinran Shōnin brings attention to his favourite epithet for Amida Buddha. It is because he's alluding to something which is itself inconceivable but which he knows to be true.

My favourite piece of useless software tells users the exact location of the moon at any moment of the day or night. All one has to do is to type in the local time, along with the exact longitude and latitude. This then gives you a wealth of detailed information, including the exact moment one can expect the moon to appear on the eastern horizon.

I like this software because I've always loved the moon. I think it's an exquisite thing to behold and I enjoy looking up at it during different times of the year, taking in its subtle changes of shadow and colour.

One of the things that delights me about this software is knowing where the moon is when not visible to the naked eye. Perhaps it is a new moon, when it's in the sky during daylight. Perhaps it's on the other side of the earth's orb, beneath the horizon. Without doubt, the best thing about the software is the way it locates the moon as it is about to rise, giving its location and distance below the horizon.

Although I know full well just how reliable this little piece of technology is, it's still fun to watch the calibration ticking down to moonrise and then to go outside and see the moon's disk beginning to break the horizon at lunar dawn; right on time! The presence of the moon just doesn't seem real until it's actually visible again.

Neither you, nor I, nor Shinran saw the events reported in the Larger Sūtra which are celebrated in this verse. It is well below the horizon of recorded history and quite intangible to us as individuals. In the same way, it is only as Amida's compassion begins to dawn in our hearts, that its truth will be affirmed for us.

Namo Fukashigikō Butsu
Homage to the Buddha of Inconceivable Light!

Jōdo Wasan 57
The light of the Buddha of Unhindered Light
Harbours the lights of purity, joy, and wisdom;
Its virtuous working surpasses conceptual understanding,
As it benefits the beings throughout the ten quarters.

UNHINDERED LIGHT

From Shinran Shōnin's point of view, 'unhindered light' (*mugekō*) is one of the most prominent attributes of Amida Buddha. It's celebrated in this verse because, in the Larger Sūtra, it appears second on the list of Amida's 'twelve lights'.[1]

It is said that Shinran used the ten-character *myōgō* ('the Name') as his *honzon* or 'principle object of reverence'. Until the time of Rennyo – the eighth *monshu* (chief abbot) of Jōdo Shinshū in the fifteenth century – the ten-character Name was generally well favoured among Shinshū followers. It was often portrayed emitting rays of light. It is a pity that copies of these *myōgō* are not available for us to use in our own home shrines, or in dōjōs and temples. It is pronounced *ki-myō-jin-jip-pō-mu-ge-kō-nyo-rai*: 'Take refuge in the Tathāgata whose light is unhindered in the ten quarters'.

As a form of nembutsu, it has value for a number of reasons. The first is that, after getting to understand the words, it proves both spiritually and intellectually satisfying – in itself, it provides a meditation on key features of Amida Buddha's reality. It reminds us of the specific significance of 'Amida' as *unhindered light*, and helps us to grow in awareness that the Buddha's wisdom penetrates to the core of our being; revealing it as it is.

It also has a more colloquial feel than *Namo Amida Butsu*, which is of Indian provenance. Somehow, there is an intimacy to it. It reminds us that the nembutsu itself is not a mere ritual – a fixed object – but has emotional, intellectual and spiritual content. Again, we are reminded of Shinran's explanation that

> *kimyō* is the command of the Primal Vow calling to and

---

[1] *The Three Pure Land Sūtras (Volume II): The Sūtra of the Buddha of Immeasurable Life*, Shin Buddhism Translation Series, 2009, p. 36.

summoning us.[2]

Thirdly, it is an intensely reassuring form of the *myōgō* because the things that stubbornly hinder our progress on the path of the Buddha are the 'three roots of evil': *lobha* (greed), *dveṣa* (anger) and *moha* (delusion); in this case, a pedestrian form of nescience, contrasted with fundamental *avidyā* (blind ignorance), that lies at the heart of existence. Amida's light of purity, joy and wisdom is the antidote to greed, anger and ignorance, respectively. In the ten-character *myōgō*, we encounter the truth of Other-Power; a power beyond the self. The self of our conditioned existence is bound by the 'three roots of evil', but the unhindered light ultimately vanquishes them.

Those who are receptive to the brilliance of Other-Power often have a glimpse of these lights of 'purity, joy and wisdom' and come to the wonderful realization that ultimate truth is not just the seemingly intractable hindrance of blind ignorance but, also, the true wisdom and compassion that fills the universe.

---

[2] CWS, p. 38.

Jōdo Wasan 58
Encouraging the beings of the ten quarters with the words,
'With sincere mind entrust yourselves and aspire for birth',
Amida established the Vow beyond conceptual understanding
And made it the cause of birth in the true and real fulfilled land.

SHINJIN

The Primal Vow is found in the Larger Sūtra as follows:

> If, when I attain Buddhahood, sentient beings of the ten quarters, with sincere mind entrusting themselves, aspiring to be born in my land, and saying my Name perhaps even ten times, should not be born there, may I not attain the supreme enlightenment. Excluded are those who commit the five grave offences and those who slander the right dharma.[1]

In these verses, which praise the significance of the Larger Sūtra, we see how Shinran interprets the sūtra with great precision. The hymns are very clear in their account of the relationship between practice (*gyō*), which is 'saying the Name' (*shōmyō*) and shinjin.

There can be no doubt that Shinran seeks to emphasize Other-Power (*tariki*), the Primal Vow (*hongan*) and shinjin. 'Raise sincere mind, serene entrusting, and desire for birth' is, in fact, the abandonment of all self-power (including any effort to be born in the Pure Land by reciting the Name), and the entrusting of ourselves wholly to Amida Buddha.

Sometimes these emphases in Shinran's writing are seen as devaluing the practice of *shōmyō*. However, all the evidence points to Shinran himself making clear that the nembutsu was a constant activity, and a celebration of spiritual relief in response to the call of Amida Buddha. This is known as *hō-on no nembutsu*, 'nembutsu of gratitude'.

In this verse, the three aspects of shinjin comprise a single internal disposition – complete abandonment of the self. The third of these, 'desire

---

[1] CWS, p. 80. The last sentence is the so-called 'exclusion clause'. However, in the *Kyōgyōshinshō*, Shinran demonstrates – by quoting extensively from his spiritual teachers – especially the Chinese masters T'an-luan (476–542) and Shan-tao (613-681), that the purport of this clause is more cautionary than literal.

for birth' (*yokushō*), means to accept the most essential dimension of the Buddha-dharma; that is, Nirvāna. Sākyamuni was reported to have said: 'I teach suffering and the release from suffering'. The primary reason for following the dharma is a yearning, however vague or ill-conceived, to find a way out of samsāra – to discover ultimate freedom (Sk. *moksa*).

Full acceptance of the dharma cannot occur until shinjin is settled. This is because the entire edifice of the teachings is underpinned by the insight that there is no self. As Dōgen Daishi (1200–1253), founder of Sōtō Zen, remarked: 'The Buddha-dharma is *anātman* – not-self'. All Buddhist teachings are cognizant of this truth, which Shinshū interprets as 'not self-power' – the abandoning of practices that involve psychological violence done to oneself.

I have always been unequivocal in my conviction that only the teaching of Shinran provides the means by which an ordinary karma-bound person can realize this fact within the mundane circumstances of daily life – something that's not well understood at the present time. But this fact cannot be avoided forever by those of true heart who genuinely seek deliverance from samsāra.

'Sincere mind, entrusting and aspiration for birth' is what the Buddha imparts to beings; once accepted, this reality floods into our hearts and emerges as *Namo Amida Butsu* from our lips.

Jōdo Wasan 59
Those who attain true and real shinjin
Immediately join the truly settled;
Thus having entered the stage of non-retrogression,
They necessarily attain Nirvāna.

JÑANA

The Buddha-dharma grew out of the yogic tradition of the Gangetic Plain and the forests of the Black Mountains, at the foothills of the Himalaya. However, it is a non-dogmatic religion of awakening that confers emancipating knowledge (Sk. *jñana*). Even the authoritative teaching of the Buddha must be proven for oneself and 'tasted'. In this sense, Śākyamuni Buddha and Shinran Shōnin were both yogins; at one with enlightenment, and shinjin, respectively.

When Shinran speaks, we hear the voice of shinjin itself. Yet this is something we can also know for ourselves: that everything Shinran wrote is the nembutsu of the Seventeenth Vow 'that all buddhas praise the Name' of Amida; that it's simultaneously the 'two aspects of the deep faith' (*nishu jinshin*): the realization of one's hopeless bondage to karmic evil and the certainty of Amida Buddha's liberation.

Shinjin should not be accepted on the basis of dogmatic authority. True shinjin (*shinjitsu shinjin*) is known as it is by the person who accepts it, although the moment of its germination in moving from seed to tree is inconceivable; indeed, it must always be so, while manifesting itself as *Namo Amida Butsu*.

When we keep in mind the *jñana* focus of the Buddha-dharma, we'll never accept anything on someone's mere say so but, rather, confirm it within ourselves. So, when we hear people make bald assertions such as 'Everyone has already received Faith from Amida', 'Everyone is already enlightened', 'This mundane world is the Pure Land' or 'the Pure Land exists in our minds', we should treat them with caution, since such sweeping statements can never be truly known; they are dogmas. In the Buddha-dharma, insights and awakenings are individual: occurring to each and every person one-by-one.

Shinran sometimes seems to use generalizations, as when he says in the *Jōdo Wasan* (No.6), 'None is there unblessed by the Light'. However, it's clear from his writing that Shinran believed that the Larger Sūtra emerged from the *jñana* of Śākyamuni. It is something that Shinran knows from his own experience, and not a matter of mere dogma or belief. When it comes to discernments stemming from his actual experience and direct knowledge, Shinran is only ever strikingly honest. He invariably relates things precisely as he sees them. He certainly did not swallow glib assurances of shinjin; for him it was truly known.

Therefore, when Amida Buddha's shinjin arises in our hearts, we actually *know* that we're 'embraced and not forsaken' by the Primal Vow of Amida Buddha. At that very time, in the midst of our busy, ordinary lives, we enter the 'rightly established state' and receive, in the present moment, the certainty that, on birth in the Pure Land, we will become a Buddha.

Jōdo Wasan 60
So profound is Amida's great compassion
That, manifesting inconceivable Buddha-wisdom,
The Buddha established the Vow of transformation into men,
Thereby vowing to enable women to attain Buddhahood.

THE ABSOLUTE EQUALITY OF WOMEN AND MEN

The Pure Land teaching is the epitome of the Mahāyāna's underlying egalitarian tendencies. Leaders like Shinran Shōnin and his wife Eshinni, give practical expression to gender equality. Each regarded the other as a bodhisattva. By virtue of Amida Buddha's shinjin given to them, both were 'equal to Maitreya Bodhisattva', who will become a Buddha at his next birth.[1]

When it comes to considerations of gender, Shinran does not acknowledge any obstacles to women becoming Buddhas just as they are. He clearly establishes this principle in the *Kyōgyōshinshō*:

> In reflecting on the ocean of great shinjin, I realize that there is no discrimination between noble and humble or black-robed monks and white-clothed laity, no differentiation between man and woman, old and young.[2]

In his other writings, he goes further. For example, Shinran had a deep sense of gratitude and profound reverence for the Prince Regent, Shōtoku Taishi (574–622) who was largely responsible for the introduction of Buddhism to Japan. In the *Hymns on Prince Shōtoku*, Shinran traces Shōtoku's spiritual lineage back to Queen Śrīmālā, a disciple of Śākyamuni Buddha:

> In India, Prince Shōtoku
> Was born as Queen Śrīmālā,
> And in China appeared
> As Master Hui-ssu.
>
> He appeared in China
> To benefit sentient beings;
> He was reborn five hundred times

---

[1] CWS, p. 122-124 *et. al.*
[2] CWS, p. 107.

As both man and woman.[3]

There is no fixed delineation here between male and female.

In the verse we are discussing now, we're told that an obstacle for women in becoming Buddhas is their morphology. Indeed, one of the titles of the thirty-fifth Vow is 'the Vow that all women attain birth in Amida's Land after becoming men'. However, it seems to me that this is out of keeping with Shinran's own attitude to gender equality, which we find in the rest of his works. It's also clear that he simply did not intend a literal interpretation of this vow.

Each of the forty-eight vows of Amida Buddha is identified by one or more titles, rather than a number. Indeed, Shinran follows this convention and I believe that is what he's doing here. In this case, he adds a footnote, as he sometimes does, to imply that the vow in question has a deeper meaning than its literal rendition.

Towards the end of the *Kyōgyōshinshō*, Shinran quotes Nāgārjuna Bodhisattva to the effect that, in reading the scriptures, we should

> Rely on the meaning, not on the words. With regard to relying on the meaning, meaning itself is beyond debate of such matters as, like against dislike, evil against virtue, falsity against truth. Hence, words may indeed have meaning, but the meaning is not the words. Consider, for example, a person instructing us by pointing to the moon with his finger. [To take words to be the meaning] is like looking at the finger and not at the moon. The person would say, 'I am pointing to the moon with my finger in order to show it to you. Why do you look at my finger and not the moon?' Similarly, words are the finger pointing to the meaning; they are not the meaning itself. Hence, do not rely upon words.[4]

The third line of the verse at the head of this essay is also the title of the thirty-fifth vow. So that line may easily be substituted for the number of the vow, thus creating an alternative title. Accordingly, it could then read: 'The Buddha established the thirty-fifth Vow/ Thereby vowing to enable women to attain Buddhahood.'

---

[3] CWS, p. 435.
[4] CWS, p. 241.

It would be quite inconsistent with everything Shinran had written if he were to consider it necessary for women to become anything other than themselves in order to attain shinjin and be born in the Pure Land.

Finally, it is worth noting that – over 600 years ago – one of the ten sub-branches of the Jōdo Shinshū tradition, Bukkō-ji-ha,[5] did not hesitate to appoint a woman as its abbot. Within the fiercely patriarchal society of that time, that in itself honours Shinran's own perspective that the Primal Vow does not discriminate in any way, whatsoever, between men and women.

---

[5] www.bukkoji.or.jp/english/

Jōdo Wasan 61

Provisionally guiding sentient beings of the ten quarters with the words,
'Aspire with sincere mind and desire to be born',
Amida revealed the temporary gate of various good acts
And vowed to appear before them [at the time of death].

SANGAN TENNYŪ

Shinran Shōnin is here referring to Amida Buddha's Nineteenth Vow, which he identifies with the Contemplation Sūtra. This vow and sūtra seem to encourage people to approach the Pure Land way by taking up practices that are hard to distinguish from the path of sages.

The way to liberation, which the sūtra posits, is a regimen of meditation and self-discipline in the form of rules for conduct or precepts. Success in these practices will be affirmed by a vision of Amida Buddha at the time of one's death.

The Nineteenth Vow reads as follows:

> If, when I attain Buddhahood, sentient beings of the ten quarters – awakening the mind of enlightenment and performing meritorious acts – should aspire with sincere mind and desire to be born in my land, and yet I should not appear before them at the moment of death surrounded by a host of sages, may I not attain the supreme enlightenment.[1]

First of all, Shinran considers this vow to be 'provisional', in that it pertains to the 'falsely settled'. The Nineteenth Vow provides a way to Nirvāna for people who rely on their own power to transcend the self. At the same time, Shinran calls this vow the 'essential gate'. This accords with the convention used by Shan-tao (613-681), the fifth dharma master of the Jōdo Shinshū lineage.

How can something that is 'provisional' also be 'essential'? Is there some kind of imperative which mandates that we must follow the stages of Shinran's personal journey in order to reach the gate of birth through Other-Power shinjin?

---

[1] CWS, p. 208.

Certainly, Shinran himself entered through this 'essential gate' on his path to freedom. Nevertheless, from the secure ground of Other-Power, he came to realize that he was actually wasting his time with something he didn't really need. Could he have moved directly through the 'inconceivable gate' of the Eighteenth Vow – the 'Vow of Sincere Mind and Entrusting' – and thus entered 'the stage of the truly settled' without first traversing the 'essential gate' of the Nineteenth Vow?

It must be said that many people have discerned evolutionary stages in spiritual development. For example, the Protestant philosopher Søren Kierkegaard identified the following three: the aesthetic, ethical and religious.

On the face of it, it would seem that Shinran underwent a similar process in his spiritual endeavours. In the sixth chapter of the *Kyōgyōshinshō*, we learn that this begins with the Nineteenth Vow, which is both ethical and aesthetic. In the graphic descriptions of the Pure Land that we encounter in the Contemplation Sūtra, Shinran sees an aesthetic moment – a kind of 'overture', a preliminary stage, a threshold between the mundane and the spiritual, that serves to attract seekers to the Pure Land way.

The Twentieth Vow, on the other hand, is very much like the 'religious' phase of Kierkegaard's thought, for it's characterized by spiritual hunger and conviction, a quest for complete liberation through active engagement in saying the nembutsu. However, the Eighteenth Vow goes beyond Kierkegaard's schema. It brings release and freedom, the life of 'naturalness' (*jinen*) and oneness with the supreme Buddha – the transcendence even of 'religion' itself as it's commonly understood.

The twentieth-century writer Hermann Hesse, in his novel *Siddhartha*, also describes a similar process of staged spiritual progress. It begins with awakening to existential pain, which then leads to the adoption of ethical practice, followed by stages that are, in turn, ritualistic, 'religious' and contemplative. This process culminates in a mystical union that is ineffable.

Shinran's own experience is known as 'turning through the three Vows' (*sangan tennyū*). As we have seen, these are:

1. the Nineteenth Vow, which is an 'expedient' and 'temporary' phase of ascetic practice, initiated by the aesthetic appeal of

images of the Pure Land;
2. the Twentieth Vow, a religious phase, in which only active engagement with nembutsu as a practice is necessary; and
3. finally – in the Eighteenth Vow of complete entrusting in absolute Other-Power – we find spiritual release through complete emancipation.

By means of the *sangan tennyū*, Shinran followed a similar pattern to Śākyamuni Buddha. He became aware of the need to transcend suffering by taking up a path of rigorous ascetic discipline. He then entered a phase of contemplation, before tasting the freedom of enlightenment.

After Shinran had reached the final stage of his own spiritual development, he spoke as though he had completely abandoned the earlier stages, and left them behind. He then entered the gate of true shinjin, which leads to the attainment of Buddhahood (in the Pure Land). So Shinran advocates shinjin first and foremost. He clearly does not see the necessity for us to follow the path of *sangan tennyū* as he did.

Shinran's reflection on his experience led to re-evaluating the Nineteenth and Twentieth Vows as expedients – compassionate means of salvation for those who struggle to accept Other-Power shinjin; who need to remain in control of their salvation; who cannot relinquish the self into the undying and trustworthy embrace of Amida Buddha.

<u>Jōdo Wasan 62</u>
Based on Amida's Vow to appear at the time of death,
Śākyamuni presented all the various good acts
In one scripture, the Contemplation Sūtra,
To encourage those who perform meditative and non-meditative
    practices.

THE LIFE OF THE NINETEENTH VOW

How does a follower of the Nineteenth Vow live? Shinran gives us a detailed account in the sixth chapter of the *Kyōgyōshinshō*. The way of 'meditative and non-meditative good' is for those who have not accepted the working of Amida Buddha's Primal Vow.

Hence, first and foremost, the purpose of the Nineteenth Vow is to attract people to the Pure Land dharma.

> How truly profound is the attempt behind this temporarily guiding Vow! How clear become the teachings of the temporary gate and [Shan-tao's] explanation [that they are for the awakening] of desire for the Pure Land![1]

While the implicit meaning of the Nineteenth Vow (and the Larger Sūtra) is 'the true diamondlike mind (of shinjin)'[2], its explicit purpose is to have us aspire for the Pure Land by revealing it to be true reality: that which is eternal, blissful, true self and pure – presented in the guise of 'Dharma-Body as Compassionate Means'.

In his teaching, Śākyamuni Buddha often revealed the way things are on 'the other shore' of enlightenment, compared to this samsāric realm of suffering. Shinran conforms to this practice in the *Kyōgyōshinshō*, when he identifies the Nineteenth Vow with the explicit meaning of the Contemplation Sūtra. This scripture presents the first intimations that there is another way of being in the world – namely, as a person of shinjin whose heart receives the Primal Vow which is 'sincere mind, entrusting and aspiration for birth'.[3]

---

[1] CWS, p. 225.
[2] CWS, p. 226.
[3] CWS, p. 341.

Although it contains implicit references to the truth of the Eighteenth Vow, the Contemplation Sūtra is also a practical guide for those who wish to pursue the way of meditative and non-meditative good. It points to precepts and visualizations as the basis for meditation practice.

The Nineteenth Vow, which Shinran praises in this verse, is also called 'the vow of appearing at the death-bed'. This is because it describes Amida coming to welcome beings, as they approach their end, to take them to the Pure Land. But in living the life of shinjin, Amida Buddha welcomes us all the time.

Jōdo Wasan 63
All the good acts and myriad practices,
Because they are performed with a sincere mind and aspiration,
Become, without exception, provisional good
That will lead to birth in the Pure Land.

VARIOUS GOOD DEEDS

Good deeds with pure intent will, as everyone knows, bring propitious results. In this verse, 'good deeds and numerous practices' means both meditation and adherence to various kinds of precepts. These were especially important for the path of sages, but the teaching of the Contemplation Sūtra and the way of Amida Buddha's Nineteenth Vow is also addressed to us.

Most people are aware of various kinds of precepts and, in the case of monks and nuns, the *Vinaya* – a list of rules that were developed, on a case-by-case basis, to address problems that arose in the early sangha. The 'five precepts' (*pañcaśīla*), for example, were apparently part of the code of conduct that prevailed in India at the time of Śākyamuni.

My reading of the Vinaya is that Śākyamuni was sensitive to public expectations for the sangha, and was concerned to curb behaviour that would bring the sangha into disrepute. This suggests that a basic rule of thumb for us all is that we should be 'good citizens' and, if we also take a monastic vow of celibacy (Sk. *brahmacharya*), we ought to be careful not to demean that way of life in our bearing and attitude.

As passed down to us, the five precepts are not killing, not stealing, not committing adultery, not lying and not using drugs that 'cloud the mind'. Another system of eight precepts is taken by lay followers on special days, and by novices in the sangha. The days of special observance are usually the 8th, 14th, 15th, 23rd, 29th and 30th days of each month (Jp. *rokusainichi*). Some people make it a weekly observance and choose the day of the week on which they were born, whereas others go further and observe eight or ten days.

The eight precepts are essentially the five mentioned above, except that complete abstinence from sex is also enjoined in addition to other restrictions, the most important of which is not eating after midday. As it is very difficult for lay people to keep these, some observe the days of abstinence by not eating meat, thus giving special emphasis to the most important precept against taking life. *The Sūtra of Upāsaka Precepts* requires the observance of at least one precept, if the others cannot be kept. For example, if one lives in a household of carnivores, abstinence from alcohol is an option, in that it will cause the least disruption to others!

When Shinran speaks of 'provisional good', he means that the Nineteenth Vow can serve as the basis for birth in the Pure Land. However, this 'birth' is constrained by one's attachment to self-power and is not the full awakening that rides on Other-Power shinjin. We will explore these ideas as we traverse the latter part of the *Shōzōmatsu Wasan*, towards the end of this cycle of essays.

Ultimately, there is no escaping the critical importance of a thoroughgoing transformation by way of awakening the entrusting heart. Shinran has salutary things to say about this in his work *Notes on 'Essentials of Faith Alone'*.

The Buddha-dharma encompasses a broad range of rules that govern the behaviour of both monks and laypeople: the 'five precepts', the 'eight precepts', the 'ten precepts of morality', all the Hīnayāna codes of conduct, the three thousand regulations of deportment, the sixty thousand regulatory practices, the 'diamond-like one-mind' precepts of the Mahāyāna, the 'threefold pure precept', the fifty-eight precepts expounded in the *Brahmā Net Sūtra*, and so on.

To maintain these is 'to uphold' and to violate them is 'to break'. Even saintly people who observe these precepts can attain birth in the fulfilled land, only after they realize the true and real entrusting heart of Other-Power. Know that it is impossible to be born in the Pure Land by simply observing precepts, or by self-willed conviction, or through good that is cultivated by oneself.[1]

---

[1] CWS, p. 458.

Jōdo Wasan 64
Provisionally guiding sentient beings of the ten quarters with the words
'Direct your merits with sincere mind, desiring to be born',
Amida revealed the true gate of the Name,
Vowing to enable beings ultimately to attain birth.

THE TRUE GATE

Shinran Shōnin here introduces us to the process of birth through the Twentieth Vow of Amida Buddha, or the 'true gate', which reads as follows:

> If, when I attain Buddhahood, the sentient beings of the ten quarters, on hearing my Name, should place their thoughts on my land, cultivate the root of all virtues, and direct their merits with sincere mind desiring to be born in my land, and yet not ultimately attain it, may I not attain the supreme enlightenment.[1]

In this verse, Shinran commends those who take up recitation of the nembutsu by 'self-power'. This effort, he says, will eventually result in birth in the Pure Land. In the *Kyōgyōshinshō*, he tells the story of his own entry through this gate of practice, on his way to the assurance of final liberation when the entrusting heart is awakened:

> Thus I, Gutoku Shinran, disciple of Śākyamuni, through reverently accepting the exposition of [Vasubandhu,] author of the Treatise, and depending on the guidance of Master [Shantao], departed everlastingly from the temporary gate of the myriad practices and various good acts, and left forever the birth attained beneath the twin *sāla* trees. Turning about, I entered the 'true' gate of the root of good and the root of virtue, and wholeheartedly awakened the mind leading to the birth that is non-comprehensible.
>
> Nevertheless, I have now decisively departed from the 'true' gate of provisional means and, [my self-power] overturned, have entered the ocean of the selected Vow.[2]

---

[1] CWS, p.229.
[2] CWS, p. 240.

The terminology that Shinran uses in this verse makes it quite clear that he sees the 'true gate', which is to recite the Name of Amida Buddha, as 'provisional' (*hōben*, Sk. *upāya*), and the resulting birth in the Pure Land as unfathomable: a manifestation of the Primal Vow's universality. *Hōben* is a well-known term which describes the way that enlightenment transforms itself in order to reach into the consciousness of the unenlightened. We will have many opportunities to explore this notion as we move through the hymns.

Listening to Shinran, one begins to realize that he understands Other-Power to be ubiquitous and tireless; working through all means to bring every being to awakening and liberation from samsāra. In describing his arrival at the 'true gate' of self-power nembutsu in this verse, Shinran is not referring to Hōnen's teaching – which is the Other-Power teaching of the Primal Vow – but to a process of abandoning 'sundry practices' and accepting only one: saying the nembutsu.

Although he recited the nembutsu in his aspiration for birth, Shinran eventually came to see that – with the awakening of shinjin – the self is illusory and powerless, because its very existence arises from the contamination of primordial ignorance (*avidyā*) and the 'three poisons' of greed, anger and delusion.

Although the process of conversion through the 'three gates' was Shinran's personal experience, it's not a requirement for the rest of us. However, like him, many seekers will, at some point, abandon 'sundry practices', having exhausted their personal resources and deciding to give themselves over to invoking the Name. Taking up the nembutsu, or entering the 'true gate', is a conscious act that we appear to do ourselves.

As Shinran discovered, the Name – *Namo Amida Butsu* – is, in fact, Amida Buddha's call to have us entrust in him. When the nembutsu becomes our own practice, we are in an analogous situation to those who heard news of Śākyamuni, decided that he was their only hope, and went to listen to him.

My understanding is that, even though we cling to the notion that the Name is something good that we do in our own cause, our efforts nevertheless place us within the ambit of the Primal Vow, whereby the awakening of the entrusting heart becomes inevitable.

Know that Śākyamuni, our loving father, and Amida, our compassionate mother, guide us – as our true parents – to the entrusting heart.[3]

---

[3] CWS, p. 464.

Jōdo Wasan 65
Based on the Vow that beings ultimately attain birth,
Śākyamuni presented, in the Amida Sūtra,
The root of good and the root of virtue,
Encouraging those of the One Vehicle.

THE AMIDA SŪTRA

Shinran Shōnin selects the Amida Sūtra as revealing the significance of the Twentieth Vow, which he calls 'the vow of sincere mind and directing of merit'. This is because this sūtra enjoins the exclusive practice of saying the Name.

> Sentient beings, each of you should accept what Śākyamuni has taught, has praised, has given witness to! It is certain beyond any doubt that when foolish beings – regardless of whether their evil or merit is great or small, or the period of time long or short – just single-heartedly practice the saying of the Name of Amida alone, for up to one hundred years or down to even one or seven days, they unfailingly attain birth.[1]

Along with the *Mahāmaṅgala Sutta*, the *Mettā Sutta* and the Heart Sūtra, the Amida Sūtra is the most widely chanted and best loved scriptures in the Buddhist world. Apart from its association with the Twentieth Vow, this text has many special qualities. The first is that it boldly proclaims Amida Buddha as a timeless reality. It merely explains his Name and does not attempt to assign a cause or origin to him.

In this way, we are led to understand the nature of Amida Buddha as ultimate reality – otherwise expressed as thusness (*tathātā*), dharma-nature (*dharmatā*), enlightenment (*bodhi*), Dharma-Body (*dharmakāya*), unconditioned (*asaṃskṛta*) and so on. Indeed, the description of the Buddha – and his Pure Land – in the Amida Sūtra simply declares the four attributes of this highest reality:

> The Dharma-Body is eternity, bliss, self and purity.[2]

Furthermore, it makes us aware of the principles outlined by Śākyamuni

---
[1] CWS, p. 231. A translation from the Amida Sūtra as rendered by Shan-tao. The passage is included in *Kyōgyōshinshō* (VI, 47).
[2] CWS, p. 188; a quotation in the *Kyōgyōshinshō* from the *Nirvāṇa Sūtra*.

in the *Kālāma Sutta* – which, in part, says that we should not accept something unless it is 'praised by the wise'. The Amida Sūtra tells us that all buddhas, throughout the universe, are one in urging us to accept its truths. And so it is that, throughout the centuries, millions of Buddhists have paid homage to Amida in response to this encouragement to have us turn to this Buddha as our only source of spiritual light.

In short, the sūtra affirms that Amida is the irresistible truth of Nirvāna[3] to which all suffering beings are drawn from the moment that the Buddha's light begins to dawn in their hearts.

---

[3] CWS, p. 184.

Jōdo Wasan 66

Those who say the Name in self-power, whether meditative or non-meditative
– Having indeed taken refuge in the Vow that beings ultimately attain birth –
Will spontaneously, even without being taught,
Turn about and enter the gate of Suchness.

TARIKI

The Vow of 'Accomplishing the Ultimate Salvation' is the Twentieth Vow.

The epic poem *Buddhacarita* tells the story of Śākyamuni Buddha's journey to enlightenment. The author, Aśvaghoṣa, lived during the first century BCE, and was spiritual advisor to the Gandhāran King, Kaniksha. Śākyamuni was enlightened 'by himself', having abandoned the guidance of teachers – notably Ārāḍa Kālāma and Udraka Rāmaputra. However, he did not create his own enlightenment. Śākyamuni was enlightened by the power of the dharma. This is how it happened.

After leaving Udraka Rāmaputra, Śākyamuni went to Magadha and undertook ascetic practices in an effort to force his enlightenment, thinking that 'no ascetic in the past, none in the present, and none in the future, ever has practiced or ever will practice more earnestly than me'. Yet, after six years of self-torment during which, it is said, he fasted so assiduously that his spine could be seen through his stomach, he realized the futility of these practices and began to eat properly and sit comfortably again.

Even so, Śākyamuni Buddha still engaged in rigorous endeavours. On taking up meditation, he declared: 'Blood may become exhausted, flesh may decay, bones may fall apart, but I will never leave this place until I find the way to enlightenment'. Still, he was assailed by confusing thoughts – 'dark shadows overhung his spirit'. He was assaulted by 'all the lures of the devils'. On examining each of these mental intrusions, one by one, he came to reject them. This process of elimination was a hard struggle, 'making his blood run thin, his flesh fall away, and his bones to crack'.

At the age of thirty-five, Śākyamuni finally reached enlightenment when the dharma dawned on him. All confusing thoughts dissipated and his demons fled, leaving his mind clear and his spirit free. The dharma, he realized, was the *only* reality.

Shinjin, in the Pure Land way, is the assurance of enlightenment and not enlightenment itself. We awaken to shinjin in this life and realize buddhahood upon passing beyond this realm of existence. In his spiritual journey, Shinran was able to discern stages of development and, like Śākyamuni, found it to be a process of elimination.

We have already seen that although the Nineteenth Vow – the way of many religious practices – portends a form of birth in the Pure Land, it nevertheless does not lead to final awakening and full realization of the Buddhist truth. So too the Twentieth Vow, which provides for 'self-power' practice of the nembutsu, leads to a 'provisional' Pure Land but does not, in itself, ensure final deliverance.

In this verse, however, Shinran asserts that 'self-power' nembutsu leads to a spontaneous (*jinen*) entry through the 'gate of True Thusness'. How so? Because, even though the nembutsu of the Twentieth Vow is a self-power endeavour, it implies a nascent faith which arises from the Vow of Amida Buddha.

Entrusting ourselves to the Name and coming to the 'gate of True Thusness' – to shinjin – seems, at first, to be something we have initiated ourselves; but in truth, we are really responding to the call of the Vow which seeks to have us take refuge in the Name. In this sense, our self-power (*jiriki*) is, in fact, the working of Other-Power.

Jōdo Wasan 67
Those who, though aspiring for the Pure Land of happiness,
Do not realize shinjin that is Other-Power,
Doubt the Buddha's inconceivable wisdom and therefore dwell
In the borderland or the realm of indolence and pride.

NAMO AMIDA BUTSU IS EVERYTHING

Shinran Shōnin goes to considerable lengths in his marginal note to this verse to explain the term 'borderland' and makes it clear that mere recitation of the nembutsu as a ritual act – in the hope of birth in the Pure Land – is very unlikely to result in permanent release from samsāra. Very few, he suggests, are able to realize buddhahood in this way, and doubt is essentially incompatible with the way of Jōdo Shinshū. This is not something of Shinran's invention; rather, he is drawing on a lengthy passage from the Larger Sūtra.

Shinran implies that awakening to *tariki no shin* – or shinjin by Other-Power – is not an 'easy way'. In fact, the lazy option is the way of self-power which leads to the 'realm of sloth and pride'. This is for the kind of reason we explored when considering the previous verse (as we watched Śākyamuni's progress towards enlightenment), in which he relinquished his attachment to false views and came to terms with his demons.

Similarly, the true way of nembutsu – that of Other-Power – is difficult, sometimes painful, yet it results in Nirvāna; that is, entry into the realm of utmost happiness. It is difficult simply because it 'runs against the stream' to use a metaphor coined by Śākyamuni when speaking of the dharma; and it's arduous because we want to live according to false views, prejudices and assumptions; because 'seeing things as they really are' is hard to do.

It seems counter-intuitive that the lazy way is to focus on practice rather than on the Name. It is ritualistic (and, therefore, basically out of step with the Buddha-dharma) rather than penetrative and reflective. In Shinran's historical context, it is to be concerned about, for example, the number of times one says the nembutsu rather than opening oneself to its call. It's to be concerned with quantity, rather than quality.

The Name – *Namo Amida Butsu* – throws up many questions for us; it sends us out looking for teachers; it encourages us to think about ourselves and our relationship to the dharma. If we take up the nembutsu for ourselves, we eventually come to see why it's described as the form of the Buddha, and as our teacher.

Amida's Vow is, from the very beginning, designed to bring each of us to entrust ourselves to it – saying *Namo Amida Butsu* – and to receive us into the Pure Land; none if this happens through our own calculation.[1]

So, the Pure Land way begins and ends in nembutsu. It is not a ritual act but something with which we develop a relationship and a dialogue. Ultimately, this is mysterious but we are told – throughout the Pure Land tradition – that the Name was the form chosen by Amida Buddha, so as to act upon us and to open our hearts to the dharma. Those who have deeply experienced the nembutsu can testify to the veracity of this path which is, by far, the most popular form of Buddhism in East Asia.

All our searching focuses on the Name. *Tariki no shin* discovers us in the process. The quality of nembutsu changes from quest to celebration when the time is ripe – and often it is both repentance (turning from self-power) and joy. We shall see this more fully when we come to explore the section on Shan-tao in the *Hymns on the Dharma Masters*. The Name itself is all-important because life is short and the quest urgent.

When it comes to our spiritual life, it's unwise to waste our time on peripheral concerns. It is through the Name that we hear the Vow and awaken to shinjin, which is the cause of birth in the Pure Land. In no other way can it be heard and we cannot be born without it. It seems to me that the value of teachings, other than those of Jōdo Shinshū, are of use only to the extent that they throw light on the Name or assist us in discussing it with others.

Let us then turn to wise nembutsu teachers – especially Hōnen, Shinran and Rennyo – and sit at their feet as we listen to the call of the Vow in *Namo Amida Butsu*. There is no more joyous thing that we can do.

---

[1] CWS, p. 427.

Jōdo Wasan 68
*It is difficult to encounter a time when a Tathāgata appears in the world,
And difficult to hear the teaching of the buddhas;
It is rare to hear the excellent dharma for bodhisattvas,
Even in a span of countless kalpas.*

THE BODHISATTVA VEHICLE

> The four vehicles are: first, the Buddha vehicle; second, the bodhisattva vehicle; third, the pratyekabuddha vehicle; fourth the śrāvaka vehicle. The Pure Land school belongs to the bodhisattva vehicle.
>
> The two collections of scripture are: first, the bodhisattva piṭaka; second, the śrāvaka piṭaka. The present teaching belongs to the bodhisattva piṭaka.[1]

In his otherwise excellent introduction to Buddhism,[2] Hans Wolfgang Schumann claims that the Mahāyāna provides several distinct paths to liberation. Among them are the bodhisattva way and that of 'faith'. He includes Jōdo Shinshū in the latter group. Generally speaking, however, almost all Mahāyāna schools are considered to be part of the bodhisattva vehicle. It's not, therefore, correct to propose a separate classification describing certain schools as 'the way of faith'.

In fact, when Schumann outlines the bodhisattva vehicle, he is unwittingly writing a summary of Jōdo Shinshū. This is not to criticize Schumann because he is a Sanskrit scholar and not a student of the Pure Land tradition in China and Japan. Yet even in the Sanskrit version of the Larger Sūtra, it's clear that the central import of Amida Buddha's vows is to support the bodhisattva path.

Schumann rightly points out that the aspiring bodhisattva sets out to secure their release from this sorrowful world of birth-and-death. This is done by undertaking the six perfections[3] for the sake of 'oneself and

---

[1] CWS, p. 534.
[2] *Buddhism: An Outline of its Teachings and Schools* (Quest Books, 1973).
[3] These are the *pāramitās*, usually translated as 'perfections'. They receive this name 'because they have arrived (*gamanāt*) at the other shore (*pāram*) of the other shore of the totality of the perfections proper to each of them.' (*Abhidharmakośa-bhāṣyam*, Vol. II, p. 694.)

others'. To achieve this goal, the assistance of the buddhas and bodhisattvas is sought and, when received, we seek to repay this debt through diligent effort. This description is an almost exact account of Shinran's thinking. In explaining the 'way of faith', Schumann alludes to it as intended for those afflicted by defiling passions and incapable of self-effort. However, in Shinran's view, Jōdo Shinshū incorporates not only the weak and needy, but also monks and sages. There are many examples of this perspective in his writings.

The idea that a bodhisattva's journey is demanding, and that the Pure Land way is just for spiritual 'failures', is often repeated by nembutsu followers. Much is made, for example, of Hōnen Shōnin's admission that he couldn't practice meditation because of his lack of mental discipline; and Shinran, too, said similar things.

But to focus on such statements is to miss the whole point of Shinran's experience and insight. In the *Kyōgyōshinshō* (and in the passages cited at the beginning of this essay), we see that there is absolutely no question that Shinran sees the Pure Land gate as an integral part of the bodhisattva vehicle.

As we closely consider – and become familiar with – Shinran's outlook, we begin to discover that his view of the Pure Land way is all-embracing; taking in those who are both 'strong' and 'weak'. It's not so much that there are those with varying capacities for whom different religious practices are needed but rather – as Shinran suggests – that there is but a single path for all.

The truth is that there's only one reality: Other-Power. Those who think of themselves as engaging in arduous practice do not, in fact, appreciate the influence of *tariki*. The way of self-power serves to deepen the understanding of ourselves and, though clearly important and legitimate, remains provisional.

It doesn't matter how such aspirants envisage their role; the fact is that *jiriki* endeavours are also embraced by the light and life of *tariki*. In this sense, there's actually no such thing as 'self-power'; only Other-Power is real. Those who awaken to this fact in shinjin – because they see reality as it is – will eventually be liberated.

Jōdo Wasan 69
It is difficult to meet true teachers
And difficult for them to instruct.
It is difficult to hear the teaching well,
And more difficult still to accept it.

THE TEACHER

This verse, like the previous one, celebrates a well-known and oft-quoted passage in the Larger Sūtra. The teacher is 'a good (virtuous) friend' (*zenjishiki*, Sk. *kalyāṇa-mitra*) who brings the dharma to life for us in their own person. A *zenjishiki* is someone we know that we can trust in spiritual matters; a person who enriches our hearts.

Such people inspire and encourage; not so much by their learning or clerical status, as through their sheer presence and by their whole-hearted attunement to the dharma that we seek; yet we are never expected to suspend our critical judgement and common sense when reflecting on our teachers. They are more an inspiration than authority figures. In his interpretation of the allegory of 'Two Rivers and a White Path', Shinran Shōnin – in the *Kyōgyōshinshō* – implies that our true teacher is none other than Amida Buddha.

A good *zenjishiki* is, of course, vital and indispensable. This is because the profound and sometimes abstruse meaning of the teaching comes to light for the seeker only when it's exemplified by a living individual. We may not meet a teacher in person, but the dharma does need a biography. Thus Shinran may be known, not just through the legacy of his written testimony, but also by the way in which his teaching comes alive when we see who he was as a person.

Anyone may be a teacher. The famous Shinshū follower Genza (1852–1930) regarded his cow as one, because the way she carried a heavy load of straw reminded him of how Amida Buddha bore the burden of Genza's own binding desires.

The person who had the greatest influence on me becoming a nembutsu follower was a friend whose courage and personal honesty helped me to see the truth of Amida Buddha's dharma. A couple of years later, Śākyamuni himself (in his recorded teaching) brought me to a further and far deeper understanding, which has never left me. Now, it is 'sitting at the feet' of Shinran and contemplating his own writing that has – for a great many years – been a daily joy.

Of course, there are bad teachers (*akujishiki*). Such people are easy to pick because their objective is to have followers rather than independent companions who are devoted to the dharma. They like to gather around them crowds of admiring people and their *modus operandi* is usually one of control.

A very telling feature about them is that they're unwilling to admit to mistakes or to change their minds from time to time; they also tend not to rejoice at the accomplishments of others. Neither Shinran nor Genza's cow manifested any of these qualities.

It's difficult to meet a good teacher – not so much because there are none available (for example, Shinran's collected works are easy to acquire) – but because our hearts and minds are closed. Meeting a good teacher (whether it's a historical figure or a living contemporary) is like falling in love. Our self-absorption is transcended and we're moved to a new stage of awareness, because we find ourselves captivated by their spirit and words. It is, indeed, difficult to progress in the dharma without such an encounter.

Jōdo Wasan 70
*More difficult even than trust in the teachings of Sakyamuni's lifetime,
Is the true entrusting of the universal Vow,
The sūtra teaches that it is 'the most difficult of all difficulties';
That 'nothing surpasses this difficulty'.*

A LESSON FROM TREES

> **osmosis** *n. ... Biology:* the diffusion of fluids through membranes or porous partitions.[1]

Difficult as it is to attain, Shinran Shōnin nevertheless expresses joyful faith (*shingyō*) in this way:

> How joyous I am, my heart and mind being rooted in the Buddha-ground of the universal Vow, and my thoughts and feelings flowing within the dharma-ocean, which is beyond comprehension![2]

In other words, he has become steeped in the Vow; imbued with it. He says elsewhere that he's grown acutely aware of his complete failure to actively eradicate his *bonnō*. In fact, the more he's steeped in the universal Vow, the more he realizes his own ignorance and incapacity. Hence, he's overcome by joy!

'Osmosis' is a good way to describe the Pure Land path. By immersing ourselves in the dharma, we can allow its influence to permeate our consciousness and overwhelm our evil karma; even though 'defiling passions' remain intact until our Nirvāna at the time of death. So, when we 'hear the dharma' (*chōmon*) well, shinjin arises and liberation is assured at that very moment. Therefore, active engagement with the teaching is essential.

Our main resources are the three Pure Land sūtras, along with the writings of T'an-luan, Hōnen, Shinran and Rennyo. Nevertheless, Shinran's hymns and the letters of Rennyo will provide us with just about everything we need to hear the dharma.

---

[1] *The Macquarie Concise Dictionary* (2001).
[2] CWS, p. 291.

When starting out on the path of *chōmon*, it's a good idea to select a single resource (like this collection of *wasan*), to become familiar with it, and then to gradually expand one's horizons. Along the way, we are sure to be intrigued by the many questions that'll come to mind – these may provoke a far-reaching exploration that could lead us into the magnificent halls of Shinran's great anthology of Pure Land teaching: the *Kyōgyōshinshō*. On exploring this vast epitome of the dharma, we soon discover a wellspring of truth and delight.

Plants grow and become healthy by being saturated with light during the day, and being firmly rooted in the soil from which they draw water and nutrients. To me, trees always stand as a metaphor of the Pure Land way. In the nembutsu, we bathe in the light of Amida Buddha's wisdom and compassion; and in paying close attention to the dharma, we receive spiritual sustenance and quench our thirst for truth.

At night, trees rest from growth and the nutrients they have absorbed become integrated into their structure.

Jōdo Wasan 71
Attaining Buddhahood through the nembutsu is the true essence of the Pure Land way;
The myriad practices and good acts are the temporary gate.
Unless one distinguishes the accommodated and the real, the temporary and the true,
One cannot possibly know the Pure Land that is naturalness (jinen).

THE TRUE TEACHING

Truly we know that without the virtuous Name, our compassionate father, we would lack the direct cause for birth. Without the light, our compassionate mother, we would stand apart from the indirect cause of birth. Although direct and indirect causes may come together, if the karmic-consciousness of shinjin is lacking, one will not reach the land of light. The karmic-consciousness of the true and real shinjin is the inner cause. The Name and light – our father and mother – are the outer cause. When the inner and outer causes merge, one realizes the true body in the fulfilled land. Therefore master [Shan-tao[1]] states:

> [Amida] takes in and saves all beings throughout the ten quarters with light and the Name; [Amida] brings sentient beings to realize shinjin and aspire for birth.

Further, [Fa-chao[2]] states:

> Attainment of buddhahood through the nembutsu: this is the true essence of the Pure Land way.

Further, [Shan-tao states:]

> Difficult to encounter is the true essence of the Pure Land way.

Let this be known.[3]

---

[1] Shan-tao (613-681) is the fifth dharma master in the Jōdo Shinshū lineage.
[2] Fa-chao (766-822) was said to be an incarnation of Shan-tao.
[3] CWS p.54ff.

The phrase *nembutsu jōbutsu kore shinshū* ('attaining Buddhahood through the nembutsu is the true essence of the Pure Land way') was first used by Fa-chao nearly four centuries before Shinran Shōnin completed the *Kyōgyōshinshō*. It was not until well after Shinran's departure, that *Shinshū* ('true teaching') was used to describe the school of Buddhism which is based on his teaching. Here, it means the teaching that will definitely lead to birth in the Pure Land and liberation from samsāra, because one has reached 'the stage of the truly settled' at the awakening of shinjin.

'Attaining Buddhahood through the nembutsu is the true essence of the Pure Land way' is an affirmation of the central place of *shōmyō* (the mindful recitation of the Name – *Namo Amida Butsu*) in the Pure Land tradition. It was Shan-tao who first identified the nembutsu as the crux of the teaching, designating other practices as 'sundry' and 'miscellaneous'. *Shinshū* then is used to distinguish the teaching of the Primal Vow of Amida Buddha from the unsettled nature of other paths, in which the nembutsu has not yet become the manifestation of shinjin – the true cause of our spiritual liberation.

The essence of Jōdo Shinshū can be encapsulated by viewing the Primal Vow as three distinct phases in the single event of awakening:[4]

1. Hearing the Name (*Namo Amida Butsu*) in association with the working of the light or wisdom of Amida Buddha;
2. The one thought-moment of shinjin; that is to say, becoming completely free of all doubt; accepting the Name with wholehearted joy and trust due to the realization that 'I am unable to be liberated, yet Amida liberates me'; and
3. Saying the Name in gratitude – *ho'on nembutsu* – which becomes one's outward disposition for the rest of our lives.

Here is another way of expressing the same event: hearing and fully understanding the call of the Primal Vow in the light of Amida Buddha, shinjin arises and we express our complete trust in the Name by calling it to mind or saying it aloud.

In the *Kyōgyōshinshō*, Shinran demonstrates – in intricate detail through his analysis of traditional texts – how this all fits together in a

---

[4] CWS, p, 80.

straightforward pattern of conversion and salvation. Thus, Shinran fulfills the axiom that the true teaching (*Shinshū*) is to become a Buddha (upon attaining birth in the Pure Land) through (the working of) nembutsu.

Each of these three phases in this single event calls for repeated reflection and elucidation. Such is the purpose of this *wasan*.

Jōdo Wasan 72
Sentient beings, having long followed the Path of Sages –
The accommodated and temporary teachings that are provisional means
– Have been transmigrating in various forms of existence;
So take refuge in the One Vehicle of the compassionate Vow.

THE ONE AND THE MANY

Here Shinran Shōnin concludes his verses dedicated to the Larger Sūtra and, with it, he summarizes all he wants to say on this topic. The purpose of the sūtra is essentially to reveal the 'One Vehicle' of the Primal Vow which, in turn, is a manifestation of the Dharma-Body.

Shinran includes an extensive section dealing with the One Vehicle in his *Kyōgyōshinshō*. In it he makes clear that he understands Amida Buddha (*Tathāgata*) to be the ultimate reality, no less, and links the other vehicles to this primary one.

These include the pratyekabuddha vehicle, in which enlightenment is attained without instruction in the dharma; the śrāvaka vehicle, in which enlightenment is possible by following the instruction of a buddha; and the bodhisattva vehicle, in which enlightenment is assured by following the course taken by buddhas. These three vehicles are not part of the One Vehicle but serve as expedients that draw disciples to it.

> In the term *ocean of the One Vehicle*, 'One Vehicle' refers to the great vehicle (Mahāyāna). The great vehicle is the Buddha vehicle. To realize the One Vehicle is to realize the highest perfect enlightenment. The highest perfect enlightenment is none other than the realm of Nirvāna. The realm of Nirvāna is the ultimate Dharma-Body. To realize the ultimate Dharma-Body is to reach the ultimate end of the One Vehicle. There is no other Tathāgata, there is no other Dharma-Body. Tathāgata is itself Dharma-Body. Reaching the ultimate end of the One Vehicle is without bound and without cessation. In the great vehicle there are no 'two vehicles' or 'three vehicles'. The two vehicles and three vehicles lead one to enter the One Vehicle. The One Vehicle is the vehicle of highest truth. There is no One Vehicle other than the One Buddha Vehicle, the Vow.[1]

---

[1] CWS, p. 60ff.

Shinran goes on to define the full phrase 'ocean of the One Vehicle'. It is an ocean because it takes in every conceivable kind of human character and personality; and does so at any kind of intellectual, moral, ethical, aesthetic, ascetic, philosophical, scientific, cultural, ethnic, national, class, caste or occupational level.

In other words, the One Vehicle carries all beings, without exception, to enlightenment. Just as an ocean ejects the floating corpses of the drowned, so the ocean of the One Vehicle ejects the putrid 'deeds' and dark minds of all people, including those who follow the 'two' and 'three vehicles'. Rather than being the ultimate goal, these vehicles serve as provisional means for final embarkation on the One Vehicle of Amida Buddha's Primal Vow.

> The ocean of the Vow does not keep within it the dead bodies of the sundry good acts of the two vehicles; that is, the middle and lower vehicles. Hardly does it keep, then, the corpses of the empty, transitory, false, and deceitful good acts and the poisoned and impure minds of human beings and devas.[2]

The dharma is a raft that is eventually abandoned. However, since there is a vehicle on offer, it's very difficult to conceive of doing without it at the outset.

The analogy of crossing a stream using one or other of these available rafts is addressed by Shinran in the *Kyōgyōshinshō* (and his letters) where he describes the One Vehicle of the Vow as being 'sudden' and entailing a 'crosswise transference'. One switches naturally (*jinen*) from one shore to the other – from that of samsāra to the certain attainment of Nirvāna – in an instant so brief as to be imperceptible; at that moment, we unequivocally relinquish the 'mind of self-effort' in *Namo Amida Butsu*.

But, apart from this, why are the 'two' and the 'three' vehicles excluded from the One Vehicle of the Primal Vow? These other vehicles are intended to have us awaken to the truth of 'no self' (Sk. *anātman*) and their practices are bent to that end. However, when compared to the One Vehicle of the Primal Vow, they are superficial; treating just symptoms and not the disease, which is blind ignorance (Sk. *avidyā*) – the source of our conditioned and suffering existence.

---

[2] CWS, p. 62.

It simply isn't possible to overcome illusion by having recourse to those things which are produced by it – for example, our conscious mind (Sk. *mano-vijñāna*) and subconscious mind (Sk. *manas*). Hence, it is clear that the 'two' and 'three' vehicles cannot fathom the Buddha-dharma's full depth.

A path in which a course is minutely laid out and which seeks rigid conformity to a host of requirements tends to exclude a vast mass of people who don't function in that way themselves. It doesn't take into account that no two people are alike.

While it's comforting for us to identify with tribes, either by seeking to comply with the expectations of a group or by following preordained patterns of behaviour, the truth is that each of us is utterly unique. Few of us can adapt ourselves to an arbitrary and inflexible formula; and, often, the attempt to do so can be very painful and even self-destructive. That is why the urge to reduce people to various external attributes – for example, skin colour – is cruel and wicked.

As ultimate reality, the Dharma-Body both transcends, and dwells within, the countless variety of life's phenomena – it is a vast 'ocean' teeming with life. Trying to grasp it by following a minutely planned path is like walking on the ocean when, in fact, we are already deep inside it. We will only become seasick and battered, tossed about in the stormy corporeality of existence, if we persist in doing so. The Primal Vow calls us to yield to the secure tranquility of the 'One Vehicle' ocean. The way to attain true emancipation is for our hearts to become flooded with the Buddha's wisdom and compassion.

> We know truly, then

says Shinran,

> that it is as a sūtra states: 'The ice of blind passions melts and becomes the water of virtues.'[3]

---

[3] CWS, p. 62.

Jōdo Wasan 73
Śākyamuni Buddha, out of vast benevolence,
Instructed Queen Vaidehī, leading her to select,
From among all the lands manifested in the pedestal of light,
Amida's world of happiness.

THE THUNDERBOLT

Chokumei is an imperial command, and yet when the word (*chokushi te*) is used in this verse, the term 'command' is carefully avoided and, in the above translation, 'leading' is used instead. The reason for this choice is quite clear and comes from a sense that this verse should be interpreted in a way that is consistent with the Contemplation Sūtra, to which it alludes.

The events detailed in the sūtra, which provide the content of this verse, refer to Queen Vaidehī's distress at being imprisoned for helping her husband – King Bimbsāra – during his incarceration by the crown prince Ajātaśatru. In her anguish, Śākyamuni comes to alleviate the queen's suffering.

He shows her all the pure lands (that is, the 'tangible' environments of the enlightened ones) and gently urges her towards Amida's realm of 'Utmost Bliss'. Surely, this story addresses – not only the way in which suffering beings turn to the dharma (as Vaidehī cries to Śākyamuni for help) – but also the spiritual choices we must make in life. In other words, the Buddha-dharma takes the way of selection and choice rather than syncretism. Choice requires a measure of courage and selflessness – and the outright abandonment of anything extraneous to our emerging sense of spiritual truth.

In the Contemplation Sūtra, we read that Śākyamuni led Vaidehī towards her eventual choice of Amida Buddha's dharma. When Shinran comes to relate this event in his hymns, he insists that it was by Śākyamuni's command. I am sure there is a reason for this; perhaps it's because awakening is often sudden, instant, immanent and spontaneous – like a thunder-clap. In this story, we encounter something of Shinran's sense of Other-Power (*tariki*), which breaks into our consciousness unexpectedly; unprompted, unplanned and without our contrivance. So it is that when Ajātaśatru himself awakens to the entrusting heart, he declares in the *Kyōgyōshinshō*:

> O, World-honored one, observing the world, I see that from
> the seed of the *eraṇḍa* grows the *eraṇḍa* tree. I do not see a
> *candana* tree growing from an *eraṇḍa* seed. But now for the
> first time I see a *candana* tree growing from the seed of an
> *eraṇḍa*. The *eraṇḍa* seed is myself; the *candana* tree is the
> entrusting heart *that has no root in my heart*.[1]

The difference between 'lead' and 'command' is very striking. To say that one is 'commanded to choose' is, of course, an oxymoron. In a command, there can be no choice except – and here's the key thing – to assent. Yes, we can always choose not to obey a command. To do this in the context of the Pure Land dharma is to choose interminable mediocrity – endless rebirths through countless aeons – and pointless wandering in samsāra. Whereas to assent means to make a decisive break with this realm of birth-and-death and attain ultimate freedom (Sk. *mokṣa*). Shinran does not see that there is any choice apart from acquiescence.

When (again in the *Kyōgyōshinshō*), Shinran examines closely the word *Namo*, in its classical translation into the Chinese term *kimyō*, he discovers a similar significance:

> ... we see that the word *namo* means to take refuge. In the term
> 'to take refuge' (*kimyō*), *ki* means to arrive at. Further, it is
> used in compounds to mean to yield joyfully to (*kietsu*) and to
> take shelter in (*kisai*). *Myō* means to act, to invite, to
> command, to teach, path, message, to devise, to summon.
> Thus, *kimyō* is the command [*chokumei*] of the Primal Vow
> calling to and summoning us.[2]

Although there are eight possible interpretations of *myō*, Shinran chooses only 'command'. The potency of Shinran's perception is overwhelming. One can almost feel his sense of Other-Power's irresistible summons. Shinran had no choice but to follow the command of the Name, which is to trust it for one's spiritual emancipation.

In every life, there arise moments when we encounter a fork in the road on which we travel. Now, in religious discourse, we are often bidden to choose a path between, say, this or that deity or one philosophy over

---

[1] CWS, p. 137ff.
[2] CWS, p. 38.

another. But, in the nembutsu, the choice is this: between *the* path or not choosing at all. The way that leads to Amida Buddha becomes clear when we find it. In the Pure Land tradition, we tell the parable of the 'Two Rivers and a White Path' where it's not a matter choosing between one path or another, but whether or not we make the only choice there is. It is, in fact, a choice between the sole reality and that which is ultimately ephemeral. It is as though the thunderbolt – the shock of realization – makes us suddenly see that this material world is transient and unreliable.

> But with a foolish being full of blind passions, in this fleeting world – this burning house – all matters without exception are empty and false, totally without truth and sincerity. The nembutsu alone is true and real.[3]

---

[3] CWS, p. 679.

Jōdo Wasan 74
*King Bimbisāra put the ascetic to death
Without waiting for the time of his rebirth as determined by
  past conditions,
And in recompense for this act of murder,
Was imprisoned in a cell seven walls thick.*

THE *NIRVĀṆA SŪTRA*

This is the second verse (in a series of nine) that draws on the Contemplation Sūtra, which begins with an incident in the life of the royal family at Rājagṛha, an important location in Śākyamuni's life. It was close to the place of his enlightenment where he delivered many of his sermons, nearby on Vulture Peak. We learn from the sūtra that King Bimbisāra has become a victim at the hands of his own son, Prince Ajātaśatru; although we come to see that this oppressive experience was the outcome (Sk. *vipāka*) of his own vicious karma (Sk. *akuśala karma*).

The account given of the karmic cause that led to Bimbisāra's distress comes from the *Nirvāṇa Sūtra*,[1] one of Shinran's most fertile resources. It's clear that one of the main reasons for Shinran's extensive use of this text is the harrowing sense of crisis and anguish that shadows the tragic events at Rājagṛha castle – and the way in which light can break into, and redeem, seemingly intractable human evil.

In the Contemplation Sūtra, Vaidehī, King Bimbisāra's consort, is acutely distressed by the cruel treatment her husband has received at the hands of their son. She receives consolation from Śākyamuni, as well as instruction in how to attain birth in the Pure Land. The *Nirvāṇa Sūtra* takes up the events that followed Bimbisāra's death. It is then that Ajātaśatru views himself as utterly incurable; he sees into the deep darkness of his heart and observes the reality of the greed, anger and depravity that imbues his every motive, taints his every love, and stains his every aspiration.

In the account of Ajātaśatru's shocking, existential pain, we are struck by the very fact that he becomes aware of his own nature with such palpable

---

[1] The only complete translation available at present is the *Mahāyāna Mahāparinirvāṇa Sūtra*, translated by Kosho Yamamoto (and edited by Tony Page), F. Lepine Publishing, 2008.

clarity, which is the first of two stages in the redemptive process. The second is his concomitant awakening to the shinjin granted by the Buddha. All this heart-breaking despair is completely, and forever, alleviated by 'shinjin that has no root in me'.[2]

The *Nirvāṇa Sūtra* expounds the great doctrine of Buddha-nature (Jp. *busshō*; Sk. *buddha-dhātu* or *tathāgatagarbha*). But without any firm basis in experience, such notions are mere empty assertions. Ajātaśatru himself was inconsolable until he heard the Buddha's call and awoke to shinjin. It is this section of the *Nirvāṇa Sūtra* – and its re-telling in the *Kyōgyōshinshō* – that bears witness to the truth of Buddha-nature, and to where the Pure Land teachings spring into life, making their fruit manifest.

---

[2] CWS, p.138. The phrase 'no root in me' means 'not something I created myself'.

Jōdo Wasan 75
King Ajātaśatru shouted, in a fit of rage,
'My own mother betrays me!'
And heinously, to strike her down,
He drew his sword against her.

ANITYA

The next four verses relate the events described in the third chapter of the Contemplation Sūtra. Indeed, for Shinran Shōnin, the first five chapters of this text are clearly the most important. In them, we encounter some of the most fearsome and terrible passions.

Shinran was certainly familiar with such vehement feelings. He not only experienced them in the course of his life – as when the nembutsu community was confronted with the fury, anger and jealousy of both the monastic and secular authorities – but the inconceivable light of Amida Buddha also cast his own inner demons into sharp relief.

In the previous verse, we saw that Ajātaśatru deposed his father, King Bimbisāra. Now, on discovering that Queen Vaidehī was taking food to him, Ajātaśatru flies into a rage. Intending to kill his mother, he declares her to be his enemy. Then he commits the cardinal offence of abusing the dharma.

> Upon hearing these words, Ajātaśatru became infuriated at his mother and shouted: 'Mother, you are my enemy because you're an accomplice to my enemy. Those vile monks with their delusive magic have enabled that wicked king to remain alive for these many days.' Immediately, he drew his sharp sword, intending to kill her.[1]

This paragraph describes some profound human truths at the heart of which is the ugliness of self-justification. No matter who we are, it's extremely difficult for us to see ourselves as being at fault in any given situation. And those of us who claim to accept our faults are very often feigning it in order to escape notice or retribution.

---

[1] *The Three Pure Land Sūtras (Volume I): The Amida Sūtra and the Contemplation Sūtra*, Shin Buddhism Translation Series, 2003, p.19.

Ajātaśatru's absurd name-calling, and hurling of accusations, are a common feature of our human life. History is full of murderous demagogues who harbour the most heinous motives while denouncing others for doing the very same thing. But even in everyday relationships and society at large, this kind of behaviour is an altogether common occurrence.

In this verse, Ajātaśatru is outspoken and enraged with the dharma itself. He is contemplating killing his mother, an evil that is inconceivable. It's impossible to see in this fuming man one who, within a few years, would become a benefactor of the Buddha-dharma; a virtuous and wise lay disciple.

Unless, of course, one is in tune with the dharma. For one of the signs (Sk. *lakṣana*) of conditioned existence is change (Sk. *anitya*). Although this truth can be threatening and fearful, it is the harbinger of positive change as well.

We learn in the *Nirvāṇa Sūtra* that the enraged and abusive Ajātaśatru later became a gentle and devoted follower of the dharma.

Jōdo Wasan 76
Jīvaka and Candraprabha earnestly admonished the king,
Saying such acts were those of an outcaste,
And that they could not remain in the castle should he persist;
Thus they tried to quell his lawless impulses.

ON VIOLENCE

Jīvaka and Chandraprabha were two devoted followers of the Buddha-dharma, wise and gentle men who were forced to take urgent action to restrain Ajātaśatru from an act of grave wrongdoing.

It is well-known that the basis of conduct enjoined by the dharma is harmlessness (Sk. *ahimsā*) and we see this reflected in prominent ethical discourses like the *Advice to Rāhula* (Śākyamuni's son) which features moral guidance based on the degree of harm inherent in any action; both to oneself and to others.

Prior to this time, we do not find a teaching that gives consideration to the outcome of actions – not just from the aspect of its karmic effect, but in terms of its impact upon others. The ethical system derived from the crucial Buddhist insight into 'not-self' (Sk. *anātman*) was the first to be other-regarding.

Consideration of karmic outcomes is a different perspective on the dharma compared to simply being ethical since, at base, the objective of any practice is to transcend karma completely, and not merely to settle for a good rebirth. The Buddha-dharma seeks to bring an end to the round of birth-and-death altogether. Self-centered concern for the personal outcomes of one's karma (or 'actions') is popular but inherently self-defeating.

When it comes to the violent conflict at the royal palace, we see a telling juxtaposition of attitudes and outcomes. Ajātaśatru, the usurper, slanders the dharma by insulting the sangha, threatens his mother's life, and takes decisions that result in his father's death. Eventually, he is the one who suffers the most as a result.

Needless to say, the purpose of the Buddha-dharma is not just to provide an ethical system, nor is it to keep followers chained to samsāra by encouraging them to practice karma that may only lead to a good rebirth.

Its sole objective is final liberation (*vimukti*).

In a striking paradox, the story of Ajātaśatru brings about the realization – through the working of the Primal Vow – that the way of nembutsu is our only option. When this realization becomes firm and unshakeable, the entrusting heart becomes settled and our spiritual emancipation is assured.

Jōdo Wasan 77
The minister Jīvaka, with hand on his sword,
Stepped backward and began to take his leave;
Ajātaśatru was thus made to discard his sword,
But he confined Vaidehī within the palace.

OUTRAGE

The tumultuous events at the palace in Rājagṛha were the occasion for the Pure Land dharma being revealed to the world. If life had treated Vaidehī fairly and justly, it's unlikely that she would have appealed to Śākyamuni for help; and then the opportunity to teach the Pure Land dharma would have passed. To explore this further, it is worth reflecting on King Bimbisāra's history.

There is a story that, before adopting the teaching of Śākyamuni, the king was a devout follower of the Vedic religion, a worshipper of fire (Sk. *agni*). One day, Siddhartha (Śākyamuni when he was still a bodhisattva and before he became a buddha) was approaching Rājagṛha when he was overtaken by some shepherds guiding a flock of sheep towards the city.

Asked why they were in such haste, a shepherd told Siddhartha that the king had proclaimed a feast and that the sheep were on their way to be slaughtered. The shepherds then hurried on. By the time Siddhartha arrived at Rājagṛha, the ceremony was well under way. He walked up to the king, and to the priests at the head of the congregation, and told them that sacrifice was a meaningless activity. He pointed out that no sentient being wanted to die so we should not kill them and, in any case, sickness and death fetches us off soon enough, so why hasten the process needlessly? He also said that it was extremely unfair to expect others to suffer on our behalf.

If one is not honestly prepared to give one's life to a particular cause, then it's disingenuous to ask others to risk their lives on our behalf. This is, of course, the *Golden Rule*, a norm of conduct common to all of humanity; except that, in the case of the Buddha-dharma, it extends to all sentient life.

As a result of that first meeting with the bodhisattva who was to become Buddha Śākyamuni, the ground was prepared for Bimbisāra's conversion to the dharma – after which he became a devout and virtuous follower to the end of his life. Now, suddenly, he is the victim of severe oppression and abuse at the hands of his own son. In her attempts to help her husband, Queen Vaidehī becomes Ajātaśatru's victim too and is imprisoned. It is this incident which – from our perspective – can only be described as one of outrage and confusion, thus serving as the occasion for the Pure Land teaching to be disclosed to the world.

In the midst of this turbulence, when darkness carries the day, the Pure Land way shines as a beacon on a moonless night – and as an oasis in a desert, fair and bright, offering the only light. This dharma is for the perplexed and the despairing.

> Let the one who seeks to abandon the defiled and aspire for the pure; who is confused in practice and vacillating in faith; whose mind is dark and whose understanding deficient; whose evils are heavy and whose karmic obstructions manifold – let such persons embrace above all the Tathāgata's exhortations, take refuge without fail in the most excellent direct path, devote themselves solely to this practice, and revere only this entrusting heart.[1]

If Queen Vaidehī had not been incarcerated and the victim of an outrage, she may not have been inclined to seek out the Pure Land dharma. And, if King Bimbisāra had thought that he would be safe and secure by following the dharma he, too, would have been wrong. Fury and bewilderment may also be the motivating force that drives us to seek out the way of nembutsu, just as it did for Vaidehī.

---

[1] CWS, p. 3.

Jōdo Wasan 78
Amida and Śākyamuni, employing compassionate means,
And Ānanda, Maudgalyāyana, Pūrṇa, Vaidehī, Devadatta, King
Ajātaśatru, Bimbisāra, Jīvaka, Candraprabha, Varṣākāra, and others –
[continued in the next hymn]

UPĀYA

Hōben (Sk. *upāya*) or 'compassionate means' is a practice of buddhas and those bodhisattvas who have attained the later stages (Sk. *bhūmi*) of spiritual development. For example, the appearance – or tangible form – of Amida Buddha as the Name (*Namo Amida Butsu*) is an upāya of the 'Dharma-Body as Suchness' (*hosshō hosshin*) which is the highest reality – formless and inconceivable – that transcends the realm of cause-and-effect. By assuming an intelligible, linguistic form, Amida Buddha emerges as the 'Dharma-Body as Compassionate Means' (*hōben hosshin*).

> All Buddhas and bodhisattvas have dharma bodies of two dimensions: 'Dharma-Body as Suchness' and 'Dharma-Body as Compassionate Means'. 'Dharma-Body as Compassionate Means' arises from 'Dharma-Body as Suchness', and 'Dharma-Body as Suchness' emerges out of 'Dharma-Body as 'Compassionate Means'. Those two dimensions of Dharma-Body differ but are not separable; they are one but cannot be regarded as identical.[1]

'Compassionate means' can be transgressive. In the Lotus Sūtra, Śākyamuni speaks of his own upāya, likening it to the father of children in a burning house whom he entices out with the promise of toys. In this case, deception and lying is involved. The significance of this is that, because unenlightened existence is rooted in ignorance (Sk. *avidyā*) and desire (Sk. *tṛṣṇā*), the enlightened ones need to transform themselves into forms redolent with the ingrained substance of our personalities. Thus, the buddhas can appeal to each of us in ways that are unique and appropriate.

We have already seen that Shinran's wife, Eshin-ni, described in a letter a dream she had in which Hōnen was revealed to her as the Bodhisattva

---
[1] CWS, p. 165.

Mahāsthāmaprāpta; a description with which Shinran readily concurred. This, too, is a manifestation of compassionate means. But the important thing to remember is that this upāya was not Hōnen's but the bodhisattva's.

Needless to say, people like us are not qualified to use compassionate means as a way to lead others to the dharma. We first need to be born in the Pure Land and to commence our career as buddhas, before this option is available to us. Any claim by an ordinary person to be an exponent of such means is quite deluded. For an unenlightened *bombu* to do this is to stoke the fires of our own hubris and desire.

Jōdo Wasan 79
All of the great sages –
By various means, brought the most foolish and lowest
Of evil people to enter the Vow
That does not neglect people of grave offences and transgressions.

INTRODUCING THE 'EVIL PERSON'

At this point, I will lay my cards on the table: there is a trend in religious discourse these days with which I disagree. It's a tendency to reduce religions to a single source or idea. I subscribe to the more recent view among scholars that religions are plural and can be quite unrelated even in traditions that have the same historical origins. I accept that this is not yet a well-received perspective, because it's disturbing for some, and out of step with the globalizing sensibilities of our time. But, since this is an acute and urgent problem that demands our attention, let's digress briefly to explore the significance of a plural – rather than a reductionist – view.

A plural view of religious revelations seeks to respect the uniqueness of each tradition and accepts that there really are irreconcilable differences. Indeed, certain religions are intended precisely as a rebuke of earlier movements.

Sometimes it's the result of clearer thought, since the differences in traditions are often quite marked. Things that look alike – as, for example, bats and birds do in flight – actually have an entirely different origin and structure. Again, this is a more generous position because it doesn't want to submerge one tradition within the worldview of another. I also believe it to be a more honest approach because it's prepared to co-exist with an uncomfortable reality.

Reductionism in the field of religious discourse is a feature of contemporary life. For example, the vast and complex reality of each individual human being is often reduced to single (and often absurd) factors such as star signs, genes, animal behaviour and so on. It's to be hoped that we'll one day grow out of this suffocating fixation and learn to celebrate again variety, difference and complexity for their own sake ... and, to be frank, admit that life is ultimately an impenetrable mystery.

I respect the fact that people are understandably concerned that the accentuation of difference may lead to conflict, yet it seems that it only does so when we seek to gain control over others. If people can be comfortable in thinking that the religion to which we subscribe represents an absolute truth while, at the same time, having sufficient respect for others to recognize their capacity to hold the same view about their own tradition, then I believe we'll have moved a long way towards genuine harmony. We'll then be able to enter into a more considerate relationship with others, wherein we may hold them in high regard, appreciating their uniqueness, dignity and spiritual sincerity.

So, when reflecting on Shinran Shōnin's teaching, we need to see it – from our position of standing 'within' it – as being unique. In his thinking, concepts like 'the evil person' have a special significance. It's a mistake to use the yardstick of non-Buddhist religions, or even related perspectives within the dharma, to understand what he means. The content of other, equally unique, religions cannot legitimately be brought to bear in discussing it.

In this verse, Shinran has left the following marginal note: 'The most foolish and the lowest are' he says 'we who have sunk to the bottom of the great sea' afflicted with 'the five grave offences and the ten unwholesome actions'. Shinran includes himself among those who can be designated as 'evil persons' and prone to depravity.

The 'five grave offences' are well-known: matricide, patricide, killing an *arhat*, destroying the harmony of the monastic community, and shedding the blood of a buddha. The ten unwholesome actions are those behaviours that lead to dire karmic outcomes as a natural consequence. They are killing, stealing, unfaithfulness in relationships, lying, speaking harshly, slander, idle chatter, greed, anger and wrong views.

The dramatic and harrowing events at the palace in Rājagṛha served, in Shinran's view, to evince this important insight. Thus, the dharma of Amida Buddha is spoken of as being especially for 'the evil person' (*akunin*). Shinran carries this theme into the next verse, so we'll have an opportunity to examine this more fully when we come to it.

Jōdo Wasan 80
Since conditions for the Pure Land teaching had matured,
Śākyamuni and Vaidehī, manifesting compassionate means,
Led the minister Varṣākāra to bear witness
And King Ajātaśatru to commit grave offences.

DROWNING

In this verse, Shinran Shōnin tells us that he sees the main players, in the events at Rājagṛha Palace, as manifesting a tide of karmic ripening whereby the fullness of time had come for the proclamation of the Pure Land teaching. This way of seeing things is most venerable in the tradition of the Buddha-dharma.

We who live in an individualistic era, tend to see Śākyamuni as a singular hero whose personal struggle led to the conquest of darkness and a personal awakening to the dharma. However, no such attitude prevails within the tradition which descends from him. From the earliest times, the birth, life and death of the Buddha are cosmic events. In the exquisite biography of Śākyamuni by Aśvaghoṣa,[1] the 'World Hero' is supported by the gods and all the natural forces of the universe.

So it is that, in this way, the dawn of the Pure Land teaching proved to be a momentous event of vast and timeless significance. In Shinran's view, an important factor leading to Śākyamuni's proclamation of the Pure Land way is the evil behaviour of Ajātaśatru, who usurped the throne of his father, Bimbisāra.

We learn, in the *Kyōgyōshinshō*, that Ajātaśatru eventually opened himself to shinjin when he repented of his wrongdoing. Repentance (Sk. *kaukṛitya*) is 'turning about' from the evils of the past to take refuge in the 'Three Treasures'. It is a determination to move on and leave the past behind. When one makes a mistake, one lets it go, prepares to take the inevitable consequences, and pushes on without any further regret. One might be wiser but neither the past, nor the future outcomes of our

---

[1] There are three readily available translations of the *Buddha-carita*: 1) E. B. Cowell's in the *Sacred Texts of the East* (Vol. LXIX); 2) Charles Willemen's (Numata Centre, 2009); and 3) Patrick Olivelle's in the Clay Sanskrit Library (NYUP & JJC Foundation, 2007).

actions, can be changed. The law of karma is inflexible.

The repeated reference to the grave wrongdoing (*gyakuaku*) of Ajātaśatru takes us back to the previous verse, in which Shinran says in his footnote that the 'most foolish and the lowest [evildoers]' are 'we who have sunk to the bottom of the great sea'. What does Shinran Shōnin mean by this intriguing phrase?

There are some nine or ten uses of the word 'sea' in the *Kyōgyōshinshō* but the two most relevant are these:

> ... sentient beings of the countless worlds, floundering in the sea of blind passions and drifting and sinking in the ocean of birth-and-death, lack the true and real mind of directing virtues; they lack the pure mind of directing virtues.[2]

The other passage is a quotation from Shan-tao:

> Beings in the ten quarters ... transmigrate within the six courses endlessly; revolving in circles, they flounder in the waves of desire and sink in the sea of pain.[3]

These two passages can be considered in concert with this quotation from the *Nirvāṇa Sūtra*:

> Good sons, there are four acts that bring evil results. What are these four? The first is to recite the sūtras in order to surpass others. The second is to observe the precepts in order to gain profit and esteem. The third is to practice charity in order to make others one's followers. The fourth is to fix and concentrate one's mind in order to reach the realm of neither thought nor no-thought. These four good acts bring evil results. Those who practice these four good acts are termed 'people who sink, then emerge again; emerge, then sink again'. Why is it said that they sink? Because they aspire to the three realms of existence. Why is it said that they emerge? Because they see brightness. To see brightness is to hear of precepts, charity and meditation. Why do they sink again?

---
[2] CWS, p. 103.
[3] CWS, p. 239.

> Because their wrong views increase and they give rise to arrogance.[4]

Shinran's reference to having sunk to the bottom of the sea is an allusion to unmitigated karmic evil, which follows from attachment to the three realms of existence.[5] There is no relieving moment of brightness; and our trajectory within samsāra is a constant downward spiral, in which nothing achieved is free from the taint of desire and ignorance. Even the good that one does is undermined by one's false assumption that samsāra is true reality. Our karma thus becomes increasingly onerous. Overwhelmed by its unremitting weight, one sinks into a pit of paralysis, unable to rise again. There is no illumination and no upward movement – the burden is too heavy, and one drowns in the painful sea of samsāra.

It's this realistic sense of our human condition that aroused such relief and joy in Shinran's heart. Being so immobilized and bogged down by evil karma, the only possibility of transcendence he could see was 'the call of the Vow' (*Namo Amida Butsu*); which, like Ajātaśatru's awakening, broke through his emotional bondage to the three realms of existence. This is the life-saving rope that appears in the stormy sea of samsāra. Since that's all there is, one has no choice but to grab hold of it. Having done so, it's not until a tug is felt from the other end that we know it can be trusted.

---

[4] CWS, p. 235.
[5] These comprise the realm of the 'five aggregates' (form, perception, conception, volition and consciousness), along with the realm of living beings and that of our environment.

Jōdo Wasan 81
Let us overturn the three minds of self-power, whether meditative
   or non-meditative,
Which vary with each practicer;
Let us aspire to enter into shinjin
That arises from Amida's benefiting of others.

OF SEEDS AND TREES

Today we will think about seeds and trees; of the way in which implicit things become explicit.

No living organism, if it's really vital, emerges into the light of day as a fully-formed, mature reality. Every thing that has life grows from a seed. Eventually, though, it grows old, tired and weary, and then dies – to be superseded by its offspring. Thus, the Buddha-dharma emerged at a time of great perplexity. This had arisen because of the irrefutable certainty in people's minds that the ruling principle of life in this world was the law of karma. This caused immense anxiety; and Śākyamuni was the one who discovered how to overcome the samsāric wandering which this law set in train.

The germ of Śākyamuni's idea was expressed in the *Sūtra on the Turning of the Wheel of the Dharma*, which revealed the Eightfold Path and the Four Noble Truths. This seed was to become a huge tree of wisdom, compassion and knowledge which, over time, encompassed almost the entire civilized world. This liberating awakening increased its light into a life-giving sun which spawned a plethora of religious movements, giving both nourishment and refuge to millions of people for more than 2,400 years now.

The great tree of the Buddha-dharma continues to draw on the germ within its original seed for the content and milieu which propels it on to ever greater heights. This is the development we can see everywhere in the world of human ideas and spirituality.

It's true that some new branches wither early; this usually happens because the pattern of the seed is violated or deformed in some way, thus cutting off the nutrients. But wherever there is growth, strength, beauty and truth it's always because some idea implicit in the original seed has become explicit. Religious movements grow and develop – they bring forth new ways and novel ideas as they manifest those things that are key to the integrity of the movement; but which may often have, at first, been hidden.

Shinran Shōnin is a genius of the spiritual life because of the clarity with which he understood this fact. Studying the dharma deeply and, having spent a lifetime contemplating its implication for the liberation of all beings, Shinran saw things which only he was able to bring to light.

In the Pure Land sūtras, he discerned an underlying significance which always referred back to the Primal Vow. Even in the Contemplation Sūtra – which is ostensibly about meditation – he saw anew things which had been dormant for a thousand years. Shinran gives prominence, not to the meditation techniques described in the sūtra, but to the events that elicited the proclamation of the Pure Land way. Also in this sūtra, we are enjoined to cultivate 'three minds' in association with our spiritual practice:

1. Sincere mind (*shijōshin*);
2. Deep mind (*jinshin*);
3. The mind that aspires for birth by transferring one's merits (*ekōhotsuganshin*).

Having established, in the previous few hymns, that we have no merits to transfer, Shinran sees in these three minds, not only the one mind of the entrusting heart, but the fact that this is grounded in Other-Power, pointing out – in his marginal note – that 'shinjin' is 'the Primal Vow's true and real *shinjin*'.

In drawing our attention to these new buds, which were implicit in the Pure Land way, Shinran's acuity sparkles and illuminates our hearts; his radiant insights free us from the constraints of our blindness and bring us joyful consolation.

Jōdo Wasan 82
Seeing the sentient beings of the nembutsu
Throughout the worlds, countless as particles in the ten quarters,
The Buddha grasps and never abandons them,
And therefore is named 'Amida'.

NEMBUTSU

This is the first in a series of five verses, which celebrate the teaching of the Amida Sūtra.

Earlier in the *Jōdo Wasan*, Shinran Shōnin suggests that Amida Buddha's light reaches everyone, everywhere, no matter who they are. However, the Contemplation Sūtra tells us that it's people of nembutsu who are actually embraced and not forsaken in the Buddha's light.

> Each ray of light shines over the worlds of the ten quarters, embracing and never abandoning those beings who are mindful of the Buddha.[1]

The pre-eminent focus of the Pure Land way is nembutsu because the Name is the form which is taken by the Primal Vow of Amida Buddha as it reaches into our lives, establishing itself in the hearts of those who accept its call. Hence, the only manifest form of shinjin is *Namo Amida Butsu*. Amida's light embraces and does not forsake 'followers of the nembutsu', and those who are aware of this naturally invoke the Name.

> Thus, although shinjin and nembutsu are two, since shinjin is to hear and not doubt that you are saved by only a single pronouncing, which is the fulfillment of practice, there is no shinjin separate from nembutsu; this is the teaching I have received. You should know further that there can be no nembutsu separate from shinjin. Both should be understood to be Amida's Vow. Nembutsu and shinjin on our part are themselves the manifestation of the Vow.[2]

There are three ways of understanding the nembutsu.

---

[1] *The Three Pure Land Sūtras (Volume I): The Amida Sūtra and the Contemplation Sūtra*, Shin Buddhism Translation Series, 2003, p.39.
[2] CWS, p. 538.

1. Thinking of the Buddha (Sk. *buddhānusmṛti*) and as a form of contemplative practice.
2. Saying the Name (*shōmyō*).
3. The Name as the form of the Vow (*myōgō*); the fulfilled form of Amida Buddha working in our lives.

Shinran Shōnin saw Shan-tao's exhortation to say the Name (*shōmyō*) 'whether standing, sitting or lying down' as an expression of deeply inconceivable factors – *myōgō* and the entrusting heart – rather than as a formal ritual designed to generate certain outcomes like birth in the Pure Land.

It seems to me that we are well advised to disabuse ourselves of any anguish about faith. The life of the Pure Land way is best seen as a straightforward proposition: absolute, single-minded trust in the Name. This is when we know for sure that the Name is the only thing that's true and real in this world of delusion; that there is no other way that we, who cannot deliver ourselves, are able to be saved. Then we'll also come to understand the ultimate source of shinjin, and be amazed to discover the power of the Buddha's Vow working in our lives.

> Therefore master [Shan-tao] states: [Amida] takes in and saves all beings throughout the ten quarters with light and Name; [Amida] brings sentient beings to realize true entrusting and aspire for birth.[3]

Adoring *Namo Amida Butsu*, we know and enjoy the embrace of Amida Buddha's light, which we can trust unconditionally and without concern for ourselves or our destiny. Shinran's understanding – that Shan-tao's advice to say the Name under all circumstances alludes to its spontaneity – removes all conditions or limitations. Everyday life is our *dōjō* (place of practice) and we can be aware of the Name, whatever we may be doing.

With *Namo Amida Butsu* as root and branch of our spiritual life, we live within Amida Buddha's light and are led to an ever-deepening awareness of his love, compassion and unremitting wisdom – along with his boundless life.

---

[3] CWS, p. 54.

Jōdo Wasan 83
The buddhas, countless as the sands of the Ganges or as particles,
Reject the small good of various practices
And all alike wholeheartedly encourage beings
To realize shinjin that is the inconceivable working of the Name.

ONLY THE NAME

In this, the second verse inspired by the Amida Sūtra, Shinran Shōnin reminds us that all the tathāgatas of the universe exhort us to take up the Name of Amida Buddha to the exclusion of all other practices. The verse especially suggests that the Name (*myōgō*) itself works upon us, to awaken the entrusting heart in a way that is imperceptible.

There is a reciprocity here: exclusive trust in the Name itself generates a feedback loop whereby our faith is nourished, sustained and enlivened in our hearts. This is why I suggested (in my reflections on the previous verse) that – for ignorant beings like us – the tangible reality is, in fact, the Name.

Remember that this verse is discussing *myōgō* as the form taken by the Vow. We hear it and it inspires trust in us. This, I think, is the reason why it's so important to deliberately limit our spiritual life to the Name alone. It seems to me that this involves 'hearing' the Name by cherishing the teachings we have received through the ages, discussing its meaning and significance with our fellow travellers in the dharma, and listening to teachers who enjoy sharing the entrusting heart of the Name with others.

In all this, the nembutsu itself resounds in the background as we say it in a spirit of taking refuge.

> Amida's Vow is, from the very beginning, designed to bring each of us to entrust ourselves to it – saying *Namo Amida Butsu* – and to receive us into the Pure Land; none of this is through our calculation.[1]

According to Shinran, the practice of the nembutsu has been fulfilled by Amida Buddha, both in the sense of its cause and effect. So there is no need for us to think that, by saying the Name, we achieve anything on our

---

[1] CWS, p. 530.

own behalf. Its invocation is a natural thing for us, said in happiness whenever we recall that we're 'embraced and not forsaken' by the Vow.

Needless to say, both active engagement with the Name, and the exclusive nature of it as the focus of our spiritual life, is problematic for many people. Some seem to feel a genuine need for other 'sundry' practices.

Lest we should think that Shinran is here talking about this or that religious practice, it's important to be aware that what he actually means is *any* practice whatsoever: *mangyō no shozen*; literally, 'small good of ten thousand practices'. For we cannot add anything to the Buddha's working, and nothing we do is able to eclipse his virtue.

So, I would like to suggest that an exclusive engagement with the Name is an aspect of Shinran's teaching that we ought to take very seriously indeed. This is because there are so many things that we do in religious life, including meditation and trying to be better people, which deflect our attention from the dharma.

The whole orientation of Pure Land Buddhism is to lead us away from ourselves. For we are *bombu*, ordinary folk who honestly recognize the limitations we have. When our self-consciousness is held in abeyance, we allow room for the blessed dharma to take root and work all by itself.

But this, necessarily, is a superficial explanation because we're discussing things here that are beyond the conditioned realms of samsāra; and we're engaging with the source of light itself, whence all wisdom and compassion arise, and from which all buddhas are conceived and born.

Jōdo Wasan 84
The buddhas of the ten quarters, countless as the sands of the Ganges,
Teach this dharma that is most difficult to accept;
For the sake of the evil world of the five defilements,
They bear witness to the teaching and protect beings who take refuge in it.

ON GOING AGAINST THE STREAM

Someone once told me that Śākyamuni had said that following the Buddha-dharma is 'to go against the stream'. I have never been able to find that reference. Of course, the entry from the status of an ordinary person (*bombu*, Sk. *pṛthagjana*) into the stages of enlightenment, or the bodhisattva career, is described as 'entering the stream'.

The only passage I have found which discusses streams is the famous allegory of the log. In it, Śākyamuni describes how just as a log becomes jammed – on its way from the mountain forest to the sea – by sticking to various kinds of obstacles, so in our journey through life we can become ensnared by attachments on our way to the great sea of Nirvāna. The image is one of flowing with the stream, rather than against it.

In any case, the verse above points again to the difficulty of accepting the dharma – especially the nembutsu way – and thereby suggests, for those who do accept it, someone who stands out from the crowd. Most of us know the story of the events that followed in the train of Śākyamuni's enlightenment. He realized just how challenging it would be to share his insights but changed his mind upon the urging of Brahmā who, acting in his compassion on behalf of suffering beings, suggested that Śākyamuni would be very remiss if he didn't make the effort to teach, as there may just be some people who would be receptive to it.

Rennyo Shōnin is reported to have said that the Shin community (*kyōdan*) exists for the sake of even just one person who awakens shinjin. The supporting texts, the Pure Land sūtras and Shinran's writing, suggest over and over again that hearing the dharma is difficult.

From the beginning, our tradition has understood that the truth is not easy for us to accept; and unlikely to be popular. History has not necessarily proved this to be true. The Buddha-dharma became a universal religion very quickly, given the constraints of the age and, at one time, spanned most of the 'civilized' world. We also know, from the inscriptions which have survived from the time of Emperor Aśoka, that a teaching which resembled the southern form of Buddha-dharma provided the communal underpinning of the great civilization over which he ruled (3rd century BCE). In seventh-century Japan, Shōtoku Taishi (574–622) adopted the Mahāyāna, and incorporated the 'Three Treasures' and certain Buddhist ideas into his constitution.

In East Asia, even today, it is striking how popular the Pure Land path continues to be; how inspiring it is for millions of people.

But I would suggest that, while the Buddha-dharma is universal, it is not really popular. It has been – and continues to be – widely accepted because it is generous and tolerant in its outlook. As a movement, its teachings have never sought to destroy the indigenous religions it met in its expansion throughout the world, and its monasteries invariably provided the masses with places of serene beauty, rest and refuge. Needless to say, followers of the dharma had their moments of unhappy derangement but – by and large – they have, throughout history, been remarkable for their serene urbanity and kindness.

The dharma has also been characterized by its generosity of spirit, freely lending its wisdom to the world at large; inspiring great movements in the development of art, literature, architecture, medicine and philosophy. The dharma has always preferred reasonable persuasion, and shunned self-righteousness and violence as arguments in its support, gaining thereby the widespread respect and affection of the masses.

Nevertheless, I think it is as true now, as ever it was, that very few people adopted the dharma as the exclusive focus of their lives, for it does come with insights which makes us all – from time to time – not a little uneasy. Such is the legacy of truth as it impresses itself on our world of illusion!

Many followers of the dharma in Australia – and I am sure this is true in every other country – lament the way in which the vast majority of those who practice it only do so in a partial and discontinuous way. Most seem to use it in a utilitarian manner and abandon it once it's fulfilled some apparently self-serving purpose.

My view is that we should be firm in insisting on the tried-and-true pattern of the dharma's relationship with the world. This is the way of seeing ourselves – and the teachings we love so much – as guests. Rather than lament the partial interest that a large number of people show in the dharma, we would do well to maintain the old generosity of spirit which has commended it throughout history to the rough and ready world at large.

Śākyamuni warned us – not just in the Amida Sūtra, which this *wasan* commemorates, but in many other places too – that what he had to teach could be baffling. Bearing this in mind, I think we should see ourselves as guests and servants of the world, being ready to offer whatever kind words, gentle wisdom, warmth, generosity and support for others that we can find within ourselves to share; no matter what their relationship with the dharma may be.

Jōdo Wasan 85
The Buddhas' protection and witness
Arise from the fulfillment of the Vow of compassion;
So let those who attain the diamond-like mind,
Respond in gratitude to Amida's great benevolence.

PRACTICING GREAT COMPASSION

The compassionate Vow animates in us the practice of great compassion, which is the very substance of the nembutsu way and its outworking in our daily lives.

In the *Kyōgyōshinshō*, Shinran Shōnin lists ten 'benefits in the present life'. Many of the remaining verses of the *Jōdo Wasan* are concerned with these, but none is more important to us, as nembutsu people, than the ninth of these: the 'benefit of constantly practicing great compassion'.

The compassionate Vow reads:

> If, when I attain Buddhahood, the countless buddhas throughout the worlds of the ten quarters do not all praise and say my Name, may I not attain the supreme enlightenment.[1]

Shinran was very conscious of how important it was to receive and accept the shinjin of Amida Buddha. This is because it results in a transformation whereby our attainment of Buddhahood becomes settled – we realize the 'diamond-like true mind', 'transcend crosswise the paths of the five courses and eight hindered existences' and attain the 'stage equal to Maitreya' (the next buddha). Shinran therefore gives strong emphasis to this being our very *raison d'être*. The compassionate vow is a vocation, a calling. As this verse says, the way to 'repay Amida's great benevolence' is to 'constantly practice the great compassion'.

There are many places in Shinran's writing where he uses strong language to impress upon us the urgency of such practice in order to repay our incalculable debt to the Buddha. He speaks of the effort as being so ardent that it will result in our 'bones being crushed'. It is easy to understand his insistence on this obligation because it's surely very hard to resist.

---
[1] CWS, p. 13.

Anyone who is deeply aware of their profound inadequacy in the matter of their own salvation – release and transcendence – knows that the idea of ever repaying the debt incurred is impossible to imagine. It's tempting to default altogether because any effort, no matter how great in our eyes, seems but a paltry irrelevance in the face of the wonder that is Amida Buddha's great Vow.

But its importance cannot be stressed enough for, without it, no one will 'hear the dharma' for one thing; furthermore, in ignoring it, we'll be oppressing our own hearts and squashing the life out of our existence; living as though we had to wear an iron mask, never expressing outwardly that which cries out to be expressed and heard from within.

'Constantly practicing the great compassion' is nothing other than *shōmyō* – saying the nembutsu. This is defined by Shinran in the first verse of the *Jōdo Wasan* collection as follows:

> Those who truly attain shinjin,
> As they utter Amida's Name,
> Being mindful of the Buddha always,
> Wish to respond to the great benevolence.[2]

Saying the Name of Amida Buddha, as we think of him, is *shōmyō* – the 'practice of great compassion'. This is, in essence, Amida's practice. And, in the Pure Land path, there is no practice of great compassion other than the Buddha's Name.

---

[2] CWS, p. 321.

Jōdo Wasan 86

To the evil beings of wrong views
In this evil age of five defilements, in this evil world
The buddhas, countless as the sands of the Ganges,
Give the Name of Amida, urging [them to entrust themselves to it].

MANY VOICES

This verse continues the theme from the last paragraph of the Amida Sūtra.

> Śāriputra, you should know that in the midst of this evil world of the five defilements, I have accomplished this difficult task.[1]

The worldview expounded in the *Abhidharma* philosophy suggests that time has a wave-like motion, not quite cyclic, but involving peaks and troughs. In the peaks, conditions are optimal, whereas troughs indicate disintegration. Favourable times support confident and easy practice but, in degenerate periods, the dharma is corrupted beyond recognition or becomes extinct altogether.

There are time measurements (*kalpas*) included in this perspective, but they are vast and of almost incalculable duration. There are also multiples of these timespans called 'great kalpas'. Śākyamuni appeared in the world almost 2,500 years ago and in a time of decline. That is why the Amida Sūtra concludes with a reference to the 'period of five defilements'.

Compounding this fluctuation in the dharma's fortunes, there is the sunset – a shadowy, dusk-like period of downturn (*mappō*, Sk. *saddharma-vipralopa*), as Śākyamuni retreats into the distant past and his teaching becomes ever more clouded. Shinran Shōnin was deeply conscious of this compounding tragedy and understood that it suffuses everything with its infection. Without a sense of the all-pervasive effects of our decadent age of dharma, it's very difficult to come to terms with much of what Shinran is telling us.

Those who overlook this reality are either scandalized by Shinran's teaching or seek to re-interpret it in such a way as to cater to the consumerist prejudices that prevail in our time. It strikes me as correct

---

[1] *The Three Pure Land Sūtras (Volume I): The Amida Sūtra and the Contemplation Sūtra*, Shin Buddhism Translation Series, 2003, p. 13.

that, without an appreciation of *mappō* as the underlying premise of Pure Land teaching, many aspects of Shinran's vision will seem unduly troubling; but I am also convinced that we do indeed live in an age of decline.

To my mind, the evidence for this is clear. However, it would be a shame to sully the *Jōdo Wasan* with such considerations. We will have ample time to explore this subject fully when we come to the *Shōzōmatsu Wasan*. For now, we may still rejoice in the resplendent effulgence of Amida Buddha – the basis of this first volume of hymns.

The important message in the last paragraph of the Amida Sūtra – to which Shinran alludes in this verse – is that, despite the obstacles, all buddhas of the 'ten directions' *do* encourage us to embrace the nembutsu way. Amida Buddha's light does fill the universe; as well as our hearts and minds.

> Nirvāna has innumerable names. It is impossible to give them in detail; I will list only a few. Nirvāna is called extinction of passions, the uncreated, peaceful happiness, eternal bliss, true reality, Dharma-Body, dharma-nature, suchness, oneness, and Buddha-nature. Buddha-nature is none other than Tathāgata. This Tathāgata pervades the countless worlds; it fills the hearts and minds of the ocean of all beings. Thus, plants, trees, and land all attain Buddhahood.[2]

It is evening now and the day is coming to rest. The sun is about to set. The storms of early spring have abated, and the season has become warm and balmy. I can hear the excited squeal of children in the distance; and somewhere, a violin. The scented air is intoxicating – damask roses, honeysuckle, gardenias, white cedars, mock orange and lilac; a silent concert celebrating the beginning of a new annual cycle of birth, stability, decay and death. The air is filled with the chorus of birds and, skimming above all this, a gentle noiseless evening breeze is turning inland from the sea, bearing news from the hills of ripening wheat and barley.

Tonight, these are the voices whispering – in enthralling unison and with resounding reassurance – that the way for us all at this time of *mappō* is *Namo Amida Butsu*.

Remorselessly, darkness is falling; but still there is light.

---

[2] CWS p.461.

Jōdo Wasan 87
Amida, full of compassion for those lost in the great night of ignorance –
The wheel of light of Dharma-Body being boundless –
Took the form of the Buddha of Unhindered Light,
And appeared in the land of peace.

THE PERSONALITY OF THE DHARMA

At this juncture, we leave behind those verses dedicated to the three canonical sūtras of the Pure Land way, because Shinran Shōnin turns next to an exploration of some other texts, which he sees as resources useful to this tradition. The nine verses that follow this one seem, in large part, to be drawn from ideas suggested by other recensions of the three Pure Land sūtras.

The other editions are surprisingly numerous and Shinran did not hesitate to use them as appropriate. One of these is quite well known to us in the form of Max Müller's translation of the *Sukhāvatīvyūha Sūtra*.[1]

The eighty-seventh verse of the *Jōdo Wasan*, above, has always been an especially arresting one because it's a sudden incursion of the personal into ideas that are often thought to be otherwise. The key words are 'compassion', 'form' and 'appeared'. No hymn that we've considered thus far has such a striking and powerful reference to the personal as a feature of the Dharma-Body.

Although the translation of this verse uses the word 'compassion', it's noteworthy that Shinran employs the Japanese *awaremu*, which has the sense of 'pitying' or 'sympathizing with'. He thereby evokes a sense of deep pathos at the heart of existence.

When we study seminal treatises like the *Abhidharmakośa-bhāṣyam* of Bodhisattva Vasubandhu, we are naturally impressed by the prominent place held by the doctrine of 'non-ego' or 'not-self' (*Sk. anātman*) within the field of concerns espoused by this teaching. Many people who encounter the dharma for the first time are intrigued by this focus and, of course, we've already seen that it's one of the three characteristics of existence which mark Buddhist orthodoxy.

---

[1] *Sacred Books of the East*, Vol. 49.

Anātman in fact attests to the complex structure of human personality; the fact that it lacks any single enduring, individual substance. The five aggregates (*Sk. skandha*) are usually presented in dharma discourses to demonstrate this – along with the complexity and evanescence of the individual attributes which contribute to our sense of character and identity.

Nevertheless, the dharma, with its emphasis on anātman, does not diminish the significance of human personhood as we experience it; neither does it deny its value or uniqueness.

The Dharma-Body as the metaphysical basis of Amida Buddha, though ineffable, has emotional qualities. A good example is compassion (Sk. *karuna*) which, in fact, is a straightforward identity with the suffering of the mass of beings and is thus concomitant with wisdom (Sk. *prajñā*) or emptiness (Sk. *śūnyatā*).

Needless, to say, the formless Dharma-Body is also *moved* (in that it manifests 'pity') – in response to the distress we endure in our 'long night of ignorance' – and thereby assumes a compassionate form as Amida, the Buddha of Unhindered Light, whose realm is 'adorned with utmost bliss' (*sukhāvatī*). So palpable and overwhelming is the tragedy of the human condition that even the inconceivable Dharma-Body – ultimate reality itself – 'feels' it and responds accordingly.

This is a telling image. Its ethos is well-attested in the life-story of the great person himself, Śākyamuni Buddha. When he was a prince, Siddhartha ventured out of a cocooned life in his father's palace to encounter the reality of 'old age, suffering and death'. His abhorrence and sorrow at such a discovery compelled him to identify and overcome the causes of these painful phenomena. Thereupon he promptly acted, abandoning his household and assuming the life of an ascetic.

When he eventually found enlightenment – the realization that he could impart a way that would benefit others – he was 'moved' to set aside his contemplative absorption (along with the enjoyment of its fruits) and return to the world of samsāra for the sake of suffering beings.

The Dharma-Body knows and shares our tears, it experiences our afflictions and is moved eternally to take the form of Amida Buddha and the Pure Land for the sake of our emancipation.

Jōdo Wasan 88
Amida, who attained Buddhahood in the infinite past,
Full of compassion for foolish beings of the five defilements,
Took the form of Śākyamuni Buddha
And appeared in Gayā.

THE TRANSMISSION OF THE DHARMA

The phrase translated as 'infinite past' (*kuon jitsujō*) in fact, reads, 'actually accomplished in the distant past'. Amida Buddha's enlightenment occurred so long ago that we did not know about him until he manifested as Śākyamuni.

When the time was ripe, Śākyamuni told Queen Vaidehī about Amida Buddha, and later delivered the Larger Sūtra to his disciples. Indeed, Amida's self-disclosure was the reason for Śākyamuni's appearance in the world. As we have already seen, the promulgation of the Pure Land teaching is Amida Buddha's contrivance, and Śākyamuni is the principal agent of its transmission in the present era. As the Seventeenth Vow says, 'All buddhas praise the Name'; all buddhas revere and declare knowledge of the true original Buddha, Amida. The actual vessel of the transmission of this truth depends on time and circumstance.

When Shinran Shōnin speaks of the 'true Buddha' he describes only the qualities of Amida, the Tathāgata of Inconceivable Light. Śākyamuni is never mentioned in that context. Hence, in our tradition, there is essentially only one Buddha who is the wellspring of all enlightenment and truth. It is here, with Amida, that the transmission of the dharma begins.

Gayā is close to the bodhi tree where Śākyamuni is said to have attained enlightenment. Therefore, this verse seems to equate that great event with his manifestation as Amida. However, it is clear – from a marginal note left by Shinran – that Śākyamuni's birth into the family of King Śuddhodana marks the entry of Amida Buddha into this world of the five defilements.

Since Śākyamuni's time, his sangha has served as the principal vehicle for the transmission of Amida's dharma from generation to generation. Throughout the ages, the light of enlightenment has flickered low, and even become extinguished. At times, it has thrived in the most impossible of situations. We, who take up the teachings of Shinran as our guide, are indebted to the devotion and perseverance of the sangha in the oases of Central Asia because it is they who conveyed the dharma from India to China, and beyond.

Transmission of the teachings has always moved at a glacial pace, facing many difficulties along the way, including misunderstanding and outright persecution. In our own time, it appears to be at a very low ebb.

Yet, in Jōdo Shinshū, we've been blessed with scholars who have devoted great efforts to study ancient languages, so that we may benefit from reliable translations. In the last few decades, Ryūkoku University and the Hongwanji International Center have produced priceless editions of Shinran's works in English. This represents the endpoint of an ancient journey, whereby the dharma has come down to us from the Primal Vow of Amida Buddha to the Anglophone world in this day and age.

Jōdo Wasan 89
Let Amida be praised for a hundred thousand koṭis of kalpas
By a hundred thousand koṭis of tongues,
Each producing countless voices,
And still that praise would be incomplete.

WHEN THE HEART IS FULL

There are ever-more urgent questions and deep matters that need resolution. I am not referring to those things that can be alleviated by talking them through, but about that nagging doubt or nameless dark brooding – inner oppression – which is constantly there; always just behind everything we think and do.

This gives us a sense of unease, especially when it persistently hints that life may actually be completely futile and meaningless. It's a continual presence, like a dark, forbidding room in a house, whose door we are terrified to open; fearful beyond endurance of what we might find inside. Our heart is full, but full of darkness.

It is impossible to open this door alone, for the contents of our inner recesses portend annihilation. These are the rapacious, reptilian things which we keep hidden because of the damage they would do, if exposed, to ourselves and to our social relations. But there is a hand that we can hold as we walk through that door, into the heart of darkness – a light that will uncover these terrors for the empty things they are, and which will set our hearts free.

Too often we are fond of describing Amida Buddha in abstruse terms and some people even venture to describe him as a symbol, metaphor or myth. But why not let go of this kind of pinched and complicated sophistry; why not tear down the walls of our fear, and open our hearts and accept Amida Buddha as he is: the Tathāgata of Inconceivable Light? How hard it is for many of us to abandon the limitations of our intellect! True, this light is inconceivable, but as we are reminded in the words of the *Shōshinge*:

> The light of compassion that grasps us illumines and protects
> us always.
> The darkness of our ignorance is already broken through;
> Still the clouds and mists of greed and desire, anger and hatred,
> Cover as always the sky of true and real shinjin.

> But though light of the sun is veiled by clouds and mists,
> Beneath the clouds and mists there is brightness, not dark.[1]

Amida, the Buddha existing from the eternal past, is as real and tangible as was the historical Śākyamuni Buddha. We always arm ourselves with doubt because, by means of it, we feel that we're protected from the irruption of deep realities – and the fullness of heart that comes from joy. Yet, there are those dark lurking things which cry out for our attention because we know that, as long as they remain so, we'll not be free – and we also certainly know that these are not symbols or myths! We're afraid to be disarmed, unsophisticated and open to the only light that can endure our inner darkness.

We should let go of our self-defeating prejudices and, in a moment of complete surrender, take hold of Amida Buddha's hand.

In the *Gobunshō*, Rennyo Shōnin says:

> For those who understand thoroughly the meaning of '*Anjin*-Faith' in our Jōdo Shinshū school, there is no necessity to possess intelligence or learning. Just become aware that, at best, you are deeply evil-prone, shameful beings, and believe that the Buddha who delivers such beings regardless is Amida Buddha only. If they cling tightly to the sleeve of Amida Tathāgata's benevolence with feelings of complete trust, without any doubt, and place faith in him for the life to come, Amida Tathāgata will be deeply joyed and, emitting 84,000 rays of Light from his person, will envelop them forever in this Light.
>
> ... Oh, how wonderful is this unobstructable Primal Vow and how welcome is this Great Light of Amida Tathāgata! Without the blessing of this Light, there is not even a remote hope that we shall be cured of this fearful sickness of ignorance and delusion, which has been ours since time immemorial.[2]

And then the heart is full!

---

[1] CWS, p. 70.
[2] *Shinshū Seiten, Jōdo Shinshū Teaching* (San Francisco; Buddhist Churches of America, 1978), p. 373, tr. Elson B. Snow (adapted).

Jōdo Wasan 90
The Great Sage Śākyamuni teaches
That Amida's land is easy to reach,
And calls the sentient being who doubts the Pure Land path
A person lacking eyes, or lacking ears.

THE NINETY-FIVE WRONG PATHS

In this verse, Shinran Shōnin draws on a section of the *Collection of Passages on the Land of Peace and Bliss* by Tao-ch'o (562–645), the fourth Dharma Master of Jōdo Shinshū:

> The land of the Buddha of Immeasurable Life is easy to go to and easy to attain. However, people cannot be born there through their own practices, which can only lead them down one of the ninety-five wrong paths. I call such people 'those without eyes' or 'those without ears'.[1]

Tao-ch'o, in turn, was quoting from the *Sūtra of Mahāmaudgalyāyana's Questions*. This passage seems to be Śākyamuni Buddha's response to an unknown inquiry.

The description of people who follow the ninety-five wrong paths is very harsh. They are characterized as being entirely bereft of sight and hearing. The ninety-five wrong paths were beliefs that held sway during the time of Śākyamuni Buddha, and many of them reflect ideas that people hold even in our own time.

We meet teachers of the ninety-five wrong paths also in the *Kyōgyōshinshō*. They hold ideas that are simply non-Buddhist, including belief in a creator God, materialism, belief in a soul, belief that death is either non-existence or eternal existence, belief that there is no law of cause-and-effect, belief that existing entities do not change; indeed, any belief that is not redolent of the Middle Way.

The essence of the Buddha-dharma can be found in Śākyamuni Buddha's own account of his experience of enlightenment:

---

[1] *Collection of Passages on the Land of Peace and Bliss* (*An Le Chi*) by Tao-ch'o; translated by Zuio Hisao Inagaki (Horai Association International, 2014).

> ... the supreme tranquility of the unageing, undecaying, the undying, the unsorrowing, and the stainless.[2]

From this realization emerged all other ideas and practices that comprise the Buddha-dharma: the Fourfold Noble Truth, the Noble Eightfold Path, and the law of dependent origination.

In the same way, those who deny or slander Amida Buddha, the Pure Land and the Primal Vow, are also to be considered without the capacity to see and hear the Dharma; for these doubts, too, are a manifestation of the same deep truth at the heart of Śākyamuni Buddha's enlightenment.

---

[2] *Ariyapariyesama-sutta*

Jōdo Wasan 91
The Supreme that is unexcelled is true emancipation;
True emancipation is none other than Tathāgata.
When we attain true emancipation,
We become free of desire and free of doubt.

STEPPING INTO THE UNKNOWN

> *Duḥkha*: Suffering; broadly explained as not having what we want, or getting what we don't want; old age, sickness and death.

The next two verses in this section of the *Jōdo Wasan* contain ideas drawn from the *Nirvāṇa Sūtra*. We know from his use of a long passage from this sūtra – which recounts the story of the crisis facing Prince Ajātaśatru – that it was especially this story of awakening to faith that most captured Shinran Shōnin's attention.

An important section of the *Kyōgyōshinshō* is the section on 'true realization' which, of course, is the goal of the Buddha-dharma. Here Shinran is keen to place the Pure Land way firmly in the context of the bodhisattva vehicle – the Mahāyāna as it came to be known. 'True realization' is the 'highest of the highest'; that is, Nirvāna which is to be 'free of desire and free of doubt'.

Nirvāna is known by many names, as we have already seen. *Tathāgata* is one of them; and, in this hymn, Shinran especially has in mind the 'Dharma-Body as Dharma-nature' (*hōsshō hosshin*) – the ineffable truth that pervades all things.

In these verses, we are discussing matters that are completely beyond our empirical grasp. We're obliged to take Śākyamuni Buddha at his word in a provisional way until we taste these realities for ourselves. Within our Pure Land sangha, there are those whose knowledge of Nirvāna and the Dharma-Body comes, indeed, from first-hand experience.

The most important of these, of course, is Śākyamuni and – in Jōdo Shinshū – Shinran revered 'the seven dharma masters', whose insights developed and refined the teaching through the ages. It's important to remember that these masters were not just clever, knowledgeable people, but profoundly wise, enlightened men who had an intimate understanding of the truths they espoused. Their teaching was not just based on studying texts or on a firm belief in their own authority; they were also experienced practitioners.

Two examples will suffice to illustrate what I mean. From my point of view, one of the strongest affirmations of Amida Buddha's reality comes from the fact that Shan-tao actually saw him while in *samādhi*. The same can be said for the Larger Sūtra, which relates the story of Amida Buddha's emergence and enlightenment.

Why should we trust Śākyamuni and Shan-tao? Because first of all, these two men (among a few others) are manifestly concerned about our ultimate well-being and, secondly, their premises begin with where we find ourselves right now.

The Four Noble Truths expound the primary concerns of the Buddha-dharma; the acceptance of which defines us as Buddhists. The Truth, as we all know, is in four parts: the nature of existence (Sk. *duḥkha*); its cause (*avidyā*, ignorance or *tṛṣṇā*, 'thirst'); the cessation of suffering (*nirodha*); and the way to this end as taught by all buddhas: refrain from all evil, turn to the dharma and clarify the mind.

When Śākyamuni expounds *duḥkha*, we know exactly what he's saying. Life is very difficult, and we understand precisely what he means by the fact that even pleasant things are painful in the end. When Śākyamuni tells us that there's a way beyond ignorance, we are being led beyond what we know – to realities that are initially obscure.

The Buddha-dharma always addresses us 'where we stand'. We can readily appreciate confronting realities such as the first of the Four Noble Truths. Having nodded in agreement with this initial contention, we are then offered a resolution. It's only in moving forward, beyond what we know, that we begin to discover, step-by-step – with increasing certainty – that this is indeed a way that can be trusted.

So it is also in our Pure Land tradition. As Rennyo Shōnin says, it's only when we 'cling onto the sleeve of Amida Buddha' that we'll eventually discover, at first hand, the supportive power of his compassion.

Jōdo Wasan 92
When a person realizes the mind of non-discrimination,
That attainment is the 'state of regarding each being as one's only child'.
This is none other than Buddha-nature;
We will awaken to it on reaching the land of peace.

THE RELIGION OF THE BOOKS

This verse is the second, in a sequence of three, that are based on the *Nirvāṇa Sūtra*. The 'state of regarding each being as one's only child' is an allusion to the mind of equality towards all sentient beings. This understanding pertains to realized bodhisattvas, since they are able to relate to all sentient beings in light of their knowledge that the constituents of existence are 'empty' (Sk. *śūnya*).

However, Shinran Shōnin is eager to bring us back down to earth, in both this and the next verse, by giving a reminder that we cannot accomplish such a sublime level of spiritual awakening in this mundane life. Not until we reach the Land of Serene Sustenance (*annyōkai*) do these truths become evident to us. Although, in the path of sages, this realm is often treated as a kind of consciousness within our mundane existence – attesting to a level of enlightenment on the part of the disciple – the Pure Land teaching does not see it that way.

In the Jōdo Shinshū tradition, there is a small collection of exquisite verses attributed to Shinran (the *Jōgai Wasan*), in which he says: "Although my defiled life is filled with all kinds of desires and delusions, my mind is playing in the Pure Land". While these verses are considered by some scholars to be of doubtful origin, even so, they do not suggest that Shinran's mind was identified with the Pure Land in the same way that this is understood in the Path of Sages. Indeed, the opposite is true.

> In the *Hymns of All Buddhas' Presence*, Shan-tao, the Master of Kuang Ming temple, explains that the heart of the person of shinjin already and always resides in the Pure Land. 'Resides' means that the heart of the person of shinjin constantly dwells there.[1]

Rather than the Pure Land being encompassed by our mind, our mind is

---
[1] CWS, p. 528.

enfolded in the Pure Land.

Needless to say, what we can know and experience as ordinary beings falls short of the full awakening that comes with complete enlightenment. Shinran took great pains to ensure that people understood that, when Amida Buddha's shinjin arises within us, we enter the stage of the 'truly settled' in this life and become buddhas when it ends.

In my previous essay, I suggested that we can approach the dharma – of which we have but a limited grasp – by way of the certainty we've found in the initial insights of a teacher. This may serve as the basis of trust for our further development in areas which are, as yet, unclear to us. But this does not, in itself, provide a sufficient basis for us to proceed along the path.

Who is to say that the teacher is not a deluded ego-maniac who gains his own sense of value and self-importance by controlling others? T'an-luan once pointed out that being misled by deceivers, whose teaching only resembles the truth, is an ever-present hazard for disciples of the dharma.[2] There is, however, a foil for this danger; and that's to be found in the high authority and reverence that the Buddhist tradition bestows upon its sacred scriptures.

Sūtras are more than mere written documents. They are a manifestation of the teacher, and buddhas. Thus, the Larger Sūtra is an embodiment of Śākyamuni; and the twentieth-century Pure Land master, Zuiken (Saizō) Inagaki (1885-1981) was able to consider the *Kyōgyōshinshō* as the Dharma-Body of Shinran. I genuinely believe that, when reading this work, we are engaging directly in a dialogue with the living Shinran, who said:

> When you alone rejoice in Faith know that you are with another. When two rejoice in Faith, know that there is still another accompanying you. I, Shinran, am that 'other' person.[3]

Exponents of Buddhism often overlook the importance of sacred texts, but I think that it's most reassuring to understand that they are the first and last recourse in our acceptance of – and progress in – the dharma. We should never be without their guidance; in fact, we would be prudent to

---

[2] CWS, p. 25.
[3] *Hanazono Bunko*.

hold them in immeasurably higher esteem than anything that belongs to this precarious *sahā* world.

> From this day on, rely on dharma, not on people who teach it. Rely on the meaning, not on words.[4]

Namo Amida Butsu

---

[4] Nāgārjuna Bodhisattva (CWS p. 241).

Jōdo Wasan 93
Tathāgata is none other than Nirvāna;
Nirvāna is called Buddha-nature.
Beyond our ability to attain it in the state of foolish beings,
We will realize it on reaching the land of peace.

ON BEING TRUE TO OURSELVES

'Foolish beings' translates the word *bombu* (Sk. *pṛthagjana*; Pali, *puthujjana*). Though we have often discussed this term, it deserves continued contemplation by those of us who follow the Pure Land way, because it is precisely for 'people like us' that this path exists.

Readers will remember that the *Contemplation Sūtra* lists nine levels of development and suggests ways in which our spiritual aptitude can be addressed accordingly. From this, the tradition presents a doctrinal analysis of the *pṛthagjana* – one who has yet to enter the stream and attain the first stage of enlightenment. The dharma delineates a hierarchy of stages – a kind of spiritual caste system – through which we move as a result of our actions or practice. A person who has not yet approached the threshold of enlightenment is a *bombu*.

'Foolish beings' have varying degrees of awareness. Some are completely ignorant and impervious to any spiritual values, while others are ready to listen to the dharma and to commence seeking the way.

It seems to me that, when Shinran Shōnin uses of the term 'foolish being' in the *Kyōgyōshinshō*, he means almost everyone: ordinary people who are preoccupied with the business of survival – of feeding themselves and their families – and who are given to all of the usual human attachments. We, who have few opportunities to know the true happiness of dharma, are the objects of a bodhisattva's boundless compassion – given our preoccupation with necessity, craving and endless commitments.

For Shinran, then, the *pṛthagjana* is an ordinary person who is given – in the usual sense – to no particular virtue or vice. He sees an 'ocean' of beings, a mass of people. Although, when Shinran comes to look within his own heart, and discovers the intractable nature of his ordinariness, he nowhere accuses individuals of ignominy. In fact, his fellow travellers are held in the highest regard and viewed with affectionate warmth, because

Shinran sees in them the working of the Primal Vow, which he adores. Furthermore, as we have already seen, he sternly admonishes us not to make value judgements in assessing others.[1]

In the context of Shinran's teaching, a *pṛthagjana* is one who belongs to 'the public' (as we say these days); one who may be considered either good or bad, wise or foolish. The Primal Vow is for us all. In medieval terms, he is speaking of 'Everyman'; not necessarily an idiot, fool or illiterate simpleton.

In the nembutsu, people become like kittens; soft and pliable enough to allow their mother to carry them to safety in her mouth. They relax into the tender care of Amida Buddha over and over again – with every breath that carries, not necessarily the sound, but the intention of *Namo Amida Butsu*. Other than that, there is nothing more that's required. We only need to become ourselves, exactly, precisely as we really are. We do not have to develop into anything other than this, and we have no special significance beyond what is imparted to us by Amida Tathāgata.

Realizing the joy and relief of Amida's support within our hearts, we may or may not become manifestly changed; any transformation is known only – with any certainty – to us and to the Buddha alone. In fact, it seems to be the case that most people who live within the happy and brilliant light of Amida Buddha became more keenly aware of their own insubstantial nature.

Neither must we struggle to become a target of Amida's compassion by playing at being something we are not. Becoming obsessed with our depravity is not only unnecessary but harmful; we only need to turn our entrusting hearts to *Namo Amida Butsu*.

It is this that gives us pause and becomes a problem for us; that causes the Pure Land way to become the 'most difficult of all difficulties'. It calls upon us to abandon our usual 'results-oriented' way of thinking. It exhorts us to abandon the kind of posing that is natural to us as human beings; the way in which we seek to find our level within society, by being this or that kind of person. We hunger for meaning and significance within a group or tribe – the fundamental unit of human society. In order to do this, we often need to deny aspects of who we are and to cast ourselves

---

[1] CWS, p. 459.

into someone else's mould.

The sad truth is, however, that all of this involves unnecessary pain and wasted effort. In fact, it's not really possible to draw any guaranteed meaning from the externalities of existence. The only abiding reality that is primarily accessible to us is *Namo Amida Butsu*.

Jōdo Wasan 94
The person who attains shinjin and joy
Is taught to be equal to the tathāgatas.
Great shinjin is itself Buddha-nature;
Buddha-nature is none other than Tathāgata.

THE FULFILMENT OF THE DHARMA

In this hymn, Shinran Shōnin is quoting from:

1. the Flower Ornament (Sk. *Avataṃsaka*) Sūtra, which taught that those who have accepted shinjin are equal to tathāgatas; and
2. the *Nirvāṇa Sūtra*, that great exposition of Buddha-nature, which it equates with emptiness (Sk. *śūnyatā*).

The idea that people of faith are 'equal to the Tathāgata' is an ancient insight, not something invented by Shinran. Yet we are reluctant to capitulate in the face of this great and unsurpassed truth, because it's something that happens when we see the reality of our inner darkness, and the futility of our raging impotence.

To awaken to faith is to submit because we are on a 'white path' between the 'two rivers' of water and fire, craving and anger, steeped in samsāra, lost from the light; heading in a direction that is unclear to us. So we just need to trust and let go; to be nothing but ourselves. This is to yield because, out there, we only feel the tug of compassion and the voice of Śākyamuni urging us on, and because there's no Pure Land that we can see, no Nirvāna that we know at first hand.

If we think we see Nirvāna, or believe the Pure Land is just in our minds, then we would do well to consider Shinran's perspective – and to think again; to look within ourselves repeatedly.

> ... priests and laymen of the Declining Age and masters of
> these days, sunken in the idea 'that one's true nature is
> Buddha' and 'that the Buddha's Pure Land exists in one's
> mind' degrade the True Enlightenment in the Pure Land; or,
> being deluded by the mind of self-power to practice meditative
> and non-meditative good deeds, they are blind to the

Adamantine True Faith.[1]

We do not see Buddha-nature, and we cannot comprehend Nirvāna; these realities work beneath the reach of our conscious minds. What we do know and hear is *Namo Amida Butsu*, especially when it's voiced for no reason at all, at the moment of capitulation; and ever afterwards, in commemoration of this great event. It's then that it becomes the sound of life, a chant of joy that is as natural to us as breathing.

In *Namo Amida Butsu*, the ancient dharma is manifest. Its light dispels the darkness and its truth breaks the bonds of what is false.

---

[1] *Kyōgyōshinshō*, Ryūkoku Translation Series (Vol. V), p. 84.

Jōdo Wasan 95
Sentient beings who, with hindered understandings,
Doubt the Buddha's unhindered wisdom,
Will sink for many kalpas in various forms of pain
In the hells of Saṃvara and Piṇḍala.

FEAR OF RELIGIOUS CONVICTION

'Religion' has not only become a rather contentious subject since the rise of industrial society a couple of centuries ago but, in recent times, it is now common – especially here in Australia – to see religious commitment as mostly a negative thing. It's often suggested that people become 'religious' because they are neurotic in some way, or weak – needing a crutch to support them in the face of life's challenges.

Treatments of religion as a phenomenon abound: social, anthropological, political, philosophical, historical, ethical and so on. Most try to analyze and understand it 'objectively'. It seems to me that seeking to come to grips with religion as a 'phenomenon' is, in the final analysis, unsatisfying and in no way convincing. Perhaps there is a need, on the part of some thinkers, to understand religion on its own terms, in order to defend it from its critics.

Religion is too much a part of the human organism, and too ingrained in our emotional make-up, to be objectively understood in any meaningful way. 'Conclusions' about its significance rarely seem to achieve much, except to reinforce the expectations of those engaged in its study. It seems likely to remain, for a long time, one of those intangibles that defy any definitive reduction. In spite of this, religious commitment has become, for a significant number of Australians, a source of fear and consternation – something that needs to be tamed.

In his study of ethics, the early twentieth-century theologian Deitrich Bonhoeffer described the deeply private nature of religious devotion and said that even he felt embarrassed, like an intruder, if he discovered someone at their prayers. There are perhaps other things that also lie behind the fear of religious conviction in our time.

One common reason that is given for this sense of repugnance is that religion is a prominent cause of violent conflict. This argument is very difficult to rebut, even though much misery has also been inflicted –

especially during the last century – in the name of irreligion. Indeed, this is confirmed by incontrovertible historical events such as the early medieval Crusades (which extended to the Middle East), the eradication of the Albigenses in Southern France, the Byzantine persecution of the Armenian Paulicians, the Hundred Years War in pre-modern Europe and, of course, the recent spate of highly publicized mass murders and suicides associated with Islam – the list is endless.

The fact that it's possible to point to these events as having been inspired by religious views is, indeed, a strong argument against all its belief systems. My feeling about this is that, since religion is so integral to human nature, it's difficult to separate it from other aspects of our personalities, such as violence. On the other hand, it's striking how prominent injunctions against violence and revenge are contained in the codes of most world religions.

Of course, the sense of well-being that's accompanied technological progress has no doubt strongly influenced the way people see religion. Here is a highly imaginative and creative endeavour which has found practical ways to ease suffering and pain, bringing many welcome material benefits and comforts to us. The fact that technology appears to be materialistic can lead people to adopt a sceptical attitude to the claims of religious traditions.

It's a pity that any religions ever allowed their teachings and practices to be used so prominently to promote the promise of material benefits. Such things may be dividends, but they are certainly not the primary objective of faith.

In any case, whatever objections may be raised, I am sure that religious conviction, of one kind or another, will remain an integral aspect of our existence – as much a part of our experience as sex and death. In a consumerist culture that is habituated to the idea that growth, acquisition, youth, productivity and ingestion are the chief requirements of a fulfilling life, perhaps anything that reminds us of weakness, diminution, idleness, relinquishment and death is terrifying. So, the negative reaction against religion that's commonly seen today, is more likely to be a question of denial.

The joy and purposefulness – along with the anguish and ambivalence – that accompany religious conviction is integral to what it means to be human. I don't know why spiritual understanding, study and pursuits are so important to many of us but I think we are the lucky ones. At least we can say that our lives are, at the very least, enriched by it.

Religious experience is part of the good life and belongs with philosophy, questions of life's meaning and purpose, and the experience of good art and craft. But merely to compare religion with these things is to weaken the significance we know it has. And it cheapens it even more when we make it a vehicle of trade, thinking that my religious conviction is only acceptable as long as it 'contributes' something to my interests or to those of society at large.

We may not quite know why it is that the nembutsu has come to hold centre-stage for us, but it's a fact that we cannot deny. In some ways, it is inconvenient, and I have often wondered whether it would be easier to give it up and live without the dharma. But the truth is that this would be to turn one's back on the very core of existence itself – the Primal Vow – and that such denial would be nothing less than hell.

Jōdo Wasan 96
Amida Tathāgata came forth and guided beings,
Teaching the 'Chapter on Life-span'
In the Sūtra of Golden Splendour
In order to end calamities and ensure long life.

THE *SŪTRA OF GOLDEN SPLENDOUR*

This is the first of fifteen verses which celebrate the benefits that beings receive in their present life as a result of entrusting themselves to the Primal Vow of Amida Buddha in his Name. The first two verses (*Jōdo Wasan* 96 & 97) are concerned with the amelioration of calamity. The next two verses (98 & 99) celebrate the power of the Primal Vow to overcome our karmic evil. And the remaining eleven verses (100–110) proclaim the benefit of being protected by gods and buddhas.

Almost all of Shinran's hymns were renditions of the *Kyōgyōshinshō* into accessible form for people who couldn't read the classical Chinese of that work. Indeed, while the *Kyōgyōshinshō* is a vast and comprehensive compendium of Pure Land teaching – including Shinran Shōnin's commentary – the *wasan* cover the same ground with greater clarity and simplicity. The *Hymns on Benefits in the Present* are no different. But they don't necessarily match specific passages from the *Kyōgyōshinshō*. Nevertheless, Shinran does sum up these benefits in the third chapter of that work.

1. The benefit of being protected and sustained by unseen powers.
2. The benefit of being possessed of supreme virtues.
3. The benefit of our karmic evil being transformed into good.
4. The benefit of being protected and cared for by all the buddhas.
5. The benefit of being praised by all the buddhas.
6. The benefit of being constantly protected by the light of the Buddha's heart.
7. The benefit of having great joy in our hearts.
8. The benefit of being aware of Amida's benevolence and of responding in gratitude to his virtue.
9. The benefit of constantly practicing great compassion.
10. The benefit of entering the stage of the truly settled.[1]

---

[1] CWS, p.112.

There is no quotation from the *Sūtra of Golden Splendour* in the *Kyōgyōshinshō*, so the reference here is unusual. It was also delivered by four buddhas, not Amida alone. But, according to Shinran, it was Amida Buddha who stood forth in his compassion to proclaim the chapter called 'Measurement of Life', which is the heart of the sūtra. This is because Amida is the original buddha and teacher of all other buddhas throughout the universe.[2]

If we are to grasp the last line of this verse, which proclaims protection from calamities and the assurance of a long life, we only need to understand the lived experience of T'an-luan (476–542), the third dharma master of Jōdo Shinshū.

Before T'an-luan converted to the Buddha-dharma – through the guidance of the central Asian Buddhist missionary Bodhiruci – he was a follower of Taoism. He suffered from fragile health and wanted to master techniques for extending his life indefinitely. On meeting Bodhiruci, he converted to Buddhism because he saw the futility of seeking a longer life in the realm of birth-and-death (*saṃsāra*). T'an-luan thus came to see the falsity of Taoist practice in that regard; discerning the wisdom of being born in the Pure Land so as to attain a liberation that was eternal and unconditioned.

This is the meaning of 'ending calamities and ensuring long life' in the Pure Land tradition. In this life we remain subject to old age, sickness and death. But people see these 'calamities' differently when the way of nembutsu has been accepted. They enter the compassionate embrace of Amida Buddha, which gives them the capacity to live this current life to the full, until its natural culmination when birth is attained in the Realm of Utmost Bliss.

---

[2] *Jōdo Wasan* 88 (CWS, p. 349).

Jōdo Wasan 97
Out of compassionate concern for the people of the land,
Master Saichō of Mount Hiei said that
One should utter 'Namo Amida Butsu'
As a spell for eliminating the seven calamities.

DENGYŌ DAISHI

This is an extension or refinement of the previous verse. The seven calamities are associated with fear of injury and death, sometimes taking the form of mere superstition. These are eclipses of the sun and moon, meteorites, lightning, wildfires, floods, storms, drought and war. As was the case for the previous verse, it is from the fear of such things that people of nembutsu are delivered.

This principle of Pure Land Buddhism is actually established in the *Sukhāvatīvyūha Sūtra* itself. Here we are told that the vast and transcendent resonance of the Bodhi tree in the Pure Land endows freedom from the fear of disease. It describes how we can still live, as best as we can, in the face of such afflictions but without being paralyzed by them. Through the power of the Primal Vow, we can accept the vicissitudes of life and live well.

Dengyō Daishi (Saichō) was born in Shiga Prefecture in 767. If it were not for him and the fact that he introduced the T'ien t'ai (*Tendai*) school of Buddha-dharma to Japan then, of course, we may never have heard of Jōdo Shinshū. Shinran Shōnin moved to Mount Hiei (the school's headquarters) to deepen his study and practice of the dharma shortly after being ordained at the age of nine by Jichin, the chief priest of Shōren-in temple in Kyoto.

It's possible that, if Shinran Shōnin had not undergone his anguished search for salvation by means of the demanding spiritual exercises on Hiei, he may never have felt the need to seek the help of Hōnen Shōnin, who introduced him to the Other-Power way.

Saichō was ordained when he was fourteen, before being sent to China to study. Upon his return, he brought back the T'ien t'ai teachings along with a knowledge of Zen and various esoteric practices. This school is named for the mountain in China where its 'northern branch' was established. After a life spent serving the imperial court, the dharma and his country, Saichō died in 822 on the holy mountain.

T'ien t'ai encompasses all developments of the Buddha-dharma through the ages, and its teaching tends more in the direction of inclusiveness rather than the rejection of ideas which may be deemed unorthodox. Thus, Saichō played a major role in the rapprochement between Shinto and Buddhism. The school bases its mission and hermeneutics on the *Lotus Sūtra* but the *Nirvāṇa Sūtra*, which was so important to Shinran, also plays a significant role.

What is noteworthy in T'ien t'ai doctrine is the identity of the apparent 'material' world with ultimate reality, the Dharma-Body. One might say that it emphasizes the immanence of the ineffable in the temporal, but I think that this kind of language – the best we have – sets up an inappropriate dualism. The doctrine is capable of serious abuse and misunderstanding, and could prove dangerous in the wrong hands. Hence, Saichō established a regime of arduous training for the monks on Mount Hiei.

I think that one can see the influence of the T'ien t'ai approach to the dharma in much of Shinran's thought. A good example of this is his appreciation of shinjin. It seems to me that Shinran sees it not as 'belief' or self-generated 'faith', but as the manifestation of the Dharma-Body in an ordinary person. This perspective seems to be very much in keeping with the T'ien t'ai spirit; indeed, it could be said that it is firm proof of it. Another striking example is Shinran's use of a broad selection of texts to support his exegesis in the *Kyōgyōshinshō*.

This reminds us of the eclectic nature of T'ien t'ai. On the other hand, it would not be correct to assert that Shinran was consciously promulgating this school's doctrine. Indeed, he was not an exponent of the *Lotus Sūtra* in any way and, of course, his principal influence was Hōnen Shōnin.

In this verse, Shinran first points to Saichō's compassion, but his main purpose is to honour the nembutsu and affirm its significance.

Jōdo Wasan 98
When we say 'Namo Amida Butsu',
Which surpasses all virtues,
Our heavy obstructions of evil – past, present and future –
Are all unfailingly transformed, becoming light.

LIGHTNESS OF BEING

Here we are not talking about mere behaviour, but something far more profound and organic. Hindrances (Sk. *nīvaraṇa*) lie at the very core of our existence, serving to exacerbate our obstacles in pursuing the way. They stop us from practicing the dharma effectively and make it difficult for us to discern the truth. Being deeply onerous, they weigh heavily upon us and cripple our ability to live effectively. They also cause us to live in a state of constant confusion and darkness. We are tossed from pillar to post, always running after this or that, driven to respond blindly to random stimuli and never knowing what to think, what to believe and what to trust.

These hindrances – mainly sensuous desire, ill-will, sloth, indolence and restlessness – cloud our judgement through the emotional turmoil they create. They cause us, for example, to be driven by unthinking prejudice and bigotry; or to respond to people on the basis of whether or not we find them attractive. We know that our life is ensnared by this debilitating fog, but we can rarely identify it with clarity.

It is only in the nembutsu, which results from the awakening of shinjin, that this grinding burden stops weighing us down and undermining our spirits. This is probably the most momentous effect of faith in everyday life – the point at which it most directly informs our mundane existence.

When hindrances cease being a millstone around our necks, we'll be able to set out cheerfully upon the way – the miasma of desire, fear and anger is dispelled and the light of Amida Buddha makes its presence felt. We then experience a palpable sense of lightness and of freedom. We can see that, though our impediments are organic, we're more able to accept ourselves as we are. Indeed, we discover that there's really nothing that truly exists except Amida Buddha.

This respite, which is the alleviation of our karmic shackles, manifests itself in different people in various ways, given the myriad diversity of human personalities and temperaments. I would suggest that the relief and joy we feel is directly related to the depth of oppression that bound us in the first place.

Jōdo Wasan 99
When we say 'Namo Amida Butsu',
The benefits we gain in the present are boundless;
The karmic evil of our transmigration in birth-and-death disappears,
And determinate karma and untimely death are eliminated.

FOLLOWING SHINRAN SHŌNIN

This verse sums up in four lines the most significant benefit of living a life of nembutsu. 'The karmic evil of our transmigration in birth-and-death disappears' implies that all our maladroit actions (Sk. *akuśala karma*) – that would normally lead to an unfavourable posthumous destiny – have had their seeds (Sk. *bīja*) destroyed. In other words, when we're overwhelmed by the pure karma of Amida Buddha (through taking refuge in the Primal Vow), we are able to live free of all anxiety. This benefit arises from the settled heart (*anjin*) in the person of Other-Power faith.

This verse refers to the 'ten benefits in the present life', which Shinran lists in the *Kyōgyōshinshō*.[1] None of these benefits offer mundane advantages. Nevertheless, they are deeply significant because they relate to matters of the heart and to our sense of spiritual security.

Is the purpose of religion to deliver comfort and material gain in this life, or to resolve profound and seemingly intractable existential questions? I believe that an authentic religion is, first and foremost, the latter. Material well-being can be delivered in other ways, independently of religion. For one thing, we can be born into wealth or gain it as a result of our efforts.

In pondering this question, perhaps it's relevant to consider why we do, indeed, follow Shinran. And is it possible for a person who lives in an entirely non-Japanese ambience to be guided by him? Is his teaching culture-bound and beyond the reach of people from varied backgrounds? These last two questions ought to be disposed of first. Obviously, if we answered either or both of them in the negative, there would be no point in exploring the first question.

The English language has seen the publication of many works on Jōdo Shinshū, which are marked by two distinct approaches. One sees

---
[1] CWS, p. 112.

Shinran's teaching as inherently universal and free of any cultural limitations, while the other is not so sure.

To suggest that Shinran's teaching represents a limited cultural perspective is patently incorrect, for it is a legacy of Buddhist culture. He knew nothing else from the time he was ordained at the age of nine. Monastic life was substantially the same from Afghanistan in the west, through the deserts of central Asia to Nara in the east, from Ulaanbator in the North to Borobodur and Sri Lanka in the south. Therefore, Shinran is the product of a universal teaching and a trans-national culture; namely, the Buddha-dharma.

While his own teaching is, in part, a response to the conditions of his time, there is little that's unique about them. War, persecution, anger, lust, political corruption, authoritarianism, poverty and family life; all these are common, universal themes.

The best way to feel comfortable with Jōdo Shinshū is to make an effort to gain a general grounding in Buddhist thought and culture, for many modern commentators assume that later cultural accretions are inherently a part of Shinran's thought. An analysis of doctrinal terms can be found in the texts of the *Abhidharma*, for example, but these may be daunting for most of us. It's the Buddha-dharma itself that will best assist us in developing our appreciation of Shinran, and enable us to find his writing familiar territory where we may feel at home.

It is best to use a variety of resources in approaching Shinran's teaching. For example, it's a good idea to consult several translations of the same text. A very helpful volume is *A Glossary of Shin Buddhist Terms* published by Ryūkoku University. This work is useful when referring to the university's own translations, which have superb footnotes, along with the text in *hiragana* and *kanji* (in addition to a *rōmaji* rendering of the original).

Why do we, then, follow Shinran? My answer is this. Śākyamuni Buddha, following his enlightenment, set in train centuries of experimentation with – and exploration of – his teaching. In the course of this, the Larger Sūtra gained prominence and the nascent 'Pure Land' tradition flickered into life. Many books were written, many problems addressed, and many experiences flowing from a life of nembutsu were recorded.

After hundreds of years, one man who was able to live in the light of the Larger Sūtra, and to find total release from within the Pure Land tradition, was Shinran. He was privileged, however, to be able to draw on what had subsequently developed, over many centuries, into a vast and rich tradition, which his incisive genius was able to assemble into a cogent and accessible form.

It is for this reason that I follow Shinran. In other words, I accept his guidance – before all others – as the principal interpreter of the Larger Sūtra, whose exegesis of this text is the most comprehensive, satisfying and accessible to have emerged since it was first delivered.

Jōdo Wasan 100
When we say 'Namo Amida Butsu'
Brahmā and Indra venerate us;
All the benevolent gods of the heavens
Protect us constantly, day and night.

GODS AND THE DHARMA

When we discuss the gods of Buddhist cosmology, we are not engaging in comparative religion. Although they may resemble the gods of Hinduism, the two systems are completely different. The gods of Buddhism have converted to the dharma, having become its guardians and protectors. Yet not all Buddhist gods are of Indian origin. According to some scholars, the image of Vajrapāṇi (Śākyamuni's protector), was modelled on either the Greek god Zeus, or the divine hero Heracles.

The most crucial point here is the fact that the Buddha-dharma does not accept the existence of a creator-deity. It's entirely non-theistic. The gods, like everything else in the universe, arise from actions (*karma*).

The *Abhidharmakośa-bhāṣyam* makes this crystal clear:

> Who created the variety of living beings and the receptacle world?
> It was not a god who intelligently created it.
> The variety of the world arises from action.
> The variety of the world arises from the actions of living beings.[1]

Several sūtras allude to the idea that all gods (Sk. *deva*), dragons, māras and other living entities, which are neither human nor animal, protect people of the nembutsu. Brahmā here refers to the greatest of many 'higher' gods who reside in the first *dhyāna*-heaven in the world of form (Sk. *rūpa-dhātu*). But even he is beset with samsāric limitations. Like all gods, his life is long and happy, but in spite of being the most exalted among them, Brahmā is also unfortunate in that he's not fully aware of his own karmic bondage.

Following his enlightenment, Śākyamuni was disinclined to go forth and teach. He is described as reflecting on the fact that there is much about the dharma that's abstract and difficult for ordinary people to understand.

---

[1] Chapter 4.

Our delusions make it difficult to see ourselves as we really are, and we're not willing to accept our need for the dharma. It was the gods Indra and Brahmā who came to Śākyamuni and persuaded him to make the effort to promulgate the teaching. Thus, Brahmā was impressed by Śākyamuni's accomplishment and could discern the precious value of his teaching. Like Brahmā, most devas are supporters of the dharma, recognizing its importance for the salvation of 'gods and humankind' alike.[2]

In the epic biography of Śākyamuni (*Buddhacarita*) by Aśvaghoṣa, devas play a major role at every stage of his movement towards awakening. It was they who arranged the events that accompanied the bodhisattva out of his palace when he encountered old age, sickness and death for the first time. The devas even guided his horse as he set forth on the great quest for enlightenment.

In keeping with this tradition, the Larger Sūtra tells us that Śakra and Brahmā attend on bodhisattvas at the time of their final birth before enlightenment, and that they always encourage newly-awakened buddhas to teach the dharma that they have discovered.

> As Śakra and Brahmā request him to turn the wheel of the Dharma, the Buddha visits various places and preaches the Dharma in his thunderous voice.[3]

In the last section of the *Kyōgyōshinshō*, Shinran Shōnin assembles passages which demonstrate that people of nembutsu are revered and protected by unseen forces throughout the universe. In fact, it's not so much nembutsu followers that are helped in this way but, rather, Other-Power faith which is the focus of this favourable attention. We have no merit that warrants such support. However, the *Namo Amida Butsu* which fills our hearts and minds attracts the same spiritual protection that the gods offer to the dharma.[4]

In this same section of the *Kyōgyōshinshō*, Shinran clearly supports the idea – inherited within the tradition – that the gods safeguard the teachings, but he also draws on many other quite uncompromising

---

[2] *Buddha Dharma* (Numata Centre for Buddhist Translation and Research, 2003), p. 27.
[3] *The Three Pure Land Sūtras*, tr. Hisao Inagaki (Revised Second Edition, Numata Center for Buddhist Translation and Research, 2003), p. 5.
[4] CWS, pp. 255-275.

passages which counsel us against the reverence and worship of gods. Shin Buddhists do not serve or pray to such beings. Amida Buddha is our only refuge.

Jōdo Wasan 101
When we say 'Namo Amida Butsu',
The four great deva-kings together
Protect us constantly, day and night,
And let no evil spirits come near.

MORE ABOUT THE GODS

The gods of the Buddha-dharma emerged in the hiatus between the era of the Vedas, and that of later Zoroastrian and Hindu developments. Both of these religions became monotheistic after the Jain and Buddhist movements had got under way.

Well before the Hindu Dharma became monotheistic, a plethora of gods (*devas*) inhabited various segments of the cosmos. Hence, from the perspective of Buddhism, these devas are powers which populate heavens and earth – and usually help human beings. Some devas, like the asuras, became literally demonized in Hindu theology but the dharma continued to accept them as a species of living and powerful being who support the dharma and are largely out of view for people – even though they are sub-human and irascible.

The devas of the Buddha-dharma belong to the old Aryan pantheon, whereas later traditions sifted them into roles consistent with a monotheistic world view. They arrived at their present status as a result of previous actions (*karma*) and the overriding outcome for them is unmitigated pleasure. Brahmā, who now resides in the first *dhyāna* heaven in the world of form (*rūpa-dhātu*) partakes of a purely intellectual and ethical pleasure but the lower gods, in various stages of the world of desire (*kāma-dhātu*), experience sensual pleasures of all kinds.

Because Brahmā is free of desire, he is often used as an exemplar of certain virtues in the Buddha-dharma. For example, chastity is described as 'the way of Brahmā' (*brahma-carya*). More famous are the sublime abodes (*brahmavihārā*), which are the norms of internal disposition for followers of the dharma in our relations with the world. They are friendliness (*maitrī*), compassion (*karuṇā*), sympathetic joy (*muditā*) and equanimity (*upekṣā*): all attitudes that tend to engender tranquility in others.

The gods of the 'Four-King Heaven' (*catur-mahārāja-kāyikas*) dwell at a very low level in the world of desire and are described by Vasubandhu Bodhisattva in his *Abhidharmakośa-bhāṣyam* as sometimes living on earth. They certainly engage in all of the sensual pleasures that we humans do – even to the extent of bearing children! In this regard, they resemble the gods of the classical Greek pantheon, who form part of the European tradition and are very much active agents in the works of Homer, for example.

For Shinran, the sense of being surrounded by the gods was no doubt very real – indeed, even quite tangible. It's comforting to know that he understood the world that way. He had been reared in a very different cultural milieu to ours. For us, a sense of living in a world replete with unseen spiritual entities is difficult. Our pattern of thought is extremely materialistic.

Even so, when one reads Homer (*Iliad* and *Odyssey*), the worldview represented there seems healthier, and happier, than the solipsism and self-obsession of our time. Our perspective is a source of misery because we believe that we're able to have ultimate control over events – an idea that simply isn't true; one that will always be defeated, thus causing frustration and disappointment.

I think that Shinran's verses on the protection that gods offer followers of the nembutsu serve as valuable lessons. First, they remind us that we human beings are not the only intelligent entities in the universe – we have no place being arrogant about our capabilities. A second useful feature of these verses is that they underscore Shinran's sense of the dharma's universality.

Shinran never takes the view that gods who aren't associated with Buddhism have anything to offer us. He was exclusively and single-mindedly dedicated to the dharma and acknowledges no other truth. Thirdly, these verses always remind me that the 'unseen powers' that be are essentially friendly.

Let us not forget that these verses are not, actually, about the gods – they are songs in praise of the nembutsu.

There is only the call of the Vow. As for spirits and gods, they have been mandated to protect the dharma and its adherents. Safely in the knowledge that this is so, we need not trouble ourselves about them, and can let them get on with their job.

Jōdo Wasan 102
When we say 'Namo Amida Butsu',
The earth-goddess called 'Firmness'
Reveres and protects us constantly, day and night,
Accompanying us always just as shadows do things.

UNEARTHING THE DHARMA

The goddess of the earth is called Prithvi, and it's said that she held the feet of anyone who preached the *Sūtra of Golden Splendour*. Perhaps she had something to do with the revival of Buddhism in the previous couple of centuries. It's almost impossible to believe now but, around two hundred years ago, the Buddha-dharma was completely unknown in the West and contact between the southern and eastern Buddhist communities was rare.

Due to the curiosity of European colonists, the dharma was literally unearthed in India, the home of its birth, where it was almost extinct. At the end of the nineteenth century, Bōdh-Gayā in Bihar – where tradition tells us that Śākyamuni attained Enlightenment – was nothing but a decrepit Hindu shrine. Now it's a massive and beautifully kept complex of gardens and hostels, along with the temples of many schools of dharma.

The gradual process of unearthing the history of the Buddhist movement, especially in India, Nepal and Sri Lanka brought new insights into the dharma; and many fine European exponents – like Arthur Schopenhauer (1788–1860) – emerged to give a worthy account of it. The dharma also gained a high level of popularity towards the end of the nineteenth century when some prominent Theosophists developed a new rationalist and secular version of the Theravāda which, today, is thriving in most Western countries.

One intriguing development that resulted from all this European and American interest was the wide acceptance of meditation as a lay practice. Public instruction in it was first introduced to Sri Lanka by Don David Hevavitherane (1864–1933) – also known as Anagārika Dharmapāla – a Theosophist and disciple of Colonel Henry Steel Olcott (1832–1907).

Anagārika Dharmapāla was a monk who eventually abandoned Theosophy, but he began a movement which completely reshaped the practice of the dharma into the form we know today. Until he began instructing ordinary monks and lay people, meditation (*dhyāna*) was usually the preserve of talented bhikṣus and was learnt and transmitted from teacher to disciple.

Of course, in Theravāda countries, meditation was practiced by yogins, not by ordinary monks or lay people. There have been some attempts to resist this new emphasis on meditation, but without success. I have heard some Thai Buddhists argue that *samādhi* does not arise in dependence on *dhyāna*; and I would concur, since the Noble Eightfold Path is not linear but concomitant in its arising.

Now that meditators are in the ascendency, especially in countries like Australia, there is a tendency for non-meditators to be disparaged. In fact, throughout the ages, a healthy dharma community has included only a few meditators. We are all quite unique and one rule should never apply to all.

These days, it is thought that meditation is the exclusive preserve of the Buddha-dharma when, in fact, it has always been practiced in, for example, Orthodox, Assyrian and Catholic Christian monasteries at various times – but only under the instruction of carefully chosen and accomplished individuals! We also find deep contemplative practices among the Sufi orders of Islam. Meditation was taught with great care because errors in this endeavour can be perilous.

It would be useful to know what it meant to follow the dharma – either for monks or lay-folk – before the time of Anagārika Dharmapāla. If many people these days believe that meditation is the practice by which we define ourselves as adherents of the way, how did those in the past identify as Buddhists? What was the distinguishing feature of living the dharma, for most of the faithful, throughout its earlier history? There can be no doubt that this was the doctrine of 'not-self' (*anātman*).

Anātman is the very core of the dharma, and informs the entire structure of its philosophy and practice. The concept of 'emptiness' (*śūnyatā*) is related to the same notion, but as extended to all 'dharmas'; that is, every particle of the cosmos. 'Not-self' thus relates primarily to the constituents of human personality, the *skandhas*. Needless to say, the whole bodhisattva tradition – and the grand philosophical schemes of Mādhyamika and Yogācāra – arise from the core fact of *anātman*. That is why, from the Hindu perspective, this doctrine is seen as heretical or 'non-dogmatic' (*nāstika*).

The intellectual systems espoused by all dharma schools are primarily for the purpose of supporting practical results. They are never mere 'philosophy'. Without a spiritually effective outcome, they have no intrinsic value. As such, they're not meant to support cosmological theories and the like, but to assist in our awakening and enlightenment; in other words, in being truly free. It is this, not *dhyāna*, that's the defining characteristic of Buddhist thought.

The practical effect of *anātman* impinges on everything in the dharma: the *Jātaka* tales, the devotional life, ethical systems, definitions of the accomplished 'saint', the bodhisattva vehicle and the six *pāramitās*. The Noble Eightfold Path begins and ends with *anātman*. Right view is 'no view' and *samādhi* – which is related to Other-Power faith – serves to undermine our ego. Indeed, the *Jātaka* tales (both of Śākyamuni and Amida Buddha) tell of nothing but the abandonment of self.

In everyday life, then, the defining feature of a Buddhist before the introduction of meditation was, more or less, nothing but generosity and a love of all people and other beings. This is the practical manifestation of *anātman* and the surrender of everything that defines us: our property, our ideas, and even our hopes and aspirations.

Followers of the dharma expressed their generosity through hospitality, which didn't judge the worth of the recipient; they also did so by way of kindness and a dedicated regime of devotional activity. Especially popular was the practice of visiting monks and giving them gifts; and of hearing the dharma by chanting the teachings, morning and night.

For those then who are interested in what might be called 'traditional Buddhism', it's easy to recommend Jōdo Shinshū. If someone wants to understand the path of Shinran as a 'process', it too is *anātman*.

Namo Amida Butsu

Jōdo Wasan 103
When we say 'Namo Amida Butsu',
Nanda, Upananda and other great nāgas,
Along with the countless nāga-gods,
Revere and protect us constantly, day and night.

NĀGAS

I have heard that, on one occasion, when the Blessed One was newly Awakened – staying at Uruvelā by the banks of the Nerañjara River in the shade of the Muccalinda tree – he sat for seven days in one session, sensitive to the bliss of release. Now, at that time a great, out-of-season storm cloud rose up, with seven days of rainy weather, cold winds and intense darkness.

Then Muccalinda the nāga king, leaving his realm and encircling the Blessed One's body seven times with his coils, stood with his great hood spread over the Blessed One, thinking: 'Don't let the Blessed One be disturbed by cold. Don't let the Blessed One be disturbed by heat. Don't let the Blessed One be disturbed by the touch of flies, mosquitoes, wind, sun and creeping things.' Then, at the end of the seven days, the Blessed One emerged from that concentration. Muccalinda the nāga king, realizing that the sky had cleared and the storm clouds had left, unravelled his coils from the body of the Blessed One, changed his appearance and, assuming the form of a youth, stood in front of the Blessed One with hands before his heart in homage.

Then, on realizing the significance of this, the Blessed One on that occasion exclaimed:

> Blissful is solitude for one who's content, who has heard the Dhamma, who sees.
> Blissful is non-affliction with regard for the world, restraint for living beings.
> Blissful is dispassion with regard for the world, the overcoming of sensuality.
> But the subduing of the conceit 'I am' – that is truly the ultimate bliss.[1]

The peace of Enlightenment, which Śākyamuni realized, was protected by the intervention of the nāga king, Muccalinda. Nāgas are snake gods. They were especially popular in the north-western part of the Indian sub-

---

[1] *Muccalinda Sutta*, tr. Thanissaro Bhikkhu.

continent, particularly in Kashmir and Gandhāra, which are now part of Pakistan and Afghanistan. They are often associated with waterways but are said to live underground in palaces. Their morphology varies from a straightforward cobra shape, like Muccalinda who used his hood to protect Śākyamuni from the elements, to a quasi-anthropomorphic form, either male or female.

According to the Hindu account of the genesis of nāgas, it was Brahmā who confined them to their underground existence because they were becoming too numerous. It is said that Brahmā assigned them the task of ending the lives of those destined for premature death. In Buddhism, nāgas are guardians of doorways, and especially oversee vaults containing sacred texts. Eight nāgas were present when Śākyamuni delivered the Lotus Sūtra,[2] including the brothers Nanda and Upananda, who are mentioned by Shinran Shōnin in this verse.

As we have already seen in the case of Brahmā, gods are viewed as defenders of the dharma. Even those who once opposed it become its supporters eventually. Buddhism does not seek to demonize its opponents, divine or human, and proudly proclaims their conversion as evidence of the tendency in 'superior beings' to seek wisdom. Gods have a capacity for omniscience, and this gives them a natural inclination to pursue the dharma and to recognize its truth when they see it. They may influence their devotees in that direction as well. So it is that, from this perspective, gods are very often viewed as teachers; and teachers as gods.

Perhaps we can see nāgas as representing those aspects of ourselves which are brooding, ominous and out of view. Our own death is perhaps such a thing. However, when we confront these hidden and troubling realities, resting within the embrace of Amida Buddha in *Namo Amida Butsu* – trusting his unfathomable wisdom and compassion – it's possible that these hidden phenomena will be seen in a different light; as small and insignificant.

And perhaps the things that we fear or regard as ugly and repellent will come to be seen as elegant and welcome; reminders, if nothing else, of the joyous fact that we are powerless and wholly in need of Amida Buddha's Vow. We may also realize that we ought not to kill the objects of our dread, but rather to accept and appreciate them – to leave them alone.

The fear is not in things themselves; but in how they are seen.

Jōdo Wasan 104
When we say 'Namo Amida Butsu',
Yama, the king of the dead, reveres us
And the officers who judge beings of the five courses of existence
All protect us constantly, day and night.

YAMA, THE DHARMA-KING

In both Hindu and Buddhist religions, the icons of Yama (Jp. Enma) are almost identical and his role is similar. He is called 'Yama, King of the Dharma' (*Yama Dharmarāja*) in both religions. At first, in the time of the Vedas, he was a rather affable character but, as people became increasingly concerned about the oppressive nature of karma, it was natural that he would be seen as developing sterner qualities. In Buddhist icons, he is almost invariably surrounded by flames and conveys a sense of fury.

In Hindu cosmology, Yama is also the ruler of the southern hemisphere, but the Buddha-dharma does not seem to attribute that role to him. For us, his function is to assess the course to which our actions (*karma*) have assigned us. That is why it's understandable that people burdened with the mistakes of their past should tremble and see him as a fierce judge. His judgement, however, is never arbitrary.

Yama himself conforms to the rigid dictates of karma and cannot override them under any circumstances. His power lies in having a knowledge of this law, but he does not frame it. The purpose of Yama, the Dharma-King, is to remind us that the operation of karma is inexorable – there is no way we can escape the results of our actions.

Yama is not alone in having the title of 'Dharma-King'. In the *Kyōgyōshinshō*, for example, Shinran Shōnin quotes a passage from Fa-chao's *Shorter Pure Land Liturgy of Nembutsu Chant in Five Stages*, in which Amida Buddha is also described as 'Dharma-King'. Yama is only a god and therefore not fully enlightened. He does not rule the dharma; the dharma rules him. In meting out judgement to the dead, he affirms the consequences of karma as discovered and taught by all buddhas.

Skillful actions lead to good results, while unskillful actions lead to unhappy outcomes. Many aspire to behave in such a way as to ensure a 'favourable rebirth' for themselves. Keeping the precepts, for example, is likely to result in a human birth which affords a further opportunity to hear the dharma.

However, the final objective in Buddhism is to transcend the round of birth-and-death (*saṃsāra*) altogether, and this is not achieved through mere virtuous actions or avoiding bad deeds. The aim is to attain 'no-birth' – to go beyond good and evil. If we heed the call of the Vow raised by Amida the Dharma-King, there should be no need for us to meet Yama. The Buddha's pure mind, which is embodied in *Namo Amida Butsu*, releases us from the bondage of samsāra. Again, there is nothing in and of ourselves that would command Yama's respect; it's just that, in seeing people of nembutsu, he perceives only the transcendent light of Amida that sustains them.

Jōdo Wasan 105
When we say 'Namo Amida Butsu',
We are protected by the great king of māras,
Residing in the sixth heaven;
This he vowed to do in the presence of Śākyamuni Buddha.

MĀRAS

Māra is the king of demons (Jp. *Daimaō*). The māras are devas who live in one of the heavens in the realm of desire (*kāma-dhātu*); the same sphere of existence to which we human beings belong. The *Paranirmitavaśavartin* is the sixth heaven of the kāma-dhātu where Māra dwells, and the devas of that particular heaven 'enjoy the things that others desire'. In other heavens, by contrast, devas may enjoy the things they have created themselves. So māras seem to be parasitic, keen to spoil other peoples' goals and even their fun. It is this that underlies the popular feeling that they are evil entities.

The malevolence of these demons is compounded by the role that their king, Māra himself, played in the well-known temptation of Śākyamuni. The *Buddhacarita* by Aśvaghoṣa is the most prominent source for this story. The original version of the text concludes at the point of the Buddha's enlightenment and, later, the story was expanded to incorporate an account of further temptations hurled by Māra against him.

The Demon-King was driven to undermine Śākyamuni's resolve while he was seated under the Bodhi tree waiting for enlightenment to dawn, having given up his efforts to force it. At that point, Māra's aim was to instill, within the bodhisattva, a completely corrosive self-doubt. He did this by first telling Śākyamuni that a usurper had taken over his father's kingdom. When that didn't move him, Māra created a shocking storm, which frightened away all the devas who had come to honour the future Buddha.

Having failed at this, Māra then tried to demoralize Śākyamuni by finding 'weaknesses' that he could exploit; suggesting, for example, that he was not worthy of Buddhahood. To this, Śākyamuni called upon the earth to witness his entire bodhisattva career of total purity and compassionate generosity. This gesture by Śākyamuni is often represented in Buddhist art.

Finally, Māra tried an appeal to Śākyamuni's sensuality by offering his 'daughters' – *tṛṣṇā* (thirst), *rati* (desire) and *rāga* (delight). After Māra had tried everything, he abandoned the effort to thwart Śākyamuni's enlightenment. He did return later, though, in order to belittle the Buddha's realization, aiming to demonstrate that no one would be able to understand and accept this teaching.

These events testify to a malicious quality that many of us share with Māra. The king of demons clearly wanted to control the events surrounding Śākyamuni's enlightenment and took delight in the prospect that the Buddha-to-be might fail in his endeavours; but Māra also feared that others might hear about the possibility of being emancipated from suffering, should Śākyamuni have succeed.

There is no greater tyranny than the kind of mean-spiritedness we find in Māra. There are those who take delight in the failure of others, who belittle their efforts and who traffic in self-doubt and guilt. They will exploit perceived vulnerabilities in a person to demoralize and humiliate them, for no purpose other than their own advantage and perverse satisfaction. That is what Māra tried to do.

From the Buddhist perspective, this is clearly wicked because it's symptomatic of a monstrously excessive egomania. Māra's depravity is not based on error, or even on a miscreant spirit; he just wants to spoil things for others – even if it means destroying beauty and truth – and he gets pleasure from doing so. When human beings behave like that, and many do, we consider it sociopathic. Such people are very unpleasant to deal with but are often successful in gaining power over human affairs.

In ordinary circumstances, a māra is one who seeks to subvert the efforts of bodhisattvas and other disciples of the dharma, so as to turn them away from the path to liberation. They may appear in human form, as spirits or as hallucinations associated with *dhyāna*. It was the *Sūtra of Golden Splendour* that reported Māra's pact with Śākyamuni to stop thwarting Buddhists and, instead, to protect them. But can this kind of being be trusted with such promises?

Even though Māra might be ambivalent about keeping his word, his ability to thwart a person of nembutsu would be as unsuccessful as were his efforts against Śākyamuni. Someone who has awakened to Amida's shinjin is unshakeable and eventually, no matter how powerful their assault, it's the māras who will fail and depart.

So, there is no need for concern at all if we take refuge in Amida Buddha, whose invincible compassion overwhelms the insidious power of demons.[1]

---

[1] CWS pp. 46-47.

Jōdo Wasan 106
The gods of the heavens and earth
Are all to be called good,
For together they protect
The person of the nembutsu.

INFLUENCE

The Icy South-Easterly and the Sun
(A fable by Aesop with an Antipodean Twist)

> A dispute arose between the Icy South-Easterly Wind and the Sun, each claiming that he was stronger than the other. At last, they agreed to try their powers upon a traveller, to see which could soonest strip him of his cloak. The Icy South-Easterly had the first try; and gathering up all his force for the attack, he came whirling furiously down from the hills upon the man, and caught up his cloak as though he would wrest it from him by one single effort: but the harder he blew, the more closely the man wrapped it around himself. Then came the turn of the Sun. At first, he beamed gently upon the traveller, who soon unclasped his cloak and walked on with it hanging loosely about his shoulders: then he shone forth in full strength, and the man, before he had gone many steps, was glad to throw his cloak right off and complete his journey more lightly clad.[1]

Well, of course, this is the story of the *North* wind and the Sun but, in the unique climate experienced by those of us who live in the southern latitudes of Australia, the North wind accompanies the short but frequent episodes of extremely warm conditions which we experience in summer. It is already hot before the wind gathers strength, and no one would be wearing a coat in the first place! Rather, towards the middle of autumn, in these parts, the south-easterlies which brought us weekly relief from the heat in summer, turn bitterly cold.

In any case, this is a story about influence, which the dictionary[2] describes

---

[1] *Æsop's Fables* (London: William Heineman, 1912), p. 23.
[2] All definitions, spelling and grammatical styles adopted in this work are guided by the most popular dictionary of Australian English usage, *Macquarie Encylopedic Dictionary* (in various editions).

as 'the invisible or insensible action exerted by one thing or person on another.' Although in the story of the North Wind and the Sun, the latter's influence is not insensible – it is at least invisible – because of its warmth. The North Wind (or the South-Easterly, here) used only force, and resistance was the result. The Sun just smiled and extended its warm grace on the battered traveller who accepted its bidding with ease.

To take this further: in the physical world of our solar system, the sun simply exists. We know it to be a system of relatively straight-forward reactions which have nuclear fusion as their ignition. Here on earth, however, the sun's energy is the very source of life. It doesn't actually create any of the plants – and the animals that feed on them – but they all receive their sustenance from its light: the plants from photosynthesis, and the animals from the plants.

While all growth and activity on earth develops into unique forms, they remain entirely dependent on the sun which does not, however, design the life-forms that emerge. The sun's role, therefore, is that of an influence.

Buddha – the wisdom that pervades all things – while not to be confused with the physical world, can be well understood by using the sun's role in relation to life on earth as an analogy. When Buddha acts, it's not to create the things that are dependent on it, but rather to emerge into the mystic (*saṃbhogakāya*) world or the sensible world (*nirmāṇakāya*) in a form that manifests enlightenment.

Yet all existing things are pervaded by Buddha as ultimate reality (or *Dharmakāya*) and all of their internal spiritual light, wisdom and compassion, derive from it. Buddha does not force itself upon beings, it just exists; our choice then is either resistance or acceptance. Self-effort to attain enlightenment is a form of defiance since it's based on force. Other-Power relies only on influence, which is the 'perfuming' of samsāric consciousness by the *Dharmakāya*. The vehicle that carries this influence is *Namo Amida Butsu*.

The gods of heaven and earth, as sentient beings with individuality and conditioned personalities, are active; always seeking to use their power to either help or hinder. But, according to Buddhist teaching, they have become friends of the dharma and now protect its followers.

Yet, influence is an important way for us to develop a proper understanding of the dharma; or anything else for that matter. I always tend to be more strongly influenced by those who are what we might call 'quiet achievers'. These are people who apply themselves with determination and self-confidence – often unremarked and unrewarded – who create something great, beautiful, enduring or useful. Their generosity of spirit and selflessness exemplifies a life of dharma. Yet, they may never know how they have influenced or helped others. And we have all been lastingly impressed by something seemingly insignificant – a brief encounter or a passing gesture.

The means by which truth is transferred is ultimately a form of influence. Force just causes hurt and resistance and is often superficial in its impact. Influence is viscerally received; sometimes even a revolution in thought can occur because of it. It's warmly received in its own time and profoundly endures.

Shinran Shōnin was and remains a man of influence. He never set out to reform the world but quietly sat at home and answered the questions of those who sought his guidance. He wrote the *Kyōgyōshinshō* as a way to account for his perspective on the teaching of Śākyamuni and Hōnen Shōnin, rather than being a noisy vehicle of propaganda.

We would do well to take a lesson from the example set by the quiet osmosis of the dharma; both by the deities who are now its guardians, and the way in which Shinran set in motion a huge spiritual movement that still endures to this day. That which abides and is warmly welcomed comes by way of influence, not by pressure or loud bluster.

As followers of Jōdo Shinshū, let us turn our attention to the dharma and live sincerely within its light. Embracing the nembutsu honestly, and with the light of Amida Buddha in our hearts, we can leave the influence of others to his pervasive presence. Needless to say, this spiritual force is invisible and we may never know the impact we have in the world.

But by just being ourselves as nembutsu followers and speaking when called upon, or from a wish to express our nembutsu-faith as an end in itself, we tell of the dharma just as we see it. Leaving aside the desire to impose our views on others, or to control the outcome of our encounters, we just let this influence play its part without interference.

Jōdo Wasan 107
Shinjin that is the inconceivable working of the power of the Vow
Is none other than the mind aspiring for great Enlightenment;
The evil spirits that abound in heaven and earth
All hold in awe the person who has attained it.

ON BEING NAKED

> The beginning of the love of wisdom... is consciousness of a man's own weakness and impotence with regard to the things of real consequence in life.[1]

Jōdo Shinshū is pre-eminently a religion of light, wisdom and truth (Sk. *satya*). The Path of Sages, on the other hand, emphasizes the bodhisattva way of compassion (Sk. *karuṇā*). This can be seen, for example, in the sublime verses of Śāntideva.

The Pure Land way urges us, above all, to stand in the light. In doing so, we strip away all pretence (*hakarai*) and artifice; and acknowledge the truth about things as they are. When this happens, we discover that there's only one reality – shinjin of the inconceivable Vow-Power (*ganriki fushigi no shinjin*), which eludes our spiritual scheming. We can never come to know this radiance unless we're willing to live under its illumination. Until that time, we can only cling blindly to hope.

To my way of thinking, being immersed in this light is to surrender everything in *Namo Amida Butsu*; but the obstacles we face are innumerable. Of course, there are the usual impediments that we find mentioned in the canons of the dharma, but there are more serious and immediate things that get in the way. The first is the widespread belief in the relativity of truth.

While the samsāric world of mind and matter may be conditioned, truth itself is not relative. We cannot flee from the reaches of the Vow forever, but one way in which people try to escape its influence is to insist that Jōdo Shinshū is one among many 'truths'. However, the Vow of Amida Buddha is absolute. If its efficacy were only relative, then it would be quite useless.

---

[1] *The Discourses of Epictetus* II, 21.

Another habit of thought, which serves as an obstacle to discovering truth, is to attach ourselves to 'views' (Sk. *dṛṣṭi*). We do this when we allow teachers and sacred texts to become objectified. Truth is most clearly revealed in dialogue, rather than by the assertion of authority. If we are reading Shinran Shōnin's writing, for example, we need to do so in such a way as to be present before him unclad. All our fears, hurts and misgivings ought to be open before the light of his wisdom. If we take his teaching as a badge to wear, a directive for our way of life, a weapon to use in an argument, or something to clothe our actual vacuity, it will be altogether ineffectual. The same can be said of the teachings of Śākyamuni or any other sage. In meeting Shinran in his work, we need to be present with our honest selves.

When I talk about being naked, I mean 'profoundly honest'. This is not the same as being truthful. An honest person knows how mendacious he can be. Veracity is one of those virtues that can be used to hurt other people, and it does indeed belong – like all conventional morality – to the realm of relativity. To be genuinely candid is to come into the light with all our scars exposed. If Shinran affronts, then be affronted; if he inspires, be inspired; if he causes us frustration and anger, be frustrated and angry.

Of course, deep self-honesty can become an artifice, a kind of garment, too. We might think that such candour involves exposure of our darkest – and most intimate – secrets to the world. This, of course, is the stuff of scandal, shock and self-assertion which has nothing to do with being completely naked. Exhibitionism is a disposition towards which many of us are inclined, but it's only a characteristic of ego-centricity, and stems from a wish to be noticed so as to make an impact on others.

True nakedness is to acknowledge things as they are, while not judging them as good or bad. For what we see, in that light, is not our moral worth, but our nothingness – only then can we discern the presence of Amida Buddha and hear the call of his Vow.

This profound personal truth, which emerges from Other-Power faith, is what evil spirits fear.

Shinnin wa isho kitamana maruhadaka.
'A true man is completely naked while fully clothed'.

Zuiken Inagaki (1885–1981)

Jōdo Wasan 108
When we say 'Namo Amida Butsu',
Avalokiteśvara and Mahāsthāmaprāpta,
Together with bodhisattvas countless as the Ganges' sands
  or as particles,
Accompany us just as shadows do things.

AVALOKITEŚVARA BODHISATTVA

'Avalokiteśvara' means 'the Lord who gazes down', although one variant of the Chinese translation of this name (adopted by Kumārajīva for example) is *Guānshìyīn* – 'Regarder of the Cries of the World'. This bodhisattva represents Amida's compassion and is, therefore, the very embodiment of life itself.

He is remarkable for being common to both Theravāda and Mahāyāna traditions. In Sri Lanka, for example, he is known as Nātha-deva. His story forms part of the *Lotus Sūtra*. He is loved throughout the Buddhist world, and many faithful see him as a close companion and friend. To my mind, Avalokiteśvara epitomizes the ongoing presence of *karuṇā* in our world, spanning the time between Śākyamuni's appearance and that of Maitreya in the future.

The *Avalokiteśvara Sūtra* describes what the bodhisattva will do to assist those who call upon him. The nature of Avalokiteśvara's help is not actually significant for its seemingly supernatural and miraculous qualities; the point is that he seeks to alleviate the symptoms of the world's suffering in order to facilitate the practice of dharma. For those who are hungry, in jail or suffering in other ways, he offers emergency assistance, as it were, so that recipients of his benevolent attention can get on with the most important thing in life: the study of the teachings so as to ensure progress along the path.

Hence, in countries where the Buddhist tradition has had a long presence, people who feel that they have been saved from some kind of disaster by the intervention of Avalokiteśvara, may dedicate more time to the dharma in order to repay the debt they owe him.

In keeping with his powers, Avalokiteśvara is the quintessential master of the 'Perfection of Wisdom' (*prajñāpāramitā*) who sees conditioned things as 'empty' (Sk. *śūnya*). Things that lack any substance are inherently impotent and thus the fear they seem to elicit is illusory. The apparently miraculous power that Avalokiteśvara appears to wield is, in reality, the dissolution of fear and the freeing of the mind from debilitating hindrances that frustrate the exercise of dharma. Thus, Avalokiteśvara delivers the *Heart of the Perfection of Wisdom Sūtra* and is honoured more for this profound offering than anything else.

Affection for Avalokiteśvara reached its height in northern India between the third and fourth centuries of our common era. He first became known in China as *Guānyīn* as early as the first century, and eventually assumed a female form. From the seventh century onwards, His Holiness the Dalai Lama has been seen as the embodiment of Avalokiteśvara (Tb. Chenrézig) by members of his lineage.

Avalokiteśvara was also a guide to Tripṭika Master Xuanzang during his perilous travels through central Asia and India (629–645 CE). Known in Japan from the very earliest days of the dharma's introduction to that country, he has come to be venerated in seven forms – the most elegant of which is *Shō-Kannon*, a seated figure holding a lotus.

Shinran Shōnin apparently had an especially close relationship with Avalokiteśvara. He wrote many verses – some of which are part of the *Sanjō Wasan* – in praise of the Prince Regent Shōtoku whom he saw as the embodiment of this bodhisattva. We know, too, that Shinran's wife, Eshinni-sama, had a dream in which she became aware that Shinran himself was also a manifestation of Kannon; but she did not tell him about the dream. In one of her letters, she describes the time in Shinran's life during which he was moving into the ambit of Other-Power faith (*tariki no shinjin*).

> Your father left Mt. Hiei, remained in retreat for one hundred days at Rokkaku-dō [where Avalokiteśvara is enshrined], and prayed for salvation in the afterlife. Then, on the dawn of the ninety-fifth day, Prince Shōtoku appeared in a vision, revealing the path to Enlightenment, after reciting a verse. Thus, he immediately left Rokkaku-dō, before dawn, and called on Hōnen Shōnin to be shown the way to salvation in the afterlife.[1]

---

[1] *The Life of Eshinni Wife of Shinran Shōnin*, Yoshoki Ohtani, p. 91.

Jōdo Wasan 109
Countless Amida Buddhas reside
In the light of the Buddha of Unhindered Light;
Each of these transformed buddhas protects
The person of true and real shinjin.

TRUE ENTRUSTING HEART

The group of verses we're considering at the moment is entitled, as you will remember, *Hymns on Benefits in the Present*. There are fifteen verses in this section, of which ten are built around the phrase *Namo-amida-butsu o tonaure ba* ('When we say *Namo Amida Butsu* ...'). Two verses are preparatory, referring to Dengyō Daishi and the *Sūtra of Golden Splendour*. Verses 106 and 107 refer to 'the person' (of the nembutsu) – people of shinjin. Now, this verse reveals just what Shinran Shōnin means by the phrase *Namo-amida-butsu o tonaure ba*.

The outward expression of true shinjin is the Name, *Namo Amida Butsu*. The passages, from which Shinran draws his inspiration for these verses, may give the impression that merely invoking the nembutsu ritualistically somehow delivers favourable results to us. However, this verse makes it clear that the source of any benefits in the present life is shinjin, which is manifested in saying the Name. The true benefit, then, is the arising of Amida Buddha's entrusting heart within us, as a secure fact of our existence.

Protection is another confusing concept in these verses. It's easy to imagine that we are shielded from misfortune, illness, or even death. This, of course, isn't what's meant at all. People of shinjin say the nembutsu which is 'the act of true settlement', because Other-Power faith is firm and cannot be dislodged. The 'entrusting heart' is, in fact, that of the Buddha – transferred to us in the Name. The source itself commands the respect and protection of unseen beings and deities.

As the Seventeenth Vow says, 'All buddhas praise the Name of Amida Buddha'. They protect those with a true entrusting heart from any damage to their faith, precisely because such people recognize and adore the Buddha of Infinite Light, who transfers his shinjin to those who accept it.

We also discover – in the final section of the *Kyōgyōshinshō* – that māras and deities throughout the universe, having been converted to the dharma, vow to protect it. Hence, they also safeguard the person of faith because shinjin is the very working of Amida in the life of an ordinary *bombu*.

Jōdo Wasan 110
When we say 'Namo Amida Butsu',
The countless buddhas throughout the ten quarters,
Surrounding us a hundredfold, a thousandfold,
Rejoice in and protect us.

THE DELIGHT OF THE BUDDHAS

We have now reached the last of the hymns on benefits in the present. It can be seen that their purport has been to celebrate the sense of abiding spiritual security and freedom that's experienced by those of true faith (Jp. *shinjitsu shinjin*). In these verses, such people are, in the main, described as those who say *Namo Amida Butsu*. Faith cannot be 'true' otherwise and, of course, the nembutsu is Other-Power.

The key thing to bear in mind in this section is that the protection of the gods and buddhas is an incidental, secondary benefit of the nembutsu way. Shinran's teaching is entirely devoid of any utilitarian content; its sole purpose is to overcome samsāra. Saying the nembutsu with the objective of securing worldly benefits is simply not in accordance with Amida Buddha's Vow.

The dharma may indeed have been used in the past by those seeking material benefits, but this motivation will not deliver the results hoped for. The Pure Land way surpasses mundane concerns altogether, which is precisely what makes it 'true and real'.

The aim of the nembutsu way, therefore, is complete transcendence; but not just for ourselves. As Tao-ch'o (562–645) remarks:

> I have collected true words to aid others in their practice for attaining birth, in order that the process be made continuous, without end and without interruption, by which those who have been born first guide those who come later, and those who are born later join those who were born before. This is so that the boundless ocean of birth-and-death be exhausted.[1]

In much of the Pure Land tradition, especially as practiced by the Ch'an (*Zen*) and T'ien-t'ai (*Tendai*) traditions in China, there is a venerable

---
[1] CWS, p. 291.

ritual in which devotees chant nembutsu while walking around an image of Amida Tathāgata and his two bodhisattva attendants, Mahāsthāmaprāpta and Avalokiteśvara. But in this hymn we see, by contrast, that it's the buddhas who surround the nembutsu follower – a complete role reversal. Shan-tao (613–681) also uses this imagery in his joyous work, *Ōjō Raisan*.

What is being commemorated here is the very heart of the dharma; in other words, its purpose is – in the words of Śākyamuni – to teach the nature of 'suffering and the release from suffering'. The role of buddhas is not that of static objects of worship, but as active agents in the liberation of all living beings. They are drawn towards us because people of nembutsu are well on the way to realizing Nirvāṇa.

We are protected because the buddhas 'crowd out' any offence against the person of true shinjin. One could even say that such a person dwells in a Buddha-focused world, and that their heart and mind inclines towards an other-worldly preoccupation. But, in any case, the peril we are contemplating here is not merely physical; it's internal. Our real threats lie within.

Are we going to close ourselves off from our true – but hidden – nature, the source of our being, the Dharma-Body? Will we, instead, let ourselves be governed by internal demons and fantasies of our own creation? Are we to be the measure of all things? Is our earthly life-span and bodily existence the sum of our existence? There is really nothing to inhibit this choice and it's one that most of us make. Many are happy to choose a warm, comfortable inner darkness; a life wherein no assumptions are challenged and no liberation is attained. Those oblivious to danger are the most vulnerable.

Nembutsu followers – who are surrounded by jubilant buddhas – have become the centre of the universe and are in tune with its joyful thrumming. And this is not because they avoid life's difficulties and challenges. The person of shinjin has confronted the demons and sees their limitations. In so doing, the light that infuses all things has been revealed. It's not people of true faith as such that the buddhas envelop but, rather, the *Namo Amida Butsu* which emerges from their lips. This is the light that adorns their lives.

Jōdo Wasan 111
*Having realized the perfect, all-pervasive truth of the nembutsu,
Mahāsthāmaprāpta, together with fifty-two bodhisattvas,
Rose from his seat and prostrated himself
At the feet of Śākyamuni Buddha.*

COURAGE

These verses, based on the *Sūtra of the Samādhi of Heroic Advance*, serve as a bridge between *Hymns on the Pure Land* and *Hymns on the Pure Land Masters*. The latter constitute Shinran Shōnin's most profound and detailed survey of the Pure Land tradition. As I have already pointed out, the *Sanjō Wasan* spiral inwards: from the brilliant light of Amida Buddha, to the working of his wisdom through history and, finally, culminating in the incisive insights into our hearts and decaying era that we find in the *Hymns on the Dharma Ages*.

The story of the nembutsu way 'in action', so to speak, begins in these next eight verses which are an account of how Bodhisattva Mahāsthāmaprāpta attained enlightenment. Then, in the subsequent set of hymns, we follow the saga of the seven dharma masters whom Shinran revered as his teachers. We, too, may see them as our living guides and dharma friends.

> Mahāsthāmaprāpta, the prince of the Dharma, rose from his seat together with fifty-two accompanying bodhisattvas, kneeled down at the Buddha's feet, and said: "As I remember the bygone days, Ganges-sands kalpas ago, a Buddha named 'Immeasurable Light' appeared in the world. Twelve tathāgatas, beginning with this Buddha, appeared in succession, each dwelling for one kalpa. The last one was called 'Light Outshining the Sun and Moon'. This Buddha taught me the nembutsu *samādhi*."[1]

This passage from the sūtra mentioned above describes the events celebrated in the ensuing verses, which relate the testimony of Mahāsthāmaprāpta Bodhisattva. They provide a link between the first two collections of hymns, because this bodhisattva stands as a sentinel at the beginning and the end of this pilgrimage; they also serve as the starting

---
[1] *Ryūkoku Translation Series*, IV, p. 166.

point for a cycle of verses that conclude with an account of Hōnen Shōnin. As far as Shinran is concerned, Mahāsthāmaprāpta Bodhisattva took the form of Hōnen – his teacher – thus becoming the embodiment of Amida Tathāgata's wisdom.

The *Śūraṅgama Sūtra* is named for the heroic valour required of a novice bodhisattva in order to set out on the path to enlightenment. Mahāsthāmaprāpta is himself an important example of this remarkable quality. Wisdom, compassion and courage are the three pillars of the bodhisattva's endeavour.

Jōdo Wasan 112
He addressed the World-honoured one, the master of the teaching,
'Ages ago, kalpas countless as the Ganges' sands in the past,
A Buddha appeared in the world
Whose name was 'Immeasurable Light'.

TIME AND THE DHARMA

The Buddha-dharma offers us a single proposition: that it's possible for us to attain a state that is not bound by time and space. Although different schools of dharma teach a variety of metaphysical doctrines, time and space (as co-relative terms) are considered a synonym for samsāra. For that reason, there's been an ongoing debate, throughout Buddhist history, about time in particular. The Sarvāstivādins saw it as real, while the Sautrāntikas did not.[1]

So, when Mahāsthāmaprāpta tells Śākyamuni that he can recall events which occurred 'as many kalpas ago as the sands of the Ganges' just what is he telling us?

A *kalpa* appears to be a unit of time, but it's not time divorced from other phenomena. As difficult as we find this idea, unless we make the effort to free ourselves from our prejudices and think out the implications of what is taught in the sūtras, the significance of the dharma will elude us.

In some important Buddhist documents – the *Abhidharmakośa*, for example – it is true that an attempt is made to calibrate kalpas as a form of linear time. However, they are more often described in extremely imaginative and colourful ways. One of the most famous of these is the suggestion that it's the length of time it would take a sparrow to wear down the Himalayas by brushing its wing against them once every hundred years.

The sūtras also often describe time as an entirely subjective phenomenon. A lifespan can be seen as a unit of chronology, even though there is a considerable difference in the length of lives in diverse species. For a god,

---

[1] That is, according to the *Satyasiddhi-śāstra* of Harivarman (c. 2nd century), which is reputedly a text of the Sautrāntika school – one of the eighteen branches of early Buddhism.

a day is fifty human years; a dog only lives an average life of around eighteen years; we humans live to an age that varies greatly between rich and poor countries; and, in East Asia, it is commonly held that cranes live for a thousand years.

It's difficult for us to see these fluctuating lifespans as a single unit because of the way we measure things. A kalpa then, in terms of measurement, is actually incalculable – not only because it is very long, but also because its significance diverges according to different forms of existence.

When the sūtras discuss time, they are speaking of origins. In them, we learn of those things that framed the world as we know it, but which are too deep to recall or remember. This idea is held in common with our actual experience as individuals. I certainly cannot remember any events before my birth and certainly nothing of my life in the womb. Worse, few adults are able remember their childhood in any clear and reliable detail. Yes, it is true that a miscellany of people, places and events float in and out of our memory, but such recollections are rarely accurate for very long.

These uncertain, nebulous events are the story we tell in giving an account of the way we are now. Likewise, Mahāsthāmaprāpta is describing his origins; not so much as he passes through a tunnel of recorded historical events, but as he gives an account of what it is that made him the bodhisattva that he is now. He's not calling up things from a list of past events, but from a deep repository of inner truth.

The past, from the point of view of the dharma, speaks not of events but of what it is that comprises our present reality. The story of Amida is not telling us about history but what it is that determines the reality and motivation of this Buddha now. History in the dharma is a matter of depth, rather than the progress of conventional time.

You will notice, in reading the sūtras of both the Pāli and the Mahāyāna canons, that explanations of the past are only revealed subjectively. Whenever Śākyamuni speaks, he does so from his own enlightened memory. He is not recounting events in the way that a modern historian might do – as a putatively 'objective' account, supported by contemporary documents.

We have to ask ourselves, then, why it is necessary to put these things into an historical framework. The answer is simple. The only way to reach into the consciousness of a deluded person is to address them in terms that conform to their delusion; the only way to converse with someone is to speak their language. In conceding the ingrained nature of our belief in time, we are hearing things in our own terms; in ways that we can understand. In teaching the dharma, buddhas speak not to themselves, but to us.

Jōdo Wasan 113
Thereafter tathāgatas succeeded each other,
Twelve in all, over a duration of twelve kalpas;
The last tathāgata was named
'Light that Outshines the Sun and Moon.'

TWELVE LIGHTS

The Pure Land Way and the Perfection of Wisdom

In the *Śūraṅgama Sūtra*, Mahāsthāmaprāpta lists twelve buddhas. Each one has a lifespan of a single kalpa. The names of each of these buddhas carries an attribute of light – exactly the same as the 'twelve lights' that characterize Amida Buddha as found in the Larger Sūtra. When Shinran Shōnin (following Mahāsthāmaprāpta, Śākyamuni, Vasubandhu and T'an-luan) speaks of 'Amida Buddha', his chief meaning is that of 'Buddha of Infinite Light' – *Amitābha*.

Light is wisdom (Sk. *prajñā*). This is the insight of an awakened one which is the 'Perfection of Wisdom' (Sk. *prajñāpāramitā*) – knowing that 'all conditioned things are empty' (Sk. *śūnya*) and that they share the same character (Sk. *lakṣaṇa*), which is 'Suchness' (Sk. *tathātā*). Accordingly, all existence is interconnected, because a buddha's awareness is grounded in 'one-ness' (Jp. *ichinyo*).

The Pure Land way, from Shinran's point of view, is a 'path of wisdom' (*prajñā-vāda*). Amida Buddha's light, pervading all things, illuminates our inner darkness, ultimately driving it out and revealing an underlying unity, which brings us to the threshold of saving truth. This is the instant in which we realize, to the very core of our being, that our own efforts at seeking the light are useless. We know that we have no option but to bathe in its incandescent embrace.

It's regrettable, therefore, that our tradition is usually said to emphasize compassion (Sk. *karuṇā*) above all else. When this occurs, the fundamental quality of wisdom tends to be forgotten, and so this teaching comes to be seen as largely sentimental in nature. In the Buddha-dharma, compassion is synonymous with wisdom and redolent with insight. The truth is often a source of dismay and even bitterness for people like us – enmeshed, as we are, in desire and delusion – for it does not discriminate in taking our preferences into account.

If there is one thing that characterizes our benighted condition, it's that we are limited, biased and prejudicial. We have likes and dislikes, fears and favours; we judge 'good' and 'evil' in ways that suit our own interests. The Buddha's light of wisdom is not prey to such limitations.

When we're tempted to make judgements based on our myopic understanding, we can be too readily influenced by current trends in thought and fashion; and by a predilection for those things elicited by our natural, human emotions. Thus, when ordinary people speak of compassion, it's always at risk of being compromised by ignorance (Sk. *avidyā*). Thus, it is sometimes taught that Amida's Primal Vow saves us 'just as we are', without qualification. But this is only partly true.

The Vow certainly 'takes in and embraces all' for it only sees oneness. But unless we freely respond to Other-Power shinjin – which at once sees our inability to emancipate ourselves – there is no likelihood of liberation for us whatsoever. Being embraced is not enough; although it's a good start, the need to turn towards and confront the light remains essential.

We cannot expect to attain Amida's enlightenment unless we are brutally honest – at least in sufficient degree to rid us of the illusion that we can somehow save ourselves. And, being *bombu*, we are never likely (nor could we) plumb the abyssal depths of our being. It's sufficient then to set aside our own efforts, and to rely unconditionally on the wisdom and compassion of the Tathāgata in *Namo Amida Butsu*.

The Twelve Lights

In the *Ōjōronchū*, T'an-luan lists thirty-seven characteristics of Amida Buddha, which include the twelve lights. These epithets are of primordial provenance and, of course, understood to have been praised by Śākyamuni himself.

The twelve lights are:

> The Buddha of Measureless Light, the Buddha of Boundless Light, the Buddha of Unimpeded Light, the Buddha of Unopposed Light, the Buddha Monarch of Flaming Lights, the Buddha of Pure Light, the Buddha of Light of Joy, the Buddha of Light of Wisdom, the Buddha of Uninterrupted Light, the Buddha of Inconceivable Light, the Buddha of Ineffable Light,

the Buddha of Light that Outshines the Sun and Moon.[1]

As we shall see in the next verse, it was Amida as 'Buddha of Light that Outshines the Sun and Moon' who became Mahāsthāmaprāpta's teacher. This last epithet sums up the final three in this list of twelve, which remind us of a vast and profound truth. The light we see with our eyes, and which sustains life on this planet, is not the ultimate illumination – it can only point to the true light.

Modern, materialistic people like us – and those of our generation – are in the habit of assuming that the physical is real, and that spiritual realities are just 'myths' and 'metaphors'. In fact, it's the other way around. The realm of the senses may be much more tangible to us but, when seen against a vista of immeasurable life, our worldly experience counts as nothing. The light of wisdom is inconceivable, not due to its limitations but because of ours. The sun and the moon are encompassed in the timeless, but they too are short-term players on the stage of eternity.

---

[1] *The Land of Bliss*, Luis O. Gómez (Higashi Honganji Shinshū Otani-ha, 1996).

Jōdo Wasan 114
The Tathāgata of Light that Outshines the Sun and Moon
Taught me the nembutsu-samādhi.
The tathāgatas of the ten quarters compassionately regard
Each sentient being as their only child.

SAMĀDHI

Samādhi is a Pāli and Sanskrit word that means, literally, 'concentration' – 'the mental state of being firmly fixed'.[1] It consists of three parts that indicate an adamantine state of mind. Traditionally, it's used to describe that part of the three-fold division of the path (Sk. *mārga*) which has to do with effort, mindfulness and concentration. Samādhi may lead to absorption (*zen*, Sk. *dhyāna*) if it's in a transcendent form that fulfills the conditions associated with enlightenment. There is also a 'weak', so-called 'worldly' form of samādhi; something akin to what we mean when referring to *serendipity*, or things 'coming together' for us.

In the *Abhidharma*, we discover that formal *dhyāna* practice is not a necessary condition for samādhi because concentration can occur unexpectedly, at any time. Samādhi does not contribute to proper awakening unless it is 'wholesome' (Sk. *kuśala*) – free of taints and attachments.

In traditional Buddhist practice, physical objects were often used as a focus of samādhi. Colours of the 'light-object' (Sk. *kṛtsna*) were selected to suit the temperament of the person using it, in order to induce concentration. Mantras and kōans are also employed for this purpose; and any activity in which the mind is focused – so as to bring about a state in which one 'forgets oneself' – can also be a form of samādhi.

This practice can very often engender a blissful condition, and the Buddha-dharma's interest in it has spread beyond its own confines to influence other spiritual paths. The martial arts, *ikebana* (flower-arranging), *sumi-e* (brush-painting), music, tea ceremonies, calligraphy and – in Japan – *haiku* poetry, have all taken up the idea of samādhi as a phase of their respective crafts. The role of samādhi extends even beyond this to other forms of study and manufacture.

---

[1] *Buddhist Dictionary: Manual of Buddhist Terms and Doctrines* by Nyanatiloka (Singapore Buddhist Meditation Centre,1970), p. 155.

The idea that samādhi has practical significance in daily life probably had its origins in the *Saṅgāti Sutta* from the Pāli canon. It suggests that the development of concentration brings four blessings to those who practice it. The first is a feeling of happiness. Secondly, one penetrates the core meaning of things with one's mind, going beyond mere notions and definitions. Also, there's a growing awareness of the evanescence of feelings and thoughts; that is to say, ideas and emotions outside the sphere of one's focus fall away easily, and attachment to them decreases.

In this verse, Shinran Shōnin reminds us of the samādhi practiced by enlightened ones, in which they regard each individual alone with complete focus. In this, and the next few verses, the 'child' spoken of is an infant: a babe-in-arms. This samādhi is likened to a father holding his only child for the first time. A newborn infant in our arms elicits extreme concentration, in which one is conscious of nothing else in the world but it. In that sense, the one-child image is quite effective.

The reference, however, is not to parent-child relationships as such. Sometimes it's suggested that Amida Buddha is our father or mother and, in Japan, a parental emphasis has become strong. However, important as such interpretations may be, the fact is that what's being discussed here is a specific moment in such relationships – one that can occur in any kind.

In this case, it speaks of mutual focal transference; something that does not occur often. It's the moment when two become one; when their concentration, or focus, is such that there's nothing else but the other. Each person in the relationship has momentarily become the other, while, of course, retaining their own inherent identity.

When beings are moved to say *Namo Amida Butsu*, that too is a kind of samādhi.

Jōdo Wasan 115
When sentient beings think on Amida,
Just as a child thinks of its mother,
They indeed see the Tathāgata – who is never distant –
Both in the present and in the future.

THINKING ON THE BUDDHA

The emphasis in this verse is on 'thinks'. We are again considering samādhi. This time, however, it's our thinking on the Buddha that's under consideration. Shinran Shōnin gives precedence to Amida's concentration on us because all nembutsu originates with the Buddha. Now, in return, we are spontaneously prompted to focus our minds on him. Furthermore, the juxtaposition of this (and the previous) verse indicates that our concentration naturally accompanies the samādhi that the Buddha directs towards us.

To recall or think on the Buddha, which is what *nembutsu* (Sk. *buddhānusmṛti*) means, is to find ourselves near to him and thus drawn effortlessly into his presence. This verse asserts that thinking brings one near to the object of our thoughts. Indeed, it draws us into an intimate bond.

This is how a baby (who has yet to realize individuation) might view such a relationship. Indeed, a child of up to about ten weeks of age has such single-minded devotion towards its mother, that it will even risk danger to reach her if she calls. However, the emphasis is not actually on the mother as such, but on the infant's unbending trust. There is no hint here that the Buddha is a 'parent' figure.

It's significant that what we find in this image is the notion of parenthood in relation to the steadfast love of the infant, who cannot do anything other than trust until he or she is rebuffed. It is inherent in the realization of *prajñā* (wisdom) that buddhas never turn their backs on those who rely on them. Therefore, any rupture in the relationship between us and the Tathāgata is always the result of a choice that we make.

Therefore, thinking on the Buddha – which is encouraged here in the analogy of a child's trust in its mother – is an imperative consistent with the natural order of things. Our dependence on the Buddha is inexorable and cannot be denied. The infant's trust is a necessity due to its circumstances. So is ours.

Given that this is such an apt metaphor – indicative of samādhi's nature when centered on the Buddha – it would be a mistake to take it literally. The resolute trust of a little child does not suggest that we adopt a puerile disposition. While it's true that some people readily have faith in others because they're child-like in nature, most of us are not. Neither do we need to become infantile to experience such confidence. The Primal Vow embraces all, forsaking none – even intelligent and sophisticated people can open their hearts and accept Amida's faith.

Our staunch adoration and trust in the Buddha also needs to be comfortable for us; intellectually as well as emotionally. Furthermore, some of us feel obliged to account for, and defend, our religious path. It is natural to yearn for the company of kindred spirits as we travel along the way. But we all belong to wider communities and networks, and our friends and loved ones deserve an explanation from us as to why we have adopted our chosen path.

We're not necessarily being encouraged here to see the Buddha as a parent-figure. The message of this verse is all about samādhi as concentration. The image of the infant's single-minded trust and the phrase 'thinking of the Buddha' (*nembutsu*) neatly draws the two parts of a unitary fact together, as Shinran so often does in his writings. The substance of our entrusting is the Name, even though we may not have the chance to utter a child's cry to draw attention to the fact that it is there.

<u>Jōdo Wasan 116</u>
Such beings are like people who, imbued with incense,
Bear its fragrance on their bodies;
They may be called
Those adorned with the fragrance of light.

NEMBUTSU SATURATION

One of the most wonderful times of my life was the first three or four years following my discovery of the nembutsu. It was indescribably liberating, as it often seems to be for so many who come to it for the first time. But it was also the period during which I became saturated with nembutsu – steeped in it. As the famous psychologist of religion, William James, once said: it's very much like falling in love.

I knew very little about the actual ecclesiology of Jōdo Shinshū at the time, and almost nothing of Shinran Shōnin. My meeting with him was some five years following my first encounter with the nembutsu, in the form of his *wasan*, copies of which I bought directly from the Ryūkoku Translation Centre. My other textbooks at that time were the *Contemplation Sūtra* and the *Amida Sūtra*. Both of these were available as offprints – published by the Prajna Temple in Sydney – of Max Müller's translations from the *Sacred Texts of the East*. I read them over and over until my copies wore out.

A Chinese monk (who worked as a prison chaplain in Malaysia) gave me a wonderful and durable *japa-mālā*. This was not the shortened kind we Shinshū followers use but a much longer set of beads – one hundred and eight of them – made of nuts from a bodhi tree. This monk also taught me how to chant nembutsu, while visualizing the Buddha as he is described in the *Contemplation Sūtra*. I made time each day for this activity, but also began taking every opportunity to recite while alone, setting up self-styled nembutsu retreats.

Those were enchanting times. I was also practicing Hatha Yoga and reading translations of the Pāli Canon, having come to see Śākyamuni as the 'greatest yogi'. It was at this time that I discovered the importance of faith (*shinjin*, Sk. *śraddha*) as the most vital step in finding release from samsāra. On one retreat, I took a newly purchased copy of *A Buddhist Bible* (edited by Dwight Goddard) and still remember the exhilaration I felt in reading the *Śūraṅgama Sūtra* and its account of Mahāsthāmaprāpta's nembutsu practice. This took me utterly by surprise, as I was just expecting to read a work of the Yogācāra tradition. It was marvellous to find the nembutsu discussed in that text as well.

Nembutsu retreats and meditation practice extended to my friends. On more than one occasion, I led sessions of nembutsu recitation and visualization based on the Larger Sūtra, which I had recently discovered. Reaching out for a tradition of like-minded individuals, I made contact with key members of the Buddhist Churches of America through whom I found, at last, the teaching of Shinran – a teacher who had plumbed the depths of practice and possessed a clear insight into the role of the nembutsu as a path to Nirvāna for ordinary people.

The most gratifying event since that time was my trip to Kyoto for ordination (*tokudo*) in 1994. It was here that I discovered that the Hongwanji is still home to many nembutsu followers. It soon became clear that the Shin Buddhist community was a suitable spiritual refuge for me. At the daily morning service (*jinjo gongyo*), I was deeply impressed when I observed many men and women of pure trust and devotion (*shinjitsu shinjin*): living embodiments of Amida Buddha's Seventeenth and Eighteenth vows.

These were people who were clearly saturated in, and perfumed by, *Namo Amida Butsu* – individuals whose very presence called out to us to follow and emulate them; to be infected by the inspiration they exuded. There was no rancid odour of sanctity or self-righteousness here; simply the demeanour of ordinary folk who perhaps knew both how to work hard, and also how to have fun and enjoy themselves. More importantly, they were aspirants who attended the daily observance every morning, to express their joy in the dharma and to reflect on the teachings of Shinran – a model for us all.

I have told this story to illustrate that there is indeed a nembutsu way of being – an active engagement with *Namo Amida Butsu* as something that is very much alive.

Jōdo Wasan 117
"When I was in the causal state,
I realized insight into the non-origination of all existence
By coming to possess the mind of nembutsu;
Hence now, in the world of Sahā...
[continued in the next hymn]

THE *SAHĀ* WORLD

This verse brings us, at last, close to the threshold of the *Kōsō Wasan* – the hymns on the Pure Land masters. It's the first reference by Shinran Shōnin to existence in this 'world of endurance' (*sahā-loka*) seeing as, throughout the *Jōdo Wasan*, we have been focused on Nirvāna, the Realm of Light.

You'll remember that one of the few points in which the teaching of Shinran is distinguished from that of his predecessors is that the Pure Land (*Jōdo*) – the focus of this first volume of hymns – is Nirvāna itself. The other is that true practice (*gyō*, the nembutsu) is of the Buddha; and that because the awakening of shinjin is the decisive cause for our ultimate attainment of Nirvāna, there is no need to be concerned about our state of mind at death.[1] It seems to me that all other aspects of the teaching are extrapolations from these core features.

As we leave behind the glorious serenity of *Jōdo*, our focus will now be confined to the constraints of the *sahā-loka*.

The 'world of endurance', of course, is not just this planet upon which we find ourselves (with our animal companions) but refers to all reality that is conditioned by impermanence and dissatisfaction. Thus it includes the realm of hells (Sk. *naraka*), ghosts (Sk. *preta*), demons (Sk. *asura*) and gods (Sk. *deva*) – in addition to our human realm and the material universe. The Pure Land transcends all of these because it's the uncreated Land of Peace and Happiness (*anrakushū*) or Nirvāna.

But now we come down to earth, so to speak. This *wasan* brings us back to our home of interminable wandering (Sk. *saṃsāra*) where we are always dogged by hardship and distress. Even though we might be born into one of the heavens, where we may remain for a very long time, our

---
[1] CWS, p. 531.

pleasure and comfort can only last for as long as the fruits of our karma continue to ripen.

We shall see, in the *Kōsō Wasan*, that all of our dharma masters knew and tasted the bitterness of the *sahā* world, this 'vale of tears'; sometimes as a result of fleeing sorrow and seeking pleasure, or in the common human experiences of loss and longing. Following that work, we shall come to the *Shōzōmatsu Wasan* which contain Shinran's hymns on the Dharma-Ages. These will bring us into our own time and condition – in which there is great affliction and where we find ourselves removed from the light of the dharma, along with the guidance of enlightened teachers.

In our time, we are prone to lose sight of the truth regarding this world, because we are now in the process of consuming the earth's resources for the sake of instant gratification; but all this bounty will no doubt be exhausted soon enough. It's also easy for people like us – who live in a so-called 'post-industrial' society – to forget that many human beings are always close to starvation; and indeed that almost half of the world's population today endures severe and frequent deprivation and misery.

Most people live under the rule of tyrannical and unjust leaders, and do not have access to proper health care or to justice through the courts. If we truly had the compassion of bodhisattvas, we would suffer with them – following that great exemplar of the bodhisattva way, Vimalakīrti. In any case, there is no iron-clad rule which says that our comfortable situation will always endure. The prosperity of our civilization is fragile.

But those of us who are affluent are rarely happy anyway. Wealth does not bring joy and, of course, neither does poverty. Many of us, who have so much, are resentful because we think we should have even more. As Śākyamuni pointed out, a sated appetite is never truly sated. So, even if we think we have everything, there is always more to want and the more possessions we have, the greater the loss should they be taken from us. Our loved ones will grow sick, become old and die; and many of us fall victim to some form of injustice. I am sure that a great majority of people are in jobs that they don't really find fulfilling, and so these have to be endured as well.

In our consumer society, there can be no greater misfortune than to be unemployed and to find ourselves deprived of the financial security we need to get by. Those without work are seen as useless *persona non grata*

– viewed only with contempt and considered by many as greedy, grasping, wasteful parasites who are underserving users of public resources. Like all wealthy people, too, we live in fear that the poor will somehow seize our goods by force, robbing us in some way.

So even those who are ostensibly comfortable and wealthy, still have much to endure.

Our human lot is subject to many vicissitudes. Illness and ageing, yearning and tragedy. There are natural disasters that are beyond our control, such as droughts, floods, fires and earthquakes. Even worse are the horrors we inflict on each other – especially war, other forms of violence, and cruelty. In the midst of these deplorable conditions, the Buddha-dharma has survived and been transmitted for nearly two and a half thousand years.

Despite the uncertainty and evanescence of human life here in this *sahā* world, innumerable seekers have been inspired to follow the Pure Land way. Of these, Shinran selected seven as being outstanding interpreters of the dharma. They were masters who showed us how to withstand this 'world of endurance' and to, ultimately, transcend it. We will now begin to explore what it is that they have to tell us, and to discover how – through them – we can find relief, salvation and the release of Nirvāna.

Jōdo Wasan 118
*I embrace persons of the nembutsu
And bring them into the Pure Land."
Let us respond with deep gratitude for the great benevolence
Of Bodhisattva Mahāsthāmaprāpta.*

This concludes the hymns to Bodhisattva Mahāsthāmaprāpta, the original state of Master Genkū.

THE GENIALITY OF THE DHARMA

In 1201, soon after joining the community of his master, Hōnen Shōnin, Shinran abandoned all practices and spontaneously entered the Eighteenth Vow of 'Sincere Mind and Entrusting', finding himself assured of ultimate enlightenment by means of the nembutsu.

From principle to embodiment, followed by effect – that is always how the dharma works. Throughout the *Jōdo Wasan*, we have been discussing ideas, doctrines, and often rather abstruse concepts. But the dharma can only be transmitted through personal encounters; either with people from the past or among those living now. When written, the dharma remains theoretical.

I have no doubt whatsoever, that when Shinran 'turned and entered the gate of True Suchness' upon meeting Hōnen, he perceived in his master the wisdom of Amida Buddha in the form of Mahāsthāmaprāpta Bodhisattva; the very wisdom that pervades all things. Of course, Hōnen did not think of himself in that way. Although he was the active agent of Shinran's awakening to shinjin, he made no such claims for himself.

It seems to me that, unlike most other religious traditions with which we are familiar, the sacred texts of the Buddha-dharma become the body of a lively reality when we accept them graciously as a meeting or conversation, which come to life as a personal encounter. It is in this sense that we're most inspired by others who embody the teachings for us.

The dharma is warm, embracing and humane. It has a smile, a twinkle in the eye, and a gentle word of encouragement. After all, it is actual people – the real individuals behind the words – who touch, move and guide us; not the purity of their hermeneutics, not the depth of their philosophy, but the ineffable light that permeates their hearts and minds.

The *Kyōgyōshinshō*, Shinran's major exposition of the Pure Land way, is certainly the doctrinal source for exegesis but it's also a living entity. It is truly Shinran himself and embodies his entire personal reality. As we listen to Shinran in this work, or in the *wasan*, we hear his voice, the ripple of his laughter and sometimes a gruff rebuke. It is this which moves and encourages us to take refuge in the Primal Vow of Amida Buddha for the sake of our spiritual welfare, just as he had done.

It would be a mistake to see the *Kyōgyōshinshō* as a treatise that was written to merely convince us of the truth of an idea by logic or reason alone. The *Kyōgyōshinshō* is the Dharma-Body of Shinran, his heart and life giving itself to us. Furthermore, when we read it, we hear the voice of a devoted disciple of Hōnen.

As we now turn to the *Kōsō Wasan*, we shall be meeting vivid, fascinating, flesh-and-blood people who were also Shinran's teachers. In these hymns we see, repeatedly, that these masters were, in themselves, as much an inspiration and encouragement to Shinran as their teaching; for he is moved, more than anything, by their relationship with Amida Buddha. He even entreats them for help in the later *Shōzōmatsu Wasan*.

The dharma is first and foremost congenial; a living and breathing corpus, forged on the anvil of sometimes bitter experience and nourished by the example, the friendship and the encouragement of others. As we embark next on a new collection of hymns, we will visit each one of Shinran's teachers in their own worlds and come to see them as kind guides; and as our warm and loving friends.

Made in the USA
Las Vegas, NV
06 April 2025